WINNING JUMPS
AND POLE VAULT

WINNING JUMPS AND POLE VAULT

ED JACOBY

EDITOR

Human Kinetics

Library of Congress Cataloging-in-Publication Data

Winning jumps and pole vault / Ed Jacoby, editor.
   p. cm.
 Includes bibliographical references and index.
 ISBN-13: 978-0-7360-7419-3 (soft cover)
 ISBN-10: 0-7360-7419-8 (soft cover)
 1. Jumping. 2. Jumping--Training. 3. Vaulting.
4. Vaulting--Training. I. Jacoby, Ed.
 GV1073.W53 2009
 796.43'2--dc22

                     2008033927

ISBN-10: 0-7360-7419-8
ISBN-13: 978-0-7360-7419-3

This publication is written and published to provide accurate and authoritative information relevant to the subject matter presented. It is published and sold with the understanding that the author and publisher are not engaged in rendering legal, medical, or other professional services by reason of their authorship or publication of this work. If medical or other expert assistance is required, the services of a competent professional person should be sought.

This book is a revised edition of *Complete Book of Jumps,* published in 1995 by Human Kinetics, Inc. ·

Acquisitions Editor: Laurel Plotzke; **Developmental Editor:** Amanda Eastin-Allen; **Assistant Editor:** Laura Podeschi; **Copyeditor:** Patsy Fortney; **Proofreader:** Anne Rogers; **Indexer:** Betty Frizzéll; **Permission Manager:** Martha Gullo; **Graphic Designer:** Joe Buck; **Graphic Artist:** Kim McFarland; **Cover Designer:** Keith Blomberg; **Photographer (cover):** Tom Roberts (main and lower left)/Kelly Huff (lower middle and lower right); **Photographer (interior):** David Harpe, unless otherwise noted. Photos on pages 8, 24, 85, 123, and 189 by Neil Bernstein; **Photo Asset Manager:** Laura Fitch; **Visual Production Assistant:** Joyce Brumfield; **Photo Office Assistant:** Jason Allen; **Art Manager:** Kelly Hendren; **Associate Art Manager:** Alan L. Wilborn; **Illustrator:** Tim Offenstein, unless otherwise noted. Illustrations on pages 9, 12, 14, 15 (top and middle), 16, 96, 102, and 105 by Paul To; **Printer:** Versa Press

We thank the University of Louisville in Louisville, Kentucky, for assistance in providing the location for the photo shoot for this book.

Human Kinetics books are available at special discounts for bulk purchase. Special editions or book excerpts can also be created to specification. For details, contact the Special Sales Manager at Human Kinetics.

Printed in the United States of America   10 9 8 7 6 5 4 3 2 1

Human Kinetics
Web site: www.HumanKinetics.com

United States: Human Kinetics
P.O. Box 5076
Champaign, IL 61825-5076
800-747-4457
e-mail: humank@hkusa.com

Canada: Human Kinetics
475 Devonshire Road Unit 100
Windsor, ON N8Y 2L5
800-465-7301 (in Canada only)
e-mail: info@hkcanada.com

Europe: Human Kinetics
107 Bradford Road
Stanningley
Leeds LS28 6AT, United Kingdom
+44 (0) 113 255 5665
e-mail: hk@hkeurope.com

Australia: Human Kinetics
57A Price Avenue
Lower Mitcham, South Australia 5062
08 8372 0999
e-mail: info@hkaustralia.com

New Zealand: Human Kinetics
Division of Sports Distributors NZ Ltd.
P.O. Box 300 226 Albany
North Shore City
Auckland
0064 9 448 1207
e-mail: info@humankinetics.co.nz

Contents

Acknowledgments

Ed Jacoby

To Jean, my wife of 50 years. She encouraged a very reluctant man to take the time and effort to gather authors and complete the material. She said, "You owe it to the sport."

My heartfelt appreciation to the contributing authors who so willingly agreed to work on the project. They are truly the best representation of teachers and coaches in the jumping events. Over the years, a great fraternity of friendship has developed among the coaching profession in track and field. These select coaches are certainly part of that group and have a strong desire to support and influence these individual jumping events. These coaches are also just great guys. They are Greg Hull, MF Athletic; Dr. Keith Henschen, University of Utah; Dr. Will Freeman, Grinnell College; Cliff Rovelto, Kansas State University; Tom and Kyle Tellez, University of Houston; and Boo Schexnayder, 2008 U.S. Olympic jump coach.

To coaches Ron Mann and Jake Jacoby, my son, and the University of Louisville, who pro- vided the athlete models and facilities at the University of Louisville. The athletes are Tone Belt, Andre Black, Rudon Bastian, Kyle Gann, Phil Feinberg, Amaka Omenyinma, Seidre Forde, and Andrea Sabbatine.

To my old friend, John Chaplin, and the USATF, who made it possible to obtain photos at the 2008 USA Olympic Track & Field Trials.

To Dr. Tom Garrett and Tartan-APS, who have allowed me employment where I am able to work with and keep in touch daily with my friends in the coaching profession. Tom has pro- vided me with much-needed encouragement to see this book project through to completion.

My primary acknowledgment goes to the Lord, who blessed me with more than 45 years in the coaching profession. I have experienced more than words can say regarding my associa- tion with young people and coaches. Hopefully, I have had a positive influence on the lives of these special individuals.

Introduction

Ed Jacoby

Through the experience of coaching jumpers, reviewing research, and using information provided by others, I have noted several commonalities as well as distinctions in the jumping events. Following are the common components:

- Running mechanics
- Sequence of the approach run, the acceleration process and postural changes during acceleration, and changes in body angles
- Transition of the approach to the takeoff
- Mechanics of the penultimate stride
- Development of impulse at takeoff and use of elastic energy, from eccentric to concentric forces
- Setting an effective approach length and speed development to the jump
- Visual steering

Here are the primary distinctions of the specific events:

- The horizontal jumps have a much higher incidence of horizontal speed at takeoff than the vertical jumps.
- Takeoff mechanics and impulse generated are specific to each event.
- Desired angles of takeoff are unique to each event.

Those elements are an outline for running speed on the runway; putting the body in the most optimal position for maximum distance or height in the jump; establishing a flight pattern that allows the least loss of runway speed at takeoff; and finally, giving direction to wanted and unwanted rotations around the hips and other joints during the flight phase of the jump. By an in-depth evaluation of these factors, a coach can identify all the mechanical needs of a jumper. It is necessary for the coach to have a good understanding and an applicable means of teaching mechanics to the athlete and taking into account each athlete's unique combinations of speed, strength, maturation, and body type.

There is always an emphasis on the mechanical aspects of jumping, and certainly this is a primary focus of coaching and learning an event. However, it is important to understand that good mechanics are not the sole factor in creating a successful jumper. Mechanical application must be prefaced by psychological and mental preparation and followed by strength and conditioning activities. Coaches must also factor in changing variables: athlete–coach issues, the individual personality and maturational level of the athlete, injuries, and even facility availability and weather. The purpose of this book is to develop a total package for the jumper and in all aspects of jump training. This book teaches more than just the mechanics of jumping; it outlines everything needed to enhance good mechanics and develop all aspects of a successful athlete.

This book presents a lineup of the best group of coaches and teachers available anywhere to provide you with mental, psychological, conditioning-planning, and individual event jump technique skills. This select group of authors are all worldly-known experts in the field of athletics. They have international experience working with elite athletes, and they all have experienced the varied problems that occur when coaching and preparing an athlete. They all have dealt with adversity as well as success. The book represents years and years of combined experience in successful study and coaching.

It is for this reason that I am so excited about this book. It contains the tools for enhancing the development of jumpers and their coaches at any level. The sharing of experiences, study, and implantation of activities by the people involved in the writing of this book have one specific goal in mind: to influence the thought process and activities of both the rookie and experienced coach and athlete.

PART I

Biomechanics of Jumping and Pole Vault

Chapter 1

The Approach

Ed Jacoby

An effective approach is the most important aspect of a jumping performance. For this reason, training should emphasize skills that provide effective acceleration, proper body position, and a good transition from the run into the takeoff. Both coach and athlete must understand the importance of the approach run in all jumping events. It alone dictates the ultimate success or failure of the jump or vault. All power, speed, impulse, and direction are developed during the run-up. Contact with the ground provides everything necessary for a successful jumping performance. Once airborne, other than controlling rotations, the athlete cannot increase the effectiveness of the jump. For this reason, in all jumping events, with the possible exception of the pole vault, as much as 90 percent of training should address approach techniques.

This chapter describes effective running mechanics and how these mechanics work together to create successful jumping performances. Only proper running technique can create the proper posture and adequate speed and force for the jump.

RUNNING MECHANICS

The most basic element of any runway event is sprinting. However, approach dynamics vary with each event. The high jump has the greatest vertical component, and the triple jump has the least. The athlete's goal is to build momentum using good approach mechanics until it peaks and then to maintain and decelerate as little as possible through the takeoff. Stride length and stride frequency, arm function, and posture are the foundations of good approach mechanics.

Stride Length and Frequency

Stride length is the distance from one foot contact to the next. It is generally measured in feet and inches or meters and centimeters. In a properly executed running approach, the stride length increases from the back of the runway through the next-to-last, or penultimate, step. Stride frequency means the rate of turnover from one foot strike to the next. This frequency is measured in hundredths of a second. Like stride length, stride frequency must increase throughout the approach, including the final step.

Running velocity, regardless of the optimal amount needed for the jumping events, is a product of stride length and frequency. At the initial push step of the approach, both stride length and stride frequency are at their lowest values. At rest, before the body starts down the runway, a great amount of force is necessary to overcome inertia and get the body moving. As that force becomes less and less, the frequency becomes faster and faster. Stride frequency becomes important at the completion of the acceleration process. It is acquired by the angular momentum of both the arms and the legs, posture, the elastic response of the driving leg, and the specific endurance of the muscles.

Stride length and stride frequency affect each other. A stride length that is too long causes overstriding (the foot landing too far ahead of the hips on ground contact). This decreases frequency and can result in breaking or slowing. It also creates the possibility for injury to the hamstrings. Too great a frequency, however (trying to pull the body along rather than pushing down and back), impedes the production of force into the ground. Frequency is actually of no value without the strong leg and hip drive providing power (Tellez 2003).

Negative foot speed is an important term in today's coaches' vernacular. Negative foot speed means that the foot is moving downward and backward, but not as fast as the hips are moving forward. Naturally, we would like these two speeds to balance out, but the best we can do is to minimize the occurrence. It becomes obvious that if the foot is placed on the ground well or even marginally ahead of the hips, slowing or braking will occur in running speed. The best preventive tool we have is aligning the tibia near 90 degrees to the ground, directly under the hips as they pass over. The heel briefly touches the ground as the ankle joint closes. This action causes a stretch on the Achilles tendon and on the calf muscles. The resulting loading action of the lower leg allows for a greater push-off of the supporting leg as a result of elastic force generation (Tellez 2003). The harder this leg pushes or applies force on the ground, the greater the speed of its recovery due to the stretch reflex. The faster this recovery, the less negative foot speed expressed. To supplement this strong pushing action, the sprinter or jumper should be taught not to run on the toes. The foot plant is a ball-to-heel action.

Some coaches stress the preactivation of the leg strike in a kind of pawing action. This is bad technique. It is true that the leg should be active, but not as a result of knee and ankle

action. The powerful extensors of the hip and the stretch reflex of the hamstrings are what create leg speed prior to foot impact. A voluntary action at the knee will only cause a reduction of angular velocity of the hip, which is the major source of force against the ground.

Arm Function

Arm action provides coordination and balance and helps the athlete apply maximal force into the ground. Sprinting requires a strong and quick backward swing of the arms. This action should be initiated from the shoulder; the forearms should be relaxed. The elbow and upper arm should move back and up on the backswing. During the backswing, when the hand is directly parallel to the hips, the elbow should open to lengthen the lever for additional force. On the forward swing, the elbow closes to 90 degrees and provides needed angular velocity. The shortened lever allows maximal speed and arm recovery.

Posture

In an effective approach, forward lean is a function of acceleration. A high degree (45 degrees) of forward lean occurs during the first stages of acceleration. As the athlete reaches top speed, the body becomes erect. Conversely, a backward body inclination occurs during deceleration. By observing the jumper's posture during the approach run, the coach can determine the efficiency of the approach. As the jumper moves along the runway, the hips naturally rise through acceleration, disregarding the slight up and down undulation caused by the running stride.

Postural changes occur regardless of how fast the athlete is running. For example, the high-jump approach is much slower than the long-jump approach. However, the athlete starts at a slow, deliberate speed and accelerates to an optimal approach speed. The body posture will undergo a forward lean and eventually reach a full upright, erect position. Athletes who slow before takeoff will have a slight backward lean, and this is not good.

Hip height also affects running. The primary purpose of the drive phase at the beginning of the run is to smoothly and progressively move the hips to a position directly above foot contact. The higher the hips are, the longer the natural stride length will be because of the longer application of force on the ground. Although athletes cannot control their height, they can learn to run tall and upright. After the initial drive phase, the foot strike must be directly under the hips. Any tendency to overstride will cause an abnormally low hip position and blocking or braking on each foot contact.

ACCELERATION PROGRESSION

All jump approach runs must incorporate a drive phase; a continuation, or maintenance, phase; and a transition phase into the jump. These phases must blend together during acceleration, which increases from the start of the runway to the last three (transition) steps into the jump. Here is an overview of the progression, which is described in more detail in the coming sections: The jumper drives out of the back of the runway by pushing hard to overcome inertia and begins to develop as much momentum as possible. The body leans approximately 45 degrees, and the hips are in a rather low position. As the hips begin to rise, the posture becomes more erect. Stride frequency begins to increase along with stride length. When the body is fully erect and maximal speed is nearly achieved, a period of maintenance is required just prior to the transition, when the penultimate foot is placed down flat and the final foot comes down flat.

An effective static start begins with the takeoff foot firmly planted at the start mark. While keeping this foot down and in contact with the ground, the athlete rocks the hips back as far as possible. By pushing the hips forward during the initial drive step, the athlete has a maximum amount of time to overcome inertia before this first foot leaves the ground. As the hips continue moving forward through

a maximum range of motion, the drive phase begins with the downward and backward push of the leg and hips using the glutes and quads. The purpose here is to keep the pushing foot on the ground as long as possible. This provides a large force application over the longest period of time.

The initial pushing action puts the body in a forward lean. The trunk angle is approximately 45 degrees, just like that of a sprinter coming out of the blocks, thus the term *drive phase*. The forward lean continues throughout the acceleration phase, but decreases somewhat during each successive stride. Step by step, the strides lengthen and the body gradually rises to a full upright position. The stride frequency also increases.

During the transition phase the athlete goes from a horizontal to a vertical trajectory. It begins with hitting the four-step check mark (see page 7), vertically aligning the body, lowering the hips with a slightly elongated penultimate step, and raising the hips with a slightly shortened last step. Deceleration should not occur during this phase of the runway.

Great sprinters running the 100-meter dash try to both maximize and minimize the events that occur over the acceleration curve. *Maximizing* means gathering as much usable speed as possible. *Minimizing* is not allowing deceleration to occur. The sprint coach uses an acceleration curve to show the acceleration over a period of time or distance. At some point during an all-out effort, the body reaches a peak speed and maintains this speed for a short time. As the nerves and muscles fatigue, the athlete begins to decelerate. Thus, the curve moves from slow to fast and then gradually to slow (figure 1.1 on page 6). This slowing is not desirable, but it is a physiological fact.

The acceleration harmonic is one of increasing stride length and stride frequency through the penultimate step. The last step should be slightly shorter, thus creating the much desired "high hips" at takeoff (figure 1.2 on page 6). Not only does stride length increase, but, just as important, the stride frequency also increases.

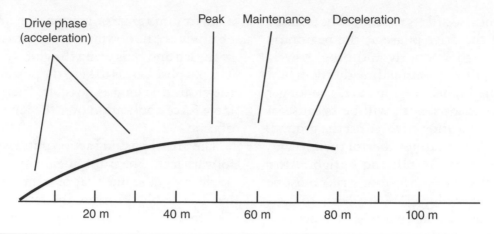

> **Figure 1.1** Acceleration curve for 100-meter sprint.

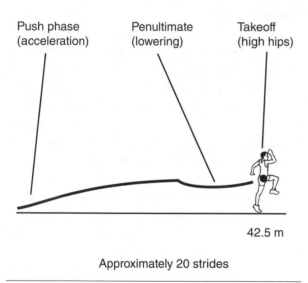

> **Figure 1.2** Push-transition foot release.

MAINTAINING SPEED AND STEERING

For an approach to be effective and consistent, the runway length should provide the greatest usable speed for the individual athlete. In addition, the coach and athlete should understand the process called steering and the need for check marks. The following sections explain how to determine the ideal approach length and how to use check marks to improve performance.

Developing Approach Length

The approach length is based on how long and how far it takes the athlete to reach top speed. A younger, less experienced athlete may reach top speed in only 12 steps; an elite athlete may take upward of 20 steps.

One way to achieve an effective runway technique for the long jump, triple jump, and pole vault is to use a 12-step learning pattern. (The high jump has a different learning pattern; this is covered in chapter 5.)

To learn the concept of tempo, the athlete stands on the track with the takeoff foot forward. From a static position, the athlete pushes out as forcefully as possible and counts each time the takeoff foot hits the ground. The count should go as follows: "1 (the step in which the takeoff foot hits the ground) and 2 and 3 and 4 (of takeoff foot)" until count 6. On "6," the athlete should pop into the air to simulate takeoff. Thus, 6 count steps equal 12 total steps.

The count system allows the athlete to visualize the push phase and increase stride frequency through takeoff. This process should take place on the track or grass away from the board or vault box. The purpose is for the athlete to become tempo and frequency oriented, rather than takeoff-spot or board oriented. All runways, from the short-approach practice runways to those at major competitions, are handled with the tempo harmonic count system so it becomes natural and automatic for athletes.

Table 1.1, developed through research, indicates a usually acceptable runway length for long and triple jumps. For example, an athlete who can run 100 meters in 13.0 seconds, or a comparable 30 meters in 4.7 seconds, should use a maximum of 12 strides during competition. On the other hand, an elite athlete who can run 100 meters in 10.4 seconds should use up to 22 strides during a competition approach run.

It is best to begin the learning process with 6 count steps (12 total steps). In competition, the elite, very fast athlete might require 10 or 11 count steps (20 to 22 total steps). Once the athlete has learned to run from 12 steps, he can add additional steps to the approach. The primary indicators of whether the athlete is using the appropriate number of steps are body alignment and peak speed at takeoff. If there is any forward lean, acceleration is still occurring, and if there is backward lean, decelerating is occurring. The body must be totally upright, and there must be no reaching for the takeoff spot. Coaches should remember that the fewer number of strides the athlete takes, the less chance there is for mistakes to occur. The coach should never increase the distance or number of steps when there is a deceleration, signified by either postural changes or an interruption of tempo and stride length at the end of the run. As the athlete improves in acceleration and transition, the runway length can be increased, but not before that.

The high-jump approach is similar to those of the other events, but because peak speed is much less, the runway distance is much shorter.

A high-jumper generally has an approach ranging from 9 to 12 total steps. The approach is shorter because excessive speed will cause the takeoff leg to buckle at ground contact. Intuitively, the body seems to understand this and therefore slows considerably in the latter part of the runway. This deceleration causes the athlete to lean back prior to takeoff, resulting in an inadequate conversion from horizontal to vertical. Although the approach is shorter, the same mechanics of pushing hard out of the back, accelerating to a peak speed, and making a takeoff transition are the same as with other jumps.

Steering and Check Marks

Steering is the ability to hit a desired takeoff point without looking directly at it. Elite athletes know that looking at the takeoff point takes them out of the correct body alignment and usually causes them to reach for the mark—both are not good.

Good steering usually occurs very subtly and is accomplished over much of the runway, not simply during the last few strides. Think of walking along a moving walkway in an airport. Prior to stepping onto solid ground, you probably take a long step or a couple of shorter steps to time your cadence and stride length to hit the nonmoving floor as you continue to walk. This disrupts the cadence of your stride. The more talented among us would naturally make subtle adjustments several or many steps back on the moving walkway, causing very little disruption

Table 1.1   Estimated Runway Distance for Individual Athletes

Speed of athlete for 30 meters	Speed of athlete for 100 meters	Suggested number of strides for approach during competition
4.7	13.0	12
4.5	12.5	14
4.3	12.0	16
4.1	11.5	18
3.9	10.5	20
3.7	10.4	22

From: *The Mechanics of Athletics* (Seventh Revised Edition) by Geoffrey H.G. Dyson (New York: Holmes & Meier, 1978). Reprinted by permission of the publisher.

of cadence from the moving walkway to the stationary floor. Similarly, good steering requires that the athlete make subtle adjustments early on the runway to avoid any major disruption in stride length late on the runway.

Check marks are tools used by both the coach and the athlete to help the athlete become consistent. In the long jump, triple jump, and pole vault, it is best to use three check marks. Normally these marks include a start mark, a coach's mark, and a takeoff mark.

The most important athlete mark is the start mark. The first step determines consistency. If the first step is off, all the remaining steps will be out of sync as well. An error at the start not only shows up at the takeoff spot, but also changes the location of the coach's mark. Thus, an accurate adjustment cannot be made to place the athlete properly to complete a success-

© Human Kinetics

ful jump. The beginning jumper should learn to use a static start (as described in the acceleration progression section on page 5) with no run-in, skipping, or bounding. Anything other than a static start allows for inconsistencies that will be magnified near the board or takeoff spot. Because 90 percent of variance at takeoff occurs in the first four steps, it is imperative that the acceleration phase be consistent.

The last mark is the actual board, or takeoff mark. Athletes who miss the takeoff mark either foul (receive no measurement) or jump behind the board and thus get no credit for the total distance jumped. In the pole vault, it is dangerous to be under or out too far from the desired takeoff spot. A high-jumper who is too close to the bar cannot time the rotation for body clearance; if too far out, the jumper will not have sufficient speed to convert, or the takeoff leg will buckle.

The athlete should never look down at the takeoff spot. As the athlete comes out of the back of the approach with pronounced forward lean, eye contact will be down toward the ground. As the body gradually rises to an upright position, the eyes will automatically pass a plane at which the board, or takeoff spot, will momentarily come into focus. However, the head and eyes keep rising with the body position, and the focal point naturally moves up and away from the board, box, or takeoff spot. Prior to takeoff, looking down is detrimental in any jump. It will cause fouling, slowing down, or being under the vault. The goal is for the athlete to become aware of the takeoff spot using peripheral sight. This is a result of many repetitions of consistent practice.

Athletes can train to know where the takeoff spot is by using the coach's mark. This mark, also called the midmark or coach's check, is critical to the coach in helping the athlete make necessary adjustments in strength and speed based on wind, track conditions, competitive emotions, fatigue, and seasonal changes. In most cases, this mark should not be a focal point for the athlete. It is placed on or near the runway, usually four steps prior to the takeoff mark or board. The well-trained athlete makes subtle stride adjustments four or six steps out from takeoff because from that point the strides become consistent. The coach's mark should therefore be in the vicinity of this natural adjustment. By placing the check mark at the fourth or sixth step, the coach can determine whether the athlete should move up or back. Sometimes pole vault coaches place this mark six steps prior to takeoff to allow for two additional steps to accommodate the pole shift and plant for these athletes.

The distance from the coach's mark to the board is basically the average of the stride length during the latter portion of the run. Normally, for elite male jumpers who run 20 steps, the distance from the coach's mark to the board will be 30 to 33 feet (9 to 10 m). For female jumpers running the same 20 steps, the distance will be 28 to 30 feet (8.5 to 9 m). Upon reaching the coach's mark, the athlete should be tall, erect, and at near or full runway speed. In a proper approach run, the stride length increases through the penultimate step. This lengthening should be very gradual and should never hinder acceleration or body posture. Reaching to hit the takeoff mark will cause deceleration and a postural lean back, thus destroying a good takeoff.

The coach's mark reveals several things that can make or break a run-up: whether the athlete is pushing out of the back in a consistent manner, whether the start mark needs to be moved forward or backward, and whether the athlete is reaching or slowing to hit the board or takeoff spot. Finally, the coach's mark gives athletes peace of mind. If they know they are on the coach's mark, they can forget about making adjustments and simply go to autopilot and jump with no reservations.

If a long-jumper fouls by, say, 6 inches (15 cm), the remedy is not simply to move the start mark back 6 inches. An athlete who is looking down at the board or the ground in the latter part of the approach will most likely be reaching

Number of total steps

	12		14		16		18		20
									R
							L–SP		L
							R		R
					L–SP	1	L	2	L
					R		R		R
			L–SP	1	L	2	L	3	L
			R		R		R		R
	L–SP	1	L	2	L	3	L	4	L
	R		R		R		R		R
1	L	2	L	3	L	4	L	5	L
	R		R		R		R		R
2	L	3	L	4	L	5	L	6	L
	R		R		R		R		R
3	L	4	L	5	L	6	L	7	L
	R		R		R		R		R
4	L–CC	5	L–CC	6	L–CC	7	L–CC	8	L–CC
	R		R		R		R		R
5	L	6	L	7	L	8	L	9	L
	R		R		R		R		R
6	L–TO	7	L–TO	8	L–TO	9	L–TO	10	L–TO

6 count = 12 steps
7 count = 14 steps
8 count = 16 steps
9 count = 18 steps
10 count = 20 steps

▶**Figure 1.3**   Step and count patterns. SP = starting point; CC = coach's check; TO = takeoff. The coach's check is shown at four steps from the takeoff, but it could be moved to six steps from the takeoff for pole vaulters.

or lengthening the last stride to hit the board or takeoff spot. Simply moving back the start mark will cause the athlete to reach even farther, almost certainly resulting in another foul.

Consider an athlete who starts down the runway and is 6 inches (15 cm) beyond the coach's mark and subsequently fouls or is under on the vault. The correct adjustment is simply to move the start mark back 6 inches. On the other hand, if the athlete is 6 inches behind the coach's mark and still fouls by 6 inches, the problem is overstriding over the last four steps. The correct adjustment is to move the start mark forward 6 inches. This technique is suitable for all jumping events except the high jump.

Coaches should periodically time athletes over the last four steps from touchdown at the coach's mark to foot release at takeoff. This should be done first on the track without a board and again after moving back to the runway during an actual jump. The two sets of times should coordinate closely. This method can also be used to determine the most efficient runway length. The runway length that consistently provides the fastest times over the last four steps is the length to use during competition. In some cases, a longer runway will not yield the fastest time over these last four steps because the athlete is not strong enough or mature enough to handle the longer distances. It is usually better for an athlete's peak speed to be less than absolute speed. This enables a controlled run, which is necessary for the transition from the run to the jump.

Figure 1.3 on page 9 provides an overview of all the check marks, showing a runway configuration for most runways using the count-step approach system. It shows the starting point, the coach's mark, and the takeoff for the long jump, triple jump, and pole vault.

Chapter 2

Takeoff and Landing

Ed Jacoby

After the athlete reaches optimal runway speed, the final two steps must mechanically position the body to jump. The speed and the angle of takeoff determine the parabola of the hips at foot release. Certain rotations, however, will affect the results of the jump. This chapter covers speed, height, takeoff angle, and balance in relation to the takeoff and the landing, as well as positioning and flight path. All coaching and technical work must center on these mechanical components; coaching areas not directly related to these items will lead to focusing on symptoms. This chapter also explains how athletes can protect themselves from injuries caused by mechanical faults.

SPEED AND POSITIONING AT TAKEOFF

The speed at which the athlete is moving—or, more mechanically, the speed of the center of mass at foot release—drastically affects the distance or height of the jump. Each athlete, regardless of strength or maturation, has a specific takeoff speed that will maximize the jump. An athlete moving at absolute speed is very unlikely to be able to negotiate a jump. An athlete's desired speed is the speed at which she can optimally convert a horizontal run into a vertical jump. Simply stated, athletes must maintain their speed as they transition into the last two steps prior to takeoff. Those who

exceed their desired effective speed experience technical breakdown at takeoff.

Every athlete also has a certain efficient distance to run during the acceleration process. Young jumpers especially suffer from increasing the length of their runs too quickly. Forcing speed too early in the run, or becoming erect too soon, will cause deceleration at the transition into the jump. It is best to learn the mechanics of a run coupled with the transition into the jump with marginal speed. A longer approach and additional velocity can come later during the training process.

An athlete is influenced by two forces when making the transition from a run to takeoff: horizontal velocity and vertical velocity. This transition must occur with as little slowdown or changeup as possible. At some point in every jump, the athlete must prepare her body to move from maximal horizontal speed (according to the event and her strength and maturation) to a large application of force in the jump. This is called *impulse*. Simply stated, impulse = force × time, meaning that we seek as much speed as possible during the leg-loading process (see the discussion later in this section on page 13) multiplied by as long a force application as possible.

The horizontal–vertical transition must be initiated by a slight lowering of the hips two steps out from the takeoff. This lowering during the penultimate stride is accomplished by landing flat-footed with a slight flexion of the ankle, hip, and knee joints. A passive or limp leg causes too much flexion and less eccentric contraction of the hips and quads. The correct action is that of amortization, flexing and stretching muscles of the hip and knee. This sets the muscles up to quickly transfer force into the next step. Individual cues for the penultimate mechanics are as follows:

- A very active hip response during the lowering process
- Moving over a slightly flexed but braced ankle
- Landing with the foot directly under the ankle

In the final takeoff step, the foot should also be placed down flat so the full force is quickly directed into the ground or board. If the last foot contact is onto the ball (plantar flexion) or the heel (dorsiflexion) of the foot, valuable time is lost before the automatically initiated full flat foot can provide force. I liken this flat-foot placement to dropping a golf ball on concrete (quick return of force) as opposed to dropping a semiflat basketball on the same surface (slow and minimal force return). The goal here is the solid, muscle-loaded, and elastic response of flat-foot placement.

One of the primary goals of any jumper is to achieve the highest possible center of mass at takeoff. As soon as an athlete leaves the ground, because of gravity, he begins to fall back to the earth. Therefore, the higher the hips are at this time, as a result of either body structure or mechanics, the greater the potential is for a longer or higher jump. The jumper's body should be totally upright (erect) three steps out from the takeoff. This provides a maximum center of mass height at takeoff. If for any reason the athlete is slowed by the body's innate knowledge that it can't complete a jump at a certain speed or the inability to reach the specified takeoff mark, there will be noticeable backward lean into the takeoff phase. This will have a negative effect on jumping ability. Another problem is the athlete leaning forward into the last steps (usually the last two) prior to takeoff. This is due to the athlete still attempting to accelerate at maximal velocity or a plantar-flexed foot placement onto the penultimate step.

Some athletes, while preparing to lower the hips in the penultimate step, incorporate forward rotation because they want to push hard with the third step out. For example, a left-footed jumper pushes hard with the last left step before the takeoff step. This inadvertently causes a surge in acceleration and creates a forward lean. A correct lowering cue for the last three steps would be: Stand up on left, flat and lower on right, and flat on last left.

Figure 2.1 demonstrates the active lowering and rising of the center of mass (hips) over the last two steps of the long jump. It is a representation of an actual jump by Carl Lewis in the USA Championships.

▶ **Figure 2.1** The lowering and rising of the hips of an elite long-jumper during the last two strides of the approach run.

We have discussed getting the jumper in the proper position with the proper momentum while preparing to leave the ground. At this point the elastic responses need to be addressed. A jump is not simply a run off the ground, although the same mechanics are employed. A jump is first a summation of all forces that are available to the athlete to effectively load the elastic components of the takeoff leg.

In the 1960s, Geoffrey Dyson, a biomechanist, noted that the more and the faster a muscle is forced into a stretch (eccentric activity), the more concentric force that muscle will yield back at the time of desired motion (Dyson 1977). In common terms, this is called *loading a muscle*. The primary pushing muscles available to the jumper are the quadriceps group, the calf muscles, and the hips.

As mentioned, the takeoff foot held in dorsiflexion stretches the Achilles area, thus loading the calf. On ground contact, the knee joint is forced to amortize, loading up the quads, and the hips are stabilized in a forward rotated position, which also sets up these muscles for a quick, strong response. Special attention should be given to the quads to load up for a quick, strong eccentric transfer to a strong pushing force against the ground. Anything that inhibits this amortization of the quads, such as pulling or pawing the leg back, weakness of the quads, or lack of initial speed through the runway transition, will have a negative effect on the ability to apply force against the ground during the jump phase.

It should also be noted that additional forces can be generated into the takeoff leg by transferring force from the arms or arm depending on the jump or jump style. The speed at which the free leg swings through is of great importance. This is why jumpers should run hard off the last step.

As noted throughout the book, opinion varies as to how the leg and hip are loaded prior to takeoff. Some say the takeoff foot should be actively brought down like a hammer; others say the foot should be grounded like a shovel. Dr. Jesus Dapena, who coined these terms, noted that there is no conclusive evidence to favor one style over the other (J. Dapena, pers. comm.). However, substantial evidence shows that the pushing muscles (quads and glutes) provide the long-lasting impulse on the ground necessary to move the center of gravity the longest possible distance.

TAKEOFF ANGLES AND FLIGHT PATH

When discussing angles at takeoff, I remember way back to my days as a budding long-jumper in high school. My coach would always say, "Get up. Get higher in the air." In fact, he would go as far as stacking a couple of bales of hay for me to jump over to achieve the height he wanted. It was a bad idea. When an athlete concentrates on vertical velocity over horizontal velocity, the jump suffers. All the jumps, including the high jump and the pole vault (the so-called vertical jumps), are achieved at much lower angles than one would imagine. In reality, the long jump is 80 percent dependent on horizontal velocity and only 20 percent dependent on the vertical component.

The jumper's center of mass moves up and down at the same angle on the flight path, or parabola. This parabola must be sufficient for the entire body to travel over the bar. In the horizontal jumps, the goal is to allow the center of gravity to complete as much of the natural parabola as possible. Unfortunately, the grounding of the feet into the pit always prevents this from happening. In the high jump, the jumper needs enough horizontal speed for the entire body to travel over the bar. A high-jumper could easily create more vertical forces to get the center of mass over the bar, but not the legs. *Sailing* is a better description of what needs to happen.

The path of the center of mass relative to the runway is called the takeoff angle. The angle of the takeoff must be thought of as a function of speed. This factor has a significant impact on hip height throughout the jump. The higher the velocity at takeoff, the higher the hips will be during the flight curve of the jump. The flight curve of a jump is analogous to that of

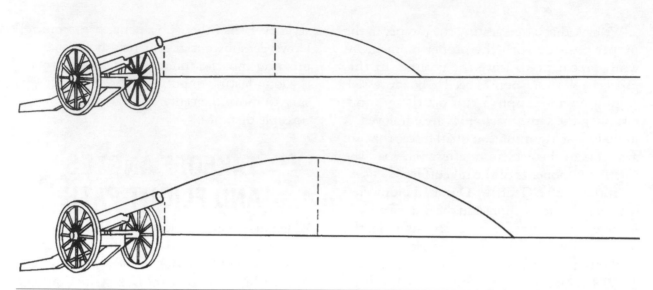

> ►**Figure 2.2** Low projectile and high projectile velocity. The projectile with the greatest velocity has a higher trajectory during flight and, therefore, a greater range.

a projectile shot from a cannon. Picture two cannons side by side and pointed at the horizon at exactly the same angle (figure 2.2). The projectiles in both cannons are identical, and the only difference between the cannons is the charge of powder placed in the barrels. In one cannon, there is a spoonful of powder, and the other contains a bucketful of powder. The projectile shot from the cannon with the most powder will have a greater velocity than the one shot from the cannon with the small charge of powder. The projectile with the greater velocity will have a much higher trajectory during flight and a far greater range.

Using the same analogy, if a runner moving at 6 meters per second leaves the ground at an angle of 20 degrees, his center of mass will rise 7 inches. If the same runner increases velocity to 10 meters per second and leaves the ground at the same 20-degree angle, his hips will rise 22 inches. Thus, the faster the athlete's approach, the more potential for a greater jump.

The flight path, or parabola, is determined just prior to and during foot release into the jump. Once the athlete is airborne, this directional path cannot be altered. The jumper travels up and down the flight path at the same angle.

Dr. Jesus Dapena provided the following ranges of takeoff angles for all the jumping events. The results are from his research of championship competitions over the years (J. Dapena, pers. comm.). The data indicate the direction of motion of the center of mass at the end of the takeoff phase, relative to the horizontal.

Long jump The range of takeoff angle for the long jump is 19 to 23 degrees (figure 2.3), based on the 12 finalists in the men's long jump at the 1983 TAC Championships (Hay, Miller, and Canterna 1983).

Triple jump Angles are important for all three phases of the triple jump (hop, step, and jump). The averages for these phases are as follows: hop, 12 to 13 degrees; step, 10 to 15 degrees; and jump, 19 to 22 degrees (figure 2.4). These data are based on the top men's finalists at the 1985 TAC Championships (Miller and Hay 1985).

High jump The range of takeoff angles for the high jump is 47 to 61 degrees (figure 2.5). This is somewhat misleading because one jumper studied had an approach that was extremely deep and perpendicular to the bar. His results were eliminated, making the usable angle range from 47 to 54 degrees. These data were collected using the nine best male jumpers ever measured at the University of Indiana lab (Dapena 2000).

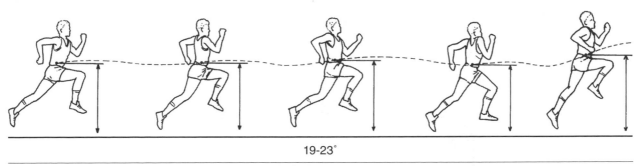

19-23°

▶ **Figure 2.3** The transition phase and takeoff of a long-jumper.

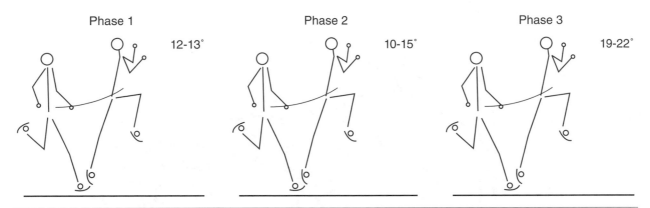

Phase 1   12-13°   Phase 2   10-15°   Phase 3   19-22°

▶ **Figure 2.4** Designated takeoff angles for the first phase (hop), second phase (step), and third phase (jump) of the triple jump.

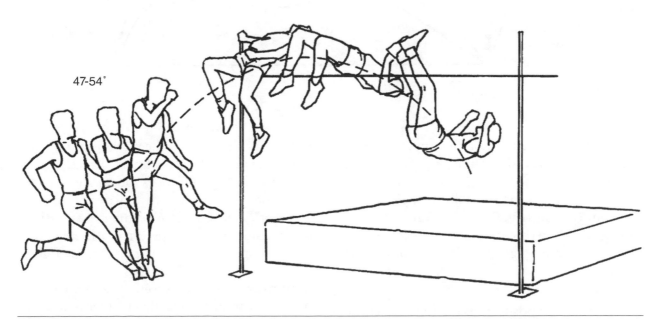

47-54°

▶ **Figure 2.5** The takeoff angle of the high jump, also showing the sailing effect along the bar.
Adapted, by permission, from J. Dapena, 1980, "Mechanics of translation in the Fosbury-flop," *Medicine and Science in Sports and Exercise* (12) 1:37-44.

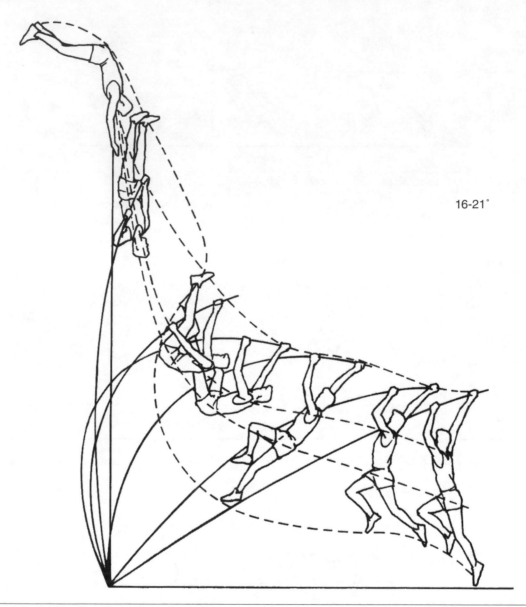

16-21°

> **Figure 2.6**   Takeoff angle in the pole vault.

Pole vault   The range of the angles of pole vaulters studied is 16 to 21 degrees (figure 2.6). These data are based on the top six finishers in the men's pole vault at the 1988 Olympic Games in Seoul (McGinnis 2006). The takeoff angle range for the top three female USA pole vaulters was 18.3 to 21.5 degrees. The angle of takeoff for the top five male jumpers ranged from 17.9 to 19.8 degrees.

As stated, the position of the foot under the hips helps determine the angle of takeoff. In the long jump and the pole vault, the foot is slightly in front of the hips. In the triple-jump hop (or first) phase, the foot is almost directly under the hips; the high-jumper's foot is ahead of the hips. Foot placement naturally determines the angle of takeoff. Foot placement has a direct relationship with the speed the athlete is running. A high-jumper must run fast enough to convert horizontal velocity into vertical velocity; if running too fast, however, the leg will buckle. As stated earlier, the real determiner is how well the athlete can maintain speed through the transition and into the jump.

BALANCE AND ROTATIONS

The final aspect of the jump has to do with balance and rotations around the hips and joints of the jumper while airborne. Rotations occur any time a jumper leaves the ground. They are controlled first by a proper takeoff angle and second by countermotions of the arms and legs. The athlete's objective is to move or adjust various parts of the body during flight to take advantage of the established parabola (which is solely determined prior to takeoff), and also to slow the forward rotation that is initiated by the hinge moment of takeoff, primarily in the long jump and triple jump. The initial rotation of the hips is determined by foot placement and the speed and angle of the takeoff. The purpose of controlling and enhancing rotations is simply to clear the bar in the high jump or to prepare for an efficient, long, and safe landing in the other events.

As stated, the parabola will never change during flight. However, manipulating the arms and legs around the center of mass can aid the jumper in establishing a good position over a crossbar or creating an optimal position for landing in the long jump and triple jump. This is due to Newton's third law of motion: For every action there is an equal or opposite reaction. For example, during bar clearance in the high jump, the head is lifted toward the chest, which causes the legs to rise. This is the result of a conscious effort by the jumper to help the legs to pass over the bar.

The rotational speed of the limbs will increase or decrease with the length of the lever. A bent limb will rotate faster, and a long limb will rotate more slowly. Visualize the figure skater: When the arms are out wide, body rotation is slow; when the arms are in near the body, body rotation is fast. Lengthening or shortening the arms, legs, and trunk very much influences the speed of rotation about the axes. The specific rotations will vary some for each event.

In the pole vault, there are two major rotations: the pole rotating in the vault box and the vaulter rotating about the pole. Pole speed is controlled by how high or how low the athlete's center of mass is on the pole itself. Consider a musical metronome. If you slide the weight up, the metronome oscillates slowly, and if you slide the weight down, the metronome oscillates quickly. The vaulter's primary goal is to maintain pole speed throughout the vault. Therefore, the hips need to stay down during the plant phase to keep the pole moving at a rapid rate. During the rotation over the bar in the high jump, a long and extended body tends to rotate slowly; therefore, the body should be shortened to enable the entire body to cross. The wise coach understands these effects on the body while it is airborne.

A problem particularly in the long and triple jumps is forward rotation of the body from the ankle joint up (the ankle is the axis) at takeoff. This is caused by the hinge moment, which is triggered by a quick deceleration of the foot and the subsequent acceleration of the upper body. As the foot performs a braking action, the momentum of the running approach is now transferred into the body above. This means that the upper body will tend to rotate forward quickly, thus shortening the completion of the parabola. The forward rotation pushes the feet prematurely into the pit. The more efficient the takeoff, the less rotation can be expected. However, some forward rotation will always occur and, if not checked, will cause a premature landing.

During the long and triple jumps, the hang or hitch-kick movements are used to diminish or eliminate undesired forward rotation. The hitch kick is a clockwise–counterclockwise rotation of the arms and legs to counter the rotation of the upper body, thus eliminating much or all of the forward rotation at takeoff. The hitch kick is covered in detail in chapter 3.

SAFE AND EFFECTIVE LANDING

Safety issues are discussed in the chapters devoted to a specific event. However, some discussion of mechanical concepts will be helpful for the prevention of injuries to all jumpers.

© Icon Sports Media

Most injuries seem to occur as a result of improper mechanics during foot contact with the ground, with either one foot or both feet. Following are the most common causes of injury in jumpers.

- Improper foot placement during the run-up phase of the jump
- Improper stabilization of the foot during the takeoff phase
- Inability to allow amortization (transfer, or the absorption, of forces) during foot contact or landing

- Inadequate strength in legs, hips, and trunk

For the sake of both safety and efficiency, athletes should not decelerate during any portion of the run-up or takeoff phase. Momentum loss generally occurs as a result of (1) grounding the foot when the body is in a lean-back position or (2) overemphasizing height (slowing and reaching) rather than runway speed during the takeoff phase. Both of these actions will place a great deal of stress on the ankle, knee, hip, and hamstrings. In addition, these activities also effectively destroy the ability to move through a jump or vault. A foot strike well ahead of the hips is often the primary cause of injuries and also leads to the most ineffective jumps.

Foot stabilization is also a major factor in injury prevention. At placement, the foot should not slide either forward or laterally. In the high jump, this means that the heel must be aligned with the ball of the foot in the direction of run-up so the total foot will summate forces along the same line and in the same direction. Sliding or slipping is usually caused by improper footwear (e.g., no heel spikes in a jump shoe), a slick surface due to water, poor surface material, a dirty surface, or even a worn-out or improperly fitted shoe. However, as mentioned before, a big problem is foot placement in relation to the athlete's center of mass. Additionally, the foot should never be jammed into the ground either heel first or toe first. If the heel touches down first, as in the high jump, the foot must rock smoothly onto its full flat surface.

Inability to allow amortization and inadequate strength actually work in tandem. Jumpers and vaulters apply very large forces into the ground to create impulse for their jumps. These forces are redirected back into the body, but not before muscle amortization takes place. Amortization is the yielding, storing, and eventually transferring of forces. This places the involved muscle group on an eccentric stretch. The body must have sufficient strength, not only to absorb, but also to transfer and summate these forces into the jump phases and landings. Generally, we tend to think of using these forces during the penultimate and takeoff phases of the jump. However, strength and the ability to transfer force are very evident during the landing phase as well. The ability to transfer and to time up muscles on opposite sides of the body is of high importance. The strength needed for single-leg bounding activities must be equal or near-equal in both the dominant and nondominant legs. Finally, the athlete and coach must remember that landing forces should be transferred throughout the entire body system and not just in individual joints. Landing should be thought of as an active sequence and not simply a crash into the pit or ground. Consideration of these concepts will allow for more productive jumps and certainly far less stress on the areas in which we see most jumpers' injuries: the ankles, knees, hips, and hamstrings.

PART II

Event Technique, Strategy, and Programming

Chapter 3

Long Jump

Kyle Tellez
Tom Tellez

The long jump could be called the most neglected field event because of the lack of attention it receives from many coaches and athletes. More often than not, the coach says to the best sprinter, "Go jump." Many do not understand the techniques that must evolve for jumpers to become effective and reach their potential.

The material contained in this chapter is a to-the-point description of the long-jumping event. It focuses on the total event, broken down into individual components, including the runway, its parts, length, transition phase, takeoff, flight, and landing. In addition, seasonal training programs and drills have been incorporated into the material.

The chapter stresses techniques that have evolved from sound biomechanical evidence and from elite athlete performance of both male and female athletes. Different techniques are addressed for individual styles of jumping, but all with a common goal of an effective performance.

WARM-UP AND COOL-DOWN

As in other events, warming up prior to competition is important not only to improve jumping performance but also to prevent injury. Warm-ups should include activity that raises the core body temperature, recruits the nerves and muscles involved in the event, and enables the athlete to have confidence in the runway and be able to cope with any adverse conditions.

Stretching should be an integral part of each day's warm-up and cool-down activity. Because stretching should be done when the muscles are warm, an easy jog should precede stretching. All stretches should be done in a slow, static manner, never forcefully or explosively, which can cause injury rather than prevent it. After every workout, either running or lifting, jumpers should cool down by stretching and jogging to alleviate tightness.

The key goals here are to remain relaxed yet focused on the total runway-jump model, which has been learned through many repetitions of training. Don't think only about individual parts, and don't think about negative problems that may have been encountered. When it becomes time to jump, the athlete should act on autopilot. Prior to a subsequent jump, light activity and acceleration strides may be helpful, but just enough to keep arousal level up and to recruit necessary nerves and muscles. It is important that each jumper considers and plans for an individual routine or warm-up activities that best suit the individual athlete's physiological and psychological needs.

© Human Kinetics

APPROACH

Most world-record performances in the jumping events in track and field have been a direct result of successful approach runs and takeoffs. Therefore, coaches and jumpers must spend time developing technically sound approach runs and takeoffs.

The first objective in the long jump is to develop a consistent, fast approach run that allows for gradual acceleration. The jumper begins the run by pushing down and back against the ground with the left foot to get the body in motion. In addition, the whole body is at a slight inclination (45 degrees) to the ground at the beginning of the run. As the jumper accelerates, the body gradually straightens into an upright position (perpendicular to the ground) by the end of the sixth stride. Once in a full sprinting position, the jumper continues

the acceleration by pushing down against the ground.

At the start of the approach run, the body must begin movement from a resting state. Once moving, the body requires time to accelerate to full speed. The approach run should be one of gradual acceleration. Many inexperienced jumpers make the mistake of accelerating too fast, too soon. This premature distribution of energy causes them to decelerate toward the end of the approach run. Thus, speed is lost going into the takeoff, resulting in a poor jump performance.

To complete a successful takeoff, longjumpers should reach their maximal controlled speed during the approach run. Maximal controlled speed is indicated by upright posture, an ongoing increase in stride length and stride frequency, and a speed that allows the jumper to make the transition from horizontal velocity to vertical velocity.

The length of the approach run should be between 12 and 19 strides. The approach run should be as long as possible depending on the jumper's experience, sprinting technique, and conditioning level. The longer the approach run, the more difficult it is to develop a consistent stride pattern. Thus, inexperienced jumpers should begin by using a shorter approach run of 12 strides. However, as jumpers gain experience, improve sprinting technique, and get stronger through conditioning programs, they can lengthen their approach runs to 14 strides and eventually to 19 strides. (Note that if a jumper's takeoff foot is the same foot that starts the run, there will be an even number of strides; if the jumper's takeoff foot is not the same as the foot that starts the run, there will be an odd number of strides.)

A successful approach run depends on the consistency of the first 2 or 3 strides. It is here that the jumper develops the rhythm of the run. If the run is inconsistent, it is usually because the first 2 or 3 strides are inconsistent. The coach and jumper can improve consistency by focusing on consistent effort in the first two or three steps through many repetitions of short and full approach runs.

The last two steps of the approach are important because they prepare, or set up, for the takeoff while conserving as much speed as possible. During the penultimate step, there is a lowering of the jumper's center of gravity (see figure 3.1, *a-c,* on page 32). This step is longer than the last step because of the acceleration curve, the lowering of the center of gravity, and the flexion of the knee and ankle of the supporting leg. Jumpers should feel the lowering, or gathering, of the body during the penultimate step. Because the penultimate step is different from a normal running stride, jumpers should not just run through this step. They must prepare the body during the penultimate step. The goal here is to be lower, but not slower. In addition, the foot is placed flat on the ground.

The last step is shorter than the penultimate step because of the raising of the jumper's center of gravity (see figure 3.1, *d-f,* on page 32). As the takeoff foot makes contact with the ground, the foot is placed flat and slightly in front of the jumper's body. In addition, there is a slight flexion of the joints of the takeoff leg. During this slight flexion, the muscles of the takeoff leg are forced into an active stretching phase, or eccentric contraction. Immediately following this active stretching phase, there is a shortening, or concentric contraction, of the muscles of the takeoff leg. When a concentric contraction is preceded by a phase of active stretching in the muscles of the takeoff leg, elastic energy is stored and the takeoff leg is "loaded up."

Jumpers should think of the last two steps as "long-short." This can help them set up the takeoff effectively. Jumpers must avoid reaching on the last step, causing the last two steps to be "long-long." Reaching, or placing the takeoff foot too far out in front of the body, will result in a braking effect and poor jump performance.

It is critical that jumpers stay relaxed and maintain approach speed through the last two steps. They must also continue to stroke their arms through the last two steps. Stopping the movement of the arms will result in a decrease in approach speed into the takeoff.

With beginning jumpers, it is best to work on the approach run without jumping. This allows them to focus on the approach run itself, developing a consistent acceleration (gradual distribution of energy), stride pattern, and rhythm through repetition. Even experienced jumpers will benefit from practicing the approach run without jumping to further develop the consistency and rhythm of the run.

To help a jumper achieve consistency in the approach run, the coach can place a check mark 4 strides out from the takeoff board. The position of the mark is determined by instructing the jumper to run a prescribed number of steps on the track and marking the point of the fourth step from the end. The jumper should repeat the run many times to ensure consistency. The coach then locates this measurement on the runway. The check mark should be between 26 and 31 feet (8 and 9.4 m) from the takeoff board. The distance from the board of the 4-stride check mark will vary depending on the jumper's height and speed and the distance of the approach run. Experienced jumpers—who are tall and fast and have 18-stride runs or more—should have check marks around 31 to 32 feet (9.4 to 9.8 m). A 32-foot check mark equals an 8-foot average step over the last 4 strides. More inexperienced jumpers—who are shorter and not as fast and have 12-stride runs—should have check marks around 26 feet (8 m). If, during a competition, a long-jumper is hitting the 4-stride mark at 27 (8.2 m) feet but is supposed to be hitting it at 31 feet (9.4 m), the jumper is probably too close to the takeoff board and is fouling or shortening the last 4 strides to get on the board.

APPROACH DRILLS

Because the long jump depends first on runway speed and second on the transition of this speed into the jump, drills should focus on developing these skills.

>> Drive Phase of the Runway <<

Purpose

To learn how to push out of a start and gradually reach a full upright position.

Performance

The drive phase is developed away from the runway. The athlete learns to push out of a standing start or rock-back start by keeping contact with the ground on the first two steps as long as possible. This places the upper body into a near-45-degree angle to the track. From this point, step by step through six to eight strides with progressing tempo, the athlete reaches a full upright position. Once the body is erect, pushing decreases as stride frequency becomes the goal.

>> Developing the Transition and Penultimate Step <<

Purpose

To get into a cadence while jogging: "right, left, right, left, flat-flat, and pop into the air."

Performance

The athlete is to develop a sequence of actions during warm-up or jogging activities. During the penultimate step, the hips lower slightly. During the takeoff, the trailing arm makes a 360-degree revolution. After becoming comfortable with this very elementary activity, the athlete can begin to incorporate the push acceleration phase with the transition phase. After practicing the sequence in six steps at medium speed, the athlete can move on to 8 to 10 steps at a higher speed, and finally to the full approach run.

TAKEOFF

The takeoff is a critical moment in the long jump. When a long-jumper breaks contact with the ground, the center of gravity forms a parabolic curve. Once in the air, nothing can be done to change this predetermined flight path. Therefore, it is important to practice correct takeoff mechanics.

The objective during the takeoff is to load up the takeoff leg to create a vertical impulse through the jumper's center of gravity. As the jumper's takeoff foot makes flat-footed contact with the ground and the leg is loaded up with elastic energy, a vertical impulse, or lift, is created through the center of gravity (see figure 3.2, *a-c,* on page 32). This vertical impulse created from the takeoff leg projects the jumper's body up and out into the air.

The takeoff foot should be placed directly in front of the body to allow for maximal vertical lift (see figure 3.2, *e-f,* on page 32). The takeoff foot must be placed flat on the board. Placing the foot heel first will cause a braking effect at takeoff. Placing the takeoff foot high up on the toes will minimize stabilization on impact, causing the leg to buckle or collapse. This also prevents the takeoff leg from loading up properly. A jumper should never try to pull back or claw the board with the takeoff foot.

The optimal position of the jumper's body at takeoff is upright and perpendicular to the ground (see figure 3.2g on page 32). In addition, the lead knee and opposite arm should be swung upward briefly to increase vertical forces against the ground (Ecker 1996; see figure 3.2, *h-i,* on page 32).

Coaches should encourage jumpers to think about bounding off the board first and then running up and out off the ground. Focusing only on running out off the ground tends to cause jumpers to not load up the takeoff leg and thus bypass a vertical impulse. As the body moves through the takeoff and up into the air, the jumper continues to run up and out off the ground.

Because of the large amount of horizontal force created during the run-up, takeoff angles in the long jump are rarely greater than 25 degrees. Jumpers should focus their eyes up and out when leaving the ground. They should not be looking down into the sand or at the takeoff board. Jumpers should not overemphasize jumping up high at the takeoff. A high angle of takeoff usually results in jumpers slowing down considerably to achieve the height, thus losing the critical speed needed at takeoff. Long-jumpers should remember to jump for distance, not for height.

A short approach run of eight strides will help jumpers work on takeoff technique. Short-run jumping allows jumpers to isolate and emphasize the takeoff mechanism at slower speeds. In addition, jumpers can take more jumps during training because they are not fatigued from too much running.

TAKEOFF DRILLS

The key to takeoff drills is to run or bound off the ground into the jump. The idea is to be very active off the ground and not lose horizontal momentum. Jumper's bodies should be fully erect, and their heads and eyes should be directed straight ahead. Emphasis must be on a forceful movement of the hips for maximum distance, both horizontal and vertical, prior to foot release at takeoff. Jumpers should create as large an impulse as possible.

▶▶ Split ◀◀

Purpose

To develop a large impulse off the ground.

Performance

This drill emphasizes a strong takeoff and balance during the forward rotation at takeoff. It is suitable for both the hang and hitch-kick styles of jump. This drill should be used only with a very short run, perhaps as little as three steps (left, right, left).

During the transition phase, the jump is initiated with very active arms. The lead arm moves forward and up to about eye level and is held at that position. The trailing arm is thrust back behind the hips and is nearly extended. Now the body is somewhat frozen, like a statue, with no forward rotation. The athlete maintains this position until landing. The only motion during the flight phase is the trailing arm, which rotates about 300 degrees. The foot of the lead leg lands in the sand simultaneously with the knee of the back leg. The jumper should maintain this split position with no rotations after landing. Sweatpants or other protective clothing can be worn to protect the knees during landing.

>> Alternate Split <<

Purpose

To develop the hitch-kick style of jump.

Performance

Athletes should use a short approach for this drill. Using the same execution as the split drill, the athlete takes off and holds the split for a short period of time, but then alternates the leading leg full cycle so it is trailing. The object is for the takeoff foot to contact the sand flat and the original leading leg to cycle back and land on the knee at the same time as the original takeoff foot is grounded. This creates an alternate leg action and at the same time a constant counterclockwise rotation of the arms. Sweatpants or other protective clothing can be worn to protect the knees during landing.

≫ Lead Arm Rotation ≪

Purpose

To develop the rotation of the lead arm in the hitch-kick style of jump.

Performance

Generally, long-jumpers have little difficulty with the rotation of the trailing arm, but many have difficulty with a counter-rotation of the lead arm. To help this rotation, the coach suspends a tether ball or other object so the athlete can touch it behind the body during the lead arm's desired 360-degree rotation. From six to eight steps and eventually farther, the jumper takes off into the pit and attempts to touch the object behind the shoulder during the lead arm rotation.

> **Figure 3.1** Single hitch-kick technique.

LANDING

Understanding the landing requires understanding the mechanics of the flight parabola. Picture the center of mass of the long-jumper as a ball. To get maximum distance out of the flight, the ball needs to complete the parabola and fall to the ground. The human body, however, has a head and arms and legs. All of these body parts reduce the distance the ball (center of mass) will travel. Rotations occur because there is weight ahead of the ball. In essence, the ball of the body cannot achieve its ultimate distance because the feet hit the sand before the ball can complete its total parabola.

When a jumper is in the air, the objective is to rotate the body into an efficient landing position that maximizes jump distance. Once contact with the ground is broken at takeoff, the jumper can do nothing to alter the flight path of the center of gravity.

The hitch-kick technique allows the jumper to counteract the forward rotation developed at the takeoff. The hitch kick is a counterrotation of the arms and legs while the athlete is airborne. It can best be described as a cycling action of both arms and legs that continues until just before the foot contacts the sand. Its function is to set up a secondary rotation counteracting the forward rotation that occurs as the long-jumper leaves the ground. Beginning jumpers should work on a single-arm and -leg revolution, whereas advanced jumpers should complete two revolutions.

Figure 3.1 represents the single hitch-kick technique. Figure 3.2 represents the double hitch-kick technique. By cycling the legs and arms through the air, the jumper can maintain an upright body position and set up for an efficient landing position. If the jumper did not counteract forward rotation by cycling the arms and legs, the body would continue

> **Figure 3.2** Double hitch-kick technique.

➤Figure 3.1, *continued*

to rotate forward into a facedown position in the sand.

Another technique for long-jumpers while in the air is the hang. This technique accomplishes the same task as the hitch kick by counteracting forward rotation in the air to achieve an efficient landing position. In the hang, the jumper keeps the body extended long after the takeoff without cycling the arms or the legs. The arms are extended high above the jumper's head, and the legs hang below the jumper's center of gravity. The hitch kick is more efficient than the hang because it reverses forward rotation more, allowing the jumper to slow down less at takeoff (Ecker 1996).

For an efficient landing, using either the hang or hitch-kick technique, the jumper extends and sweeps the arms down and backward toward the ground (figures 3.1, *m-n,* and 3.2, *m-n*). This action of the arms raises the legs up toward the torso and closer to the jumper's center of gravity.

Thus, the action of the arms causes an equal and opposite reaction with the legs. As the jumper makes contact with the sand, the knees bend and flex to cushion the impact (figures 3.1, *o-p,* and 3.2, *o-p*). In addition, the arms are brought forward to assist the jumper's forward momentum and keep the jumper from falling back.

The best jumps are the direct result of well-executed approach runs and takeoffs. Thus, jumpers having problems with undesirable rotation in the air and inefficient landings should always look to their approach runs and takeoffs. Improper placement of the takeoff foot can cause an inefficient landing. Reaching, or overstriding, into the takeoff causes a braking effect. Placing the foot too far under the hips causes too much forward rotation and cannot be efficient as a force application. The key is for the center of gravity to be as low as possible. Premature grounding of the feet caused by unchecked forward rotation is the culprit.

➤Figure 3.2, *continued*

LANDING DRILLS

▶▶ Elevated Takeoff and Landing ◀◀

Purpose

To practice proper takeoff, push-off of hips, arm activity, or landing.

Performance

This drill can be used directly from the runway or off a 6-inch (15 cm) box. From a short approach, the athlete—using any technique, hang or hitch kick—jumps into a padded pit or pole vault or gymnastics pad. Prior to landing, the athlete lifts the knees as high as possible and lands on the butt, feet, and hands at the same time. This prevents forward rotation, allows the arms and hands to move back behind the hips (thus shifting the center of mass back on the parabola), and gives the athlete a feeling of sliding the hips forward toward the feet.

▶▶ Slide to Feet ◀◀

Purpose

To allow for continued forward movement of the body.

Performance

This is an advanced version of the previous drill. The athlete uses a faster running speed and jumps directly into the long-jump pit. The goal is to not allow anything but the feet to contact the sand. The arms are back behind the hips, and the legs immediately flex, allowing the hips to slide up even with the feet before contacting the sand.

COMPETITION STRATEGY

Adverse weather conditions affect jump performances. More than anything, bad weather disrupts what happens on the runway. Therefore, when the weather is bad, jumpers should complete several full-effort approach runs prior to the competition. Most problems are detected at the coach's mark. If the athlete is coming down the runway with the same effort as in good weather conditions, adjustments should be made to get her on the coach's mark. This is done by having her move forward or backward from the starting point. Adverse winds especially can cause major changes in reaching the coach's mark.

In cold and windy conditions, athletes should spend more time warming up and should be sure to stay warm during the competition. In some cases, coaches may decide not to have the athletes complete all of the competition jumps. It is very difficult to stay warm during extremely cold and windy conditions.

The athlete and coach must make adjustments depending on the wind, rain, or cold weather. If there is a strong headwind during the competition, the jumper's approach run might need to be moved up 6 to 12 inches (15 to 30 cm) to allow him to reach the coach's mark and takeoff board at the right time. In a strong tailwind, the athlete might need to compensate by moving back 6 to 12 inches (15 to 30 cm).

Whatever the conditions may be, the coach and athlete must be able to adjust accordingly. Also, the athlete must listen to and trust the coach, focusing on the coach rather than on the other competitors.

PRACTICE CONSIDERATIONS

Generally speaking, long-jump training is sprint training, and vice versa. Sprint technique and speed are certainly the major components of a long-jumper's success. A specific progression of training speed, strength, and technique should always be adopted into the short-term and long-term training program.

As with any other event, the long-jump skills must be trained in progressions. Early in the season there is a need for general fitness, as in endurance and strength. Over time, this changes to specific endurance and specific strength activities and culminates in speed and technique applications specifically needed in the long jump.

Regardless of the level—high school, collegiate, or beyond—a program design is necessary. The idea is to build this program from the major competition backward to the beginning of training. Some athletes will have a year to prepare, but a younger athlete may have only two or three months to prepare. Regardless, general conditioning, specific training techniques, and speed must be incorporated into athletes' seasonal preparation. Remember, especially when dealing with younger athletes, that the individual techniques of jumping and sprint mechanics can and should be developed during warm-up activities. Warm-up activities should contain basic drills that emphasize the individual technical aspects incorporated into the long-jump event. Specifically, drills can be included for teaching the acceleration phase, the transition phase, the takeoff, and in-air activity.

Keep in mind the important factors: sprint mechanics, postural concerns, transition from horizontal speed to takeoff, foot placement, and in-flight activity and landing. All of these factors can and should be broken down and developed as single components. When working with and developing specific drills, remember that all athletes are unique and have specific strengths and weaknesses.

SAMPLE LONG-JUMP PROGRAM

	September to Mid-October (General Preparation Phase)	
Monday	Long-jump drills Weight training: Power cleans, bench presses, squats, pull-ups, bar dips, and leg curls (3 × 10 on all exercises, 60% of max effort)	Example of Tuesday workout during the general preparation phase: • Warm-up: 800 m, 10 minutes of stretching, 4 × 60 m buildups • 500-400-300 m: Run should be easy, with an 8- to 10-minute rest between efforts • Cool-down: 800 m
Tuesday	500-400-300 m or 2 × 500 and 4 × 100	
Wednesday	Circuit training: Step-ups, push-ups, jump rope, body squats, medicine ball seesaw, medicine ball overhead throw, medicine ball chest pass (2 × 30 seconds on each exercise with 20 seconds between exercises) Plyometrics: Hurdle hops (2 × 8 hurdles), box jumps (2 × 8 boxes)	
Thursday	6 × 150 or 8 × 100	
Friday	Stadium steps Weight training: Power cleans or hang cleans, incline presses, front squats, pull-ups, arm curls, leg curls, and bar dips (3 × 10 on all exercises, lighter than Monday) 8 × stadium steps	
Saturday	Rest	
Sunday	Jog 10 to 15 minutes	
	Mid-October to December (Specific Preparation Phase)	
Monday	Long-jump approach runs Weight training: Power cleans, bench presses, squats (4 × 5 on these exercises, 80% of max effort); pull-ups, bar dips, leg curls (3 × 10 on these exercises)	Example of Monday workout during the specific preparation phase: • Warm-up: 800 m, 10 minutes of stretching, 4 × 60 m buildups • 8 to 10 long approach runs, working on acceleration; establish coach's mark • Cool-down: 800 m • Weight training session
Tuesday	400-300-200 or 2 × 400 and 4 × 100 m	
Wednesday	Circuit training: Step-ups, push-ups, jump rope, body squats, medicine ball seesaw, medicine ball overhead throw, medicine ball chest pass (3 × 30 seconds on each exercise with 30 seconds between exercises) Plyometrics: Hurdle hops (3 × 8 hurdles), box jumps (2 × 8 boxes)	
Thursday	6 × 150 or 8 × 100 m	
Friday	Short-run jumps, stadium steps Weight training: Power cleans or hang cleans, incline presses, front squats (4 × 5 on these exercises, lighter than Monday); pull-ups, arms curls, leg curls, bar dips (3 × 10 on these exercises)	
Saturday	Rest	
Sunday	Jog 10 to 15 minutes	

January (Competition Phase—Indoor Season)		
Monday	Long-jump approach runs Weight training: Power cleans, bench presses, squats (4 × 5 on these exercises, 80% of max effort); pull-ups, bar dips, leg curls (3 × 10 on these exercises)	Example of Wednesday workout during the competition phase: • Warm-up: 800 m, 10 minutes of stretching, 4 × 60 m buildups • 8 to 10 short-run jumps, 6 to 10 strides, working on penultimate stride and getting takeoff foot down • Cool-down: 800 m • Weight training session
Tuesday	300-200-100 m	
Wednesday	Short-run jumps Weight training: Power cleans or hang cleans, incline presses, front squats (4 × 5 on these exercises, lighter than Monday); pull-ups, arm curls, leg curls, bar dips (3 × 10 on these exercises)	
Thursday	90-80-70-60 or 6 × 60 m	
Friday	Rest	
Saturday	Competition	
Sunday	Rest	

February (Competition Phase, Peak—Indoor Season)		
Monday	Long-jump approach runs Weight training: Power cleans, bench presses, squats (4 × 1, 2, or 3 on these exercises, 85 to 100% of max effort); pull-ups, bar dips, leg curls (3 × 10 on these exercises)	Example of Wednesday workout during the competition phase: • Warm-up: 800 m, 10 minutes of stretching • 6 to 8 medium-length runways and jumps, 12 to 14 strides • Cool-down: 800 m • Weight training session
Tuesday	4 × 150 m	
Wednesday	Short-run jumps	
Thursday	90-80-70-60 or 6 × 60 m	
Friday	Rest	
Saturday	Competition	
Sunday	Rest	

Early to Mid-March (Specific Preparation Phase—Following Indoor Season, Early Outdoor Season)		
Monday	Long-jump approach runs Weight training: Power cleans, bench presses, squats (4 × 5 on these exercises, 80% of max effort); pull-ups, bar dips, leg curls (3 × 10 on these exercises)	Example of Tuesday workout during the specific preparation phase: • Warm-up: 800 m, 10 minutes of stretching • 1 × 400 m, full recovery • 1 × 300 m, full recovery • 1 × 200 m, full recovery • Cool-down: 800 m
Tuesday	400-300-200 m	
Wednesday	Weight training: Power cleans or hang cleans, incline presses, front squats (4 × 5 on these exercises, lighter than Monday); pull-ups, arms curls, leg curls, bar dips (3 × 10 on these exercises)	
Thursday	6 × 150 or 8 × 100 m	
Friday	Stadium steps	
Saturday	Rest	
Sunday	Rest	

(continued)

(continued)

Mid-March to April (Competition Phase)		
Monday	Long-jump approach runs Weight training: Power cleans, bench presses, squats (4 × 1, 2, or 3 on these exercises, 85 to 100% of max effort); pull-ups, bar dips, leg curls (3 × 10 on these exercises)	Example of Monday workout during the competition phase: • Warm-up: 800 m, 10 minutes of stretching • 6 to 10 long-jump runways, stressing push phase and posture • Cool-down: 800 m • Weight training session
Tuesday	300-200-100 m	
Wednesday	Short-run jumps Weight training: Power cleans, bench presses, squats (4 × 1, 2, or 3 on these exercises, 85 to 100% of max effort); pull-ups, bar dips, leg curls (3 × 10 on these exercises)	
Thursday	90-80-70-60 or 6 × 60 m	
Friday	Rest	
Saturday	Competition	
Sunday	Rest	
May to June (Competition Phase)		
Monday	Long-jump approach runs Weight training: Power cleans, bench presses, squats (2 or 3 × 1 to 4 on these exercises, 80 to 100% of max effort, plus 1 × 10 at 70%); pull-ups, bar dips, leg curls (3 × 10 on these exercises)	Example of Thursday workout during the competition phase: • Warm-up: 800 m, 10 minutes of stretching • 6 × 60 m with full recovery • Cool-down: 800 m
Tuesday	4 × 150 m	
Wednesday	Short-run jumps	
Thursday	90-80-70-60 or 6 × 60 m	
Friday	Rest	
Saturday	Competition	
Sunday	Rest	

Chapter 4

Triple Jump

Boo Schexnayder

The triple jump is one of the most graceful events in athletics, and one of the most physically demanding, requiring high levels of physical preparation and technical skill. No event is more graceful when done well or more brutal to the competitor when done poorly. This chapter examines the triple jump in depth, addressing the demands, requirements for success, biomechanics and techniques, and schemes for teaching.

WARM-UP AND COOL-DOWN

A well-planned warm-up routine is important to ensuring top triple-jump performances. It can be broken down into two parts: the general warm-up and the specific warm-up. Following are guidelines for the content and timing of each.

The purpose of the general warm-up is to prepare the body for the intensity of the specific warm-up. It should begin at least one hour before the competition and should last from 20 to 30 minutes, depending on the level of the athlete. The general warm-up should be done in sweats and flats, be punctuated by the periodic intake of fluids, and contain the following:

1. A warm-up jog of approximately 800 meters with mild movement exercises such as skipping, backward jogging or skipping, and lateral shuffles mixed in periodically.
2. Five to six minutes of mild static stretching. Athletes should be very careful not to overdo this or to stretch too aggressively.

3. Five to six minutes of dynamic flexibility exercises and other challenging ballistic, range-of-motion exercises, such as leg swings, trunk twists, and arm circles.
4. Eight to 10 repetitions of various sprint development drills, with periodic 30-meter buildups mixed in.
5. Athletes requiring additional warm-up can do dynamic flexibility or sprint development drills.

The purpose of the specific warm-up is to prepare the body for the intensity of competition. It should begin 20 to 30 minutes before the competition, depending on the level of the athlete and the level of competition. The specific warm-up should be done in light warm-up gear and spikes and should contain the following:

1. Two aggressive buildup runs on the track, including one of at least 50 meters in length
2. Two repetitions of 15 meters of mild bounding
3. Two or three approach runs

4. Two or three triple jumps performed from approach runs of 8 to 10 steps

When waiting for later flights, athletes should stay active with sprint drills or dynamic flexibility exercises. Those jumping in a very late flight should consider postponing the start of the warm-up and beginning the specific warm-up as the previous flight is ending. Championship meets often have more formal check-in procedures that take more time. Athletes should be prepared for them and adjust their warm-up start times if necessary. Special sports medicine needs may also necessitate an earlier arrival time or warm-up start time.

After the competition, proper closure should take place. This closure should consist of several parts:

- A discussion and evaluation of the competition between the coach and athlete
- An evaluation of any minor injuries
- A proper cool-down

The cool-down itself can take many forms, depending on the athlete's state of health and other upcoming competitions. Generally speaking, postmeet cool-down procedures should include the following:

1. Jogging in sweats until perspiration occurs
2. Local icing of any acute injury sites
3. Continued proper hydration and nutrition, depending on any upcoming competitions
4. A later lukewarm Epsom salt bath to facilitate muscle relaxation

DEMANDS OF THE TRIPLE JUMP

A good place to begin the design of a training program for any event is to thoroughly examine the demands of the event and identify the qualities needed for successful performances. As we examine the triple jump, several obvious (and many not-so-obvious) demands surface. These are listed and discussed individually next. The triple-jumper must be capable of handling all these demands before great performances can be expected.

Speed and the ability to accelerate Speed contributes directly to good triple-jump performances. The velocity attained prior to takeoff might be the most important determinant of success. The importance of velocity, combined with the fact that the nature of the event limits approach distances, points out the importance of acceleration capabilities. The jumper must be able to overcome inertia and accelerate in a powerful, efficient manner. Athletes with good speed abilities are not necessarily good accelerators, though, and vice versa. Both of these qualities must be developed in the training program. The quality of acceleration also determines momentum values, so acceleration capabilities must be technically sound as well.

Ability to handle impact Throughout the phases of the triple jump, the jumper must manage large impact forces with each landing and takeoff. The ability to handle these impacts without undue duress or breaking down is essential to achieving good performances in the event.

External force production External forces are forces the jumper applies to the ground during performance—specifically, the pushing applied to the ground during the run and jump. The ability to create large external forces enables the performer to accelerate well, achieve high velocities, and create great takeoff forces. Large external force production is necessary for achieving good performances, but the time available to apply these forces in the triple jump is short.

Ability to handle internal forces Throughout all phases of the triple jump, forces generated within the body are high. The ability to generate and control these internal forces enables successful performance. The core of the body must be capable of harnessing and controlling the torques created by the limbs.

The musculoskeletal system is primarily a system of third-class levers. Anchoring the fulcrums of these levers is essential to the efficient operation of these lever systems. This anchoring function is critical to the body's ability to handle internally generated forces. The body must also be able to withstand the transmission of these internal forces. For example, the muscles of the core of the body must stabilize so that the body can maintain alignment as the limbs move during sprinting. Connective tissue structures such as ligaments, tendons, and fascia must be strong enough to withstand the forces they are subjected to as internal forces are generated.

Large ranges of motion Attaining large ranges of motion in the triple jump assists in producing powerful takeoffs and controlling unwanted rotations. Large ranges of motion enable high levels of displacement and good performances. Therefore, flexibility can have a great bearing on the technical aspects of the event.

Coordination The high speeds involved in performing the triple jump require that precise movements be performed in extremely short periods of time. For this reason, coordination is important. The athlete must possess coordination in a general sense and be able to execute the techniques of the event flawlessly and repetitively.

Elastic energy The ability to create force via the stretch reflex, especially at takeoff, is essential to high performance in the triple jump. Stretch reflexes are also created in other body parts and situations, including postural musculature. High levels of elastic energy production are a hallmark of great performances in this event.

APPROACH

The approach run in the triple jump, as in any other jumping event, plays a critical part in performance. The approach run should serve the following three purposes:

- Provide the velocity needed for good performances

Andy Lyons/Getty Images

- Provide accuracy, delivering the jumper to the board without excessive adjustments in stride, to maximize distance

- Place the jumper in a good physical position and in a correct cyclic pattern of movement from which to execute the takeoff

Approach runs in the triple jump typically vary from 12 to 18 steps in length, with higher-level performers typically using longer runs. The number of steps is of more concern than the actual distance, because the number of steps determines the potential velocity at takeoff. Longer runs provide more velocity, but if an athlete's technique is not sound and the velocity achieved exceeds the athlete's coordination capabilities, then good performances will occur only by chance.

Acceleration is the fundamental component of all jump approaches. All approaches, in their simplest form, are accelerations to maximal desired velocity. In the final stage of the approach, the athlete achieves maximal velocity mechanics. There may be unique distributions and patterns of frequency development, but the process remains the same.

For the sake of discussion, the approach run is broken down into four phases. Although each phase has unique features and presents unique coaching challenges, we divide the approach run for the sake of discussion; in fact, these phases must blend smoothly, with no radical mechanical changes. These phases are, in order, as follows:

1. Start
2. Drive phase
3. Continuation phase
4. Transition phase

The triple-jumper should employ a start that not only places the jumper in the correct position to execute the remainder of the approach, but is also consistent enough to meet accuracy goals. Typically, crouch starts and rollover starts fit these needs and are the best choices.

In a crouch start, the jumper separates the heel of the front foot and the toe of the rear foot by 6 to 8 inches (15 to 20 cm). The knee of the front foot is located over the toe of that foot, placing that shin at an acute angle to the runway. The shoulders should be positioned very close to the front thigh, the head low and neck relaxed, and the hips elevated so that they are at least as high as the shoulders. From this position, the jumper pushes upward and outward forcefully into the first step.

The primary disadvantage of the crouch start is that the jumper has no visual contact with the board or pit prior to the start. This can be remedied with a rollover start. In this start, the jumper stands upright, rocks back onto the rear foot, then shifts the weight and bends forward, flexing at the waist. From this position, the jumper drives forcefully upward and outward into the first step.

With either start, the goal is to create a powerful displacement of the jumper's body. This displacement should occur at an angle of about 50 degrees, and at the completion of the start, the jumper should display a body lean of the same degree. Although standing up or pushing too hard is an error and results in poor momentum development, pushing out at too low an angle causes stumbling, poor displacement, and other problems as well.

The drive phase comprises approximately the first third of the approach. The primary goal of the drive phase is momentum development. To achieve this goal, the jumper should exhibit low stride frequency and high displacement values. The steps are powerful driving-type steps. Most of the acceleration achieved in the approach should be accomplished in this phase. In addition, the drive phase is characterized by a smooth progression from the forward body lean at the completion of the start to a nearly upright posture. This progression of body angles should result from the legs powerfully and repeatedly pushing the hips upward into a position of good posture. With each step, the direction of force application becomes less horizontal and more vertical.

It is critical that the coach understand the value of the drive phase as a momentum development tool. Many faults at takeoff result because the jumper senses inadequate momentum; these can be traced to failure to develop momentum during the drive phase.

The continuation phase follows the drive phase. It is characterized by continued (but less pronounced) acceleration and the attainment of maximal velocity mechanics. Running postures are upright, and force application to the ground with each step is primarily vertical.

The transition phase consists of the final four steps of the approach, as the athlete makes the transition into takeoff. It is characterized by good maximal velocity mechanics. Although the mechanics in the transition phase are not very different from those in the continuation phase, they are separate because of the special problems athletes experience as takeoff nears.

The transition phase is critical to triple-jump success. These last four steps provide the environment from which the jump is performed and are the site of many common errors. A good triple-jump coach understands that good mechanics in this phase contribute to good performance, and that errors in this phase relate to errors in other phases of the event.

In the final few steps, adherence to good running mechanics is key. Not only do good running mechanics place the body in the proper position to take off, but they also establish patterns of movement that easily blend into proper takeoff and jumping mechanics. Here we address the mechanics of these steps and how they relate to triple-jump performance.

The jumper should preserve good running mechanics, velocity, posture, and amplitude of movement in the final few steps of the run. These processes should continue up to and through takeoff. The jumper's primary concern should be to position the body for an effective takeoff.

The jumper should focus on smooth continuation of the acceleration process. Deceleration is a frequent error. Accelerating too aggressively in the transition phase is another frequent mistake. This fault can result in forward lean, reduced amplitudes of movement, and an inability to time the movements of the hop phase. An increase in frequency in the final few steps should not occur at a rate greater than the natural increase displayed earlier in the approach.

A common reason jumpers make the mistake of accelerating too aggressively in the final steps is that they sense inadequate momentum. The remedy for this situation is to improve the quality of the drive phase so the jumper feels comfortable in the final steps. Momentum should be developed early in the approach so that the jumper can relax and position for takeoff as takeoff nears.

One special aspect of the transition phase is the penultimate step. In other jumping events, the penultimate step differs from a normal sprint step. The way the foot contacts the ground is altered, and the body's center of mass is lowered to set up an increased angle of takeoff.

The takeoff angles desired in the triple jump, however, are considerably lower than those in other jumping events. In fact, these takeoff angles do not differ greatly from the takeoff angles in typical sprint strides. For this reason, unlike in other jumping events, the penultimate step in the triple jump should display no radical mechanical difference from other steps of the approach.

Although not typically considered, vertical movements during the approach have a great effect on the jumper's ability to execute the takeoff and subsequent movements correctly. Efficient runners, when viewed from the side, exhibit a very slight bounce as they run. The body's center of mass traces a sinusoidal path. High points of this wavelike path correspond to periods of flight, and low points correspond to periods of ground contact.

This path of the body's center of mass is critical because it sets up an environment of vertical undulation as the jumper approaches the board. Good triple-jumpers amplify this vertical undulation to create the three phases of the jump. The necessity of this vertical undulation also emphasizes the need for the pushing kinetics previously discussed. This type of force application to the ground best ensures the development of a vertical force component with each step. Triple-jumpers can be taught to display and maintain vertical undulation by staying relaxed in the final steps of the approach, keeping the hips elevated, and pushing vertically against the ground with each step.

Triple-jumpers who lack vertical undulations inherently alter the run and takeoff, compromising the jump. Mistakes such as exaggerated penultimate steps, lowering in the final steps, and excessively high hops are all maneuvers triple-jumpers frequently use to compensate for a lack of vertical undulation.

Clearly, preserving these vertical undulations of the center of mass in the final few steps is crucial. Also, in the final steps, horizontal velocities are almost completely established. For this reason, the jumper should attempt to aggressively push the body upward with each final step.

Perhaps the best way for the coach to evaluate vertical undulation is to observe the jumper's shin angles in the final few steps. At contact, the angle the shin shows with respect to the track should be nearly vertical (the knee should be only very slightly in front of the ankle). Two errors are noticeable when examining shin angles and the direction of force application. In one case, the feet begin to contact the ground in front of the body's center of mass, and shin angles become obtuse. This results in deceleration and excessively high takeoffs. In the other case, the jumper begins to push off from each step in a more horizontal direction. Shin angles become more acute, and vertical undulation is compromised. This often happens because the jumper begins to anticipate the flat takeoff from the board prematurely. The triple-jumper should not be concerned with developing horizontal takeoff forces until the takeoff foot contacts the board.

Triple-jumpers should not show any deviation in normal running arm action in the final steps. It is a frequent error for triple-jumpers (especially those using a double-arm technique) to gather the arms early, causing deceleration and unwanted lowering of the body's center of mass.

Jumpers inherently adjust the lengths of their final steps to arrive at a good takeoff location. This is commonly called *steering*. Although rehearsal of the approach is essential to minimize the need for excessive steering, it is important to accept that steering does and should take place. For this reason, proper visual focus patterns should be taught to facilitate steering. In the drive phase, as soon as the body angle permits, the jumper should look directly at the board. Later, in the continuation phase, the jumper should keep the head upright but continue to maintain visual contact with the board using peripheral vision. In the transition phase, the jumper should keep the head upright. This necessitates losing visual contact with the board. However, if the jumper has been tracking the board visually up to this point, a sense of perceived velocity and the board's location has been established, and tracking the board without visual contact in these last few steps is typically not difficult.

APPROACH DRILLS

Although space dictates that this discussion of teaching strategies for the triple jump center on the takeoff phase of the jump, clearly, we cannot neglect the importance of developing acceleration capability, running mechanics, and the approach. The following drills can also be used for the long jump, because the long jump and the triple jump employ the same approach mechanics.

>> Wall <<

Purpose

To learn the positions involved in starting, accelerating, and using the force generated by the legs throughout the approach to push the body from its initial lean into an upright running posture.

Procedure

The athlete is in a starting position 4 to 5 feet (1.5 m) from a wall. The athlete fires forward toward the wall as in a start, places the hands out in front of the body to catch the wall, and braces the body at arm's length. This should position the body so that it is leaning against the wall at a 45-degree angle, with the hands on the wall and the arms extended. After a brief pause, the athlete takes five or six small steps with high knees so the body's angle of incline gradually decreases until the body is upright and the athlete's toes are against the wall.

>> Resisted Runs <<

Purpose

To assist in power development; helps to enhance acceleration abilities and drive phase mechanics.

Procedure

The athlete performs short, fast sprints of 20 to 50 meters using some type of resistance to increase the demand. Pulling a sled, running uphill, and using a harness can all provide the needed resistance.

>> Track Approaches <<

Purpose

To eliminate the distractions of the board and sand pit so the athlete can focus on the approach.

Procedure

The athlete performs actual meet-length approach runs on the track, away from the distractions of the board and the sand pit. Once consistency is established, the athlete can move to the runway.

TAKEOFF

The takeoff from the board in triple jumping is one of the most difficult skills to master in track and field. When taking off from the board, the triple-jumper must achieve several goals: conserve horizontal velocity, maintain good jumping posture, and set up mechanically correct subsequent movements.

The triple-jumper arriving at the board must conserve good posture. Head and pelvic alignments should be maintained as described previously. Dropping the head to look at the board, titling the head back, and leaning back are all frequent errors. Ideal pelvic alignment is both difficult and crucial; initiating takeoff with poor pelvic alignment makes this task nearly impossible.

The position of the takeoff leg with respect to the body is important when the jumper's foot touches the takeoff board. Generally speaking, the takeoff foot should be grounded underneath the body's center of mass to best maintain horizontal velocity. A good coaching practice is to note the position of the shin as the foot touches down. A vertical shin at this point is consistent with the best takeoff. An obtuse shin angle (knee behind the ankle) is consistent with excessive deceleration at takeoff, whereas an acute shin angle introduces too much forward rotation too soon into the jump effort.

Prior to impact with the board, the jumper should stabilize the ankle to best accept impact and amortize forces. Placing the ankle in a dorsiflexed position prior to the foot's touchdown accomplishes this stabilization. The heel should lead the movement of the foot to the board prior to contact, and foot contact should be nearly flat. During the support phase, the jumper should initiate a rolling action of the foot against the surface, using the entire surface of the foot to absorb impact forces.

Late in the support phase of takeoff, the ankle should bridge. This bridging consists of flexion at the ball of the foot as body weight moves onto the forefoot, with the ankle remaining stable at a 90-degree angle. Failure to bridge and collapse of the ankle (the ankle moves to an angle less than 90 degrees) typically result from poor ankle stabilization prior to ground contact. An absence of bridging may also result from the jumper's failure to displace and execute the takeoff correctly. This fault will be discussed in more detail shortly.

Proper leg-firing sequences and timing during takeoff are critical. Takeoff velocities and trajectories are determined by these actions of the takeoff leg. More important, correct firing patterns during takeoff elicit reflexes that allow the jumper to perform the hop and step much more effectively.

The jumper should remain patient for a fraction of a second once the foot touches the board and wait for the shin to rotate forward until the knee is positioned significantly in front of the ankle (over the toes) and the foot begins to bridge. This rotation of the shin may even be associated with a very slight lowering of the body's center of mass as the jumper moves past the board. Once this position is reached, the jumper should aggressively push off the board in a forward direction by extending the hip. This hip extension should be timed so that the force application is directed along the axis of the shin. If this is done correctly, the jumper will feel a sensation of pushing off the board and feel pressure on the ball of the bridged foot throughout takeoff.

A common error of triple-jumpers is to initiate the hip extension too early in the takeoff. Rather than waiting for the shin to rotate and then pushing, the jumper pulls or grabs the board early. This error frequently results when the jumper has failed to perform the proper pushing kinetics in the final steps of the approach. These pushing strides set up patterns of movement that are easily modified into a good push-off from the board. Pulling-type steps yield faulty, pulling-type takeoffs.

Continuous displacement is important at takeoff. The triple-jumper should continue to move horizontally throughout this entire sequence of movement. If the jumper does this correctly, he should move a great distance beyond the planted takeoff foot before the foot leaves the ground. A good coaching landmark is the position of the jumper's hips as the take-off foot loses contact with the board. The hips should be located a great distance beyond the foot. Good, sustained ankle bridging is also characteristic of good displacement.

High degrees of horizontal displacement at takeoff are essential to good triple jumping, but they do pose one problem. When displacing to such great degrees, the body is subject to forward rotation, and the pelvis tends to rotate forward into a position of poor posture.

During takeoff, these problems are countered by the action of the free leg. In coordination with the push-off from the board, the jumper should aggressively move the front surface of the thigh forward, effectively creating a great split between the thighs as takeoff is completed. This movement of the free leg counters the forward rotation of the pelvis. A common error in the free-leg action is driving the knee upward rather than the thigh forward. This elicits the body's flexion reflex, resulting in hip flexion that introduces even more pelvic misalignment. A forward movement of the thigh enables that side of the pelvis to move forward more freely into a position of good alignment.

At takeoff, arm actions should increase in amplitude and coordinate smoothly with take-off. Two types of arm movements are typically used at takeoff. In the first, the single-arm technique, the jumper leaves the board with the arms moving in the same alternating fashion displayed during the approach—one arm moving forward and the other backward. In the double-arm technique, both arms are pushed forward simultaneously as the jumper leaves the board. Athletes using a single-arm takeoff should split the arms forcefully and extend at the elbow in concert with takeoff. Athletes using a double-arm technique should push the arms forward smoothly in concert with the push-off from the board.

Takeoff drills can be found on page 57 in the fundamental drill series section later in this chapter.

BOUNDING SKILLS

Teaching the bounding skills associated with triple jumping is an important part of coaching the event. Many coaches teach the hop, step, and jump phases separately. However, these phases have many technical elements in common, and these are addressed in this section. A discussion of the unique aspects of the individual phases follows. Bounding skills can be grouped into three categories: posture, ground contact patterns, and swinging segment usage.

Posture

As in the approach run and takeoff, conservation of postural integrity throughout the phases of the triple jump is essential to good performance. Stability is an important component of postural integrity. Triple-jumpers are subject to huge impact forces from each phase as they land, and the core of the body must remain stable under this impact. Alignment is important as well. The head should remain aligned in a neutral position with respect to the spine, and forward and backward lean should be avoided.

Alignment of the pelvis is the most critical element of posture in bounding. As mentioned previously, the pelvis should be aligned in a neutral position with respect to the spine. In triple jumping, the pelvis acts as the rudder of the body, directly determining the ability to create flight in each phase. Without fail, faulty triple-jump phases (including the common poor step phase problem) are caused by anterior pelvic tilt and an excessively lordotic posture. Even small misalignments can have a great effect on performance. For this reason, establishing and maintaining mobility and flexibility in this area are very important.

Pelvic alignment (and posture in general) should not be associated with total rigidity. Small movements of the pelvis are important in initiating leg movements and fighting forward rotation. Throughout the phases, even the best triple-jumpers lose postural alignment slightly and regain it repeatedly. It is best to think of proper pelvic posture throughout the phases as pelvic movement within a certain range of movement, rather than as a static position.

Many technical aspects of the triple jump are geared toward preserving pelvic alignment. We have already discussed how proper free-leg action at takeoff assists in this goal, and we point out several other posture-preserving techniques as our discussion continues.

Ground Contact Patterns

Before discussing the specifics of contact patterns in triple jumping, we examine muscle function during jumping. Efficient jumping involves the following three phases of muscular activity:

1. *Stabilization of the joints of the takeoff leg.* Stabilization of the joints of the takeoff leg is accomplished by isometric muscle contractions in the extensor muscles of the leg. These contractions are developed during the flight phase prior to contact and enable the leg to withstand impact without buckling.

2. *Eccentric activity.* On impact, the joints of the leg flex slightly, placing a stretch on the extensor muscles, particularly the quadriceps,

of the leg. This enables the leg to develop stretch reflexes that increase takeoff forces. The quality of this eccentric phase depends on the quality of the isometric stabilization.

3. *Concentric activity.* At the end of the eccentric phase, the leg extends powerfully to propel the body into flight. This push-off is assisted by stretch reflexes activated during the eccentric phase.

Because of the high-impact forces encountered in the phases of the triple jump, proper stabilization of the takeoff leg prior to impact is crucial. During the flight time prior to impact, stabilization in the form of isometric muscle contractions should be developed about the knee and the ankle. The jumper should stabilize the knee by isometrically contracting the quadriceps. He should stabilize the ankle by placing it in a position of dorsiflexion.

Because impact and force amortization needs in bounding resemble those in the takeoff from the board, the mechanics of ground contact are similar. The athlete's heel should lead the movement of the foot to the board prior to contact, and foot contact should be nearly flat. During the support phase, the jumper should initiate a rolling action of the foot against the surface, using the entire surface of the foot to absorb impact forces.

A frequent error in triple jumping (especially during the hop phase landing) is plantar-flexing the foot, pointing the toe just prior to impact, which results in a toe-first landing. This is an interesting dilemma, because dorsiflexion and correct ground contact patterns are usually inherent even in untrained individuals. The answer to fixing this error lies in understanding the body's stability reflex. When humans in flight experience excessive forward rotation, they tend to hasten ground contact to regain stability. The plantar flexion we see in triple-jump phases is almost always a reaction to excessive forward rotation. Interestingly, anterior pelvic tilt introduces instability and results in the same plantar flexion problem. Good coaching practice calls for repairing the cause of the forward rotation or postural problem rather than directly addressing plantar flexion of the foot.

When bounding, the foot should contact the ground only slightly in front of the body's center of mass—this is defined as *front-side distance*. Although velocity and impulse demands dictate that the foot land slightly in front of the center of mass, excessive front-side distance results in deceleration, and buckling in extreme cases. Conversely, absence of a slight front-side distance creates excessive forward rotation.

The jumper should balance eccentric and concentric activity. As discussed earlier, the body creates force best when isometric preparation, eccentric activity, and concentric work take place in sequence. The backward movement of the foot as it approaches the ground, which is seen in triple-jumpers, is a result of natural continued cyclic movement; it does not result from actively pulling back against the ground. When jumpers use aggressive grabbing or clawing movements, premature concentric work results. The isometric and eccentric phases are bypassed. This excessive emphasis on concentric work in the form of aggressive hip extension weakens the isometric preparation of the quadriceps, diminishes gains from the stretch reflex, and frequently causes injury. For these reasons, jumpers should not use grabbing or clawing actions.

Swinging Segment Usage

Swinging segments are the limbs (both arms and the free leg) that execute swinging movements during the takeoff of a jump. Much of the power developed during the takeoff of each triple-jump phase is a result of the movement of these body parts.

During the takeoff of each phase, the arms should execute a strong, powerful swinging movement. When swinging the arms, the jumper should use large ranges of motion at the shoulder. Also, the arms should be extended at the elbow. A jumper using a single-arm technique should display an exaggerated, alternating swinging movement. The arms should be swung in an extended position, so that the front arm reaches a position roughly parallel to the ground while the rear arm moves back into a position that places that hand behind the body,

just above the waist. Jumpers using a double-arm technique should begin in an extended position with the hands located behind the body about waist high. The arms should then be swung powerfully to a position that places the hands in front of the face and the elbows at 90 degrees, slightly wider than the shoulders.

The free leg should display large amplitudes of movement as well. This free-leg action should not be purely angular. The hip should advance while the free leg swings. The swing should be initiated with the leg in an extended position. Although the leg need not be completely straight, triple-jumpers frequently err by bending the knee prematurely. In these cases, the knee is driven upward rather than the leg being swung in an extended position. This extended position of the free leg when starting the swing is critical because it preserves and may even improve pelvic alignment and posture.

The reason for using this technique with the free leg becomes apparent when we consider the flexion reflex. When abrupt flexion occurs in a joint, other joints in the limb tend to flex as well. When the swing is initiated with flexion of the knee, the hip tends to flex also. This hip flexion blocks that side of the pelvis from moving forward, creates anterior pelvic tilt, and accelerates forward rotation. It is true that triple-jumpers often display flexed knees in the phases, particularly during the step phase. This knee lift and knee flexion is permissible, but the knee flexion should occur later in the swing.

Finally, blocking is an important part of proper swinging segment usage. At the instant the body leaves the ground, the arms and free leg must stop swinging and then naturally reverse direction. This imparts the momentum of these swinging segments to the body.

PHASES OF THE TRIPLE JUMP

Examining bounding skills as a group is a good introduction to the phases of triple jumping. However, the phases themselves are unique and should be studied individually as well. This section examines the phases of the triple jump—the hop, the step, and the jump—and the unique techniques and coaching practices that apply to them. Mastery of these aspects of the jump is frequently the difference between good and great performances.

Hop

The first phase of the triple jump is the hop phase (figure 4.1). Rules dictate that the triple-jumper land on and take off from the same foot that was used in the takeoff from the board. The goal of the hop phase is to achieve distance, conserve horizontal velocity, and position the body to execute the next phase (the step) correctly.

A prerequisite to successfully coaching or performing the hop phase is an understanding of reflexive action and its effect on the movements of the hop. Proper running mechanics and a good takeoff set up reflexive actions that greatly improve the quality of movement in the hop and give the jumper a much better chance of executing the hop correctly.

The leg activity during the hop phase is actually very simple. It consists of a forward movement of the thigh once the takeoff from the board is essentially complete. Much of this forward movement of the thigh is an elastic reaction to stretch reflexes set up in the hip flexor muscles. As the athlete displaces during takeoff, the hip flexors stretch. The rebound from this stretch initiates the thigh movement.

Other than this forward movement of the thigh, the hop cycle is a very passive, reflexive activity. Perhaps the most common fault in triple jumping is pulling the hop leg through too soon or too aggressively. Cuing triple-jumpers to simply allow the hop leg to fall to the ground after takeoff is complete can be very valuable at times.

Many triple-jumpers display a high recovery of the foot during the hop cycle. The foot passes very close to the buttocks as it moves forward.

Figure 4.1 The hop.

This high recovery should not be a goal unto itself. This recovery is the result of a transfer of angular momentum in the lower leg, not deliberate flexion of the knee. When the knee is deliberately flexed, the body's flexion reflex causes hip flexion to occur as well. This hip flexion creates anterior pelvic tilt and accelerates forward rotation.

Late in the hop phase, the leg should stabilize and prepare for impact as discussed earlier. Isometric stabilization of the quadriceps is an important part of this stabilization. Excessive knee flexion and excessively high recoveries delay this preparation of the quadriceps. For this reason, teaching these techniques is questionable with beginners who lack adequate flight time to prepare properly for impact. Emphasizing low recovery heights during the hop phase is a good practice with beginning triple-jumpers.

The free-leg movement during the hop phase is frequently neglected, but plays an important part in conserving posture and balance at this time. Unlike the hop-leg cycle, the free-leg cycle is an active movement that plays an important role in the timing of the hop phase movements. After completing takeoff, the hip should extend and the knee should straighten somewhat so that the leg extends and falls. Although the knee need not extend completely, some straightening is important here. The foot of the free leg should be in front of the body for an instant during this movement. This movement resembles a hitch kick and serves the same purpose in controlling forward rotation. These active movements of the free leg also delay the cycling action of the hop leg, improving the timing of the phase.

The human body is designed to walk and run using a left-right-left-right pattern. Movement becomes confused with successive rights or lefts. This fact provides further rationale for an active free leg after takeoff. Although the free leg does not touch the ground, actively performing this hitch-kick-like motion preserves the alternating left-right pattern.

Figure 4.1, *continued.*

Figure 4.2   The step.

Step

The second phase of the triple jump is the step phase (figure 4.2). Rules dictate that the triple-jumper land on and take off from a different foot than was used during the takeoff from the board and the hop phase. The goal of the step phase is to achieve distance, conserve horizontal velocity, and preserve posture.

The step phase is a relatively simple maneuver for any athlete with adequate bounding skills. Cause-and-effect coaching is perhaps more applicable here than in any other instance in track and field, because nearly all poor steps are caused by poor pelvic alignment, resulting from faults in the takeoff or hop phase.

When moving from the hop to the step phase, here more than any other instance, the jumper

Figure 4.3   The jump.

must initiate the swing with the free leg in a lengthened position. This is a critical moment in which pelvic alignment can be gained or lost; proper swinging mechanics here can make a big difference in performance distances. Although many jumpers display a high knee during the step, it is a common fault to bend and drive the knee prematurely. It is frequently good coaching practice to deemphasize high knees with beginners, so they can more easily swing the leg in an extended position. The athlete should not attempt to flex the knee until the swing leg is positioned approximately perpendicular to the ground.

A key coaching point of the step phase is developing a high takeoff angle. The takeoff angle in the step phase should be higher than that of the takeoff from the board. Because this is an inherently unnatural act for the triple-jumper, a concerted effort must be made to achieve consistency in performing this aspect of the jump correctly. This is accomplished by good isometric preparation of the limb prior to the hop landing and a concerted attempt to push up early and vertically. At this point in the event, horizontal forces are already established, so it is good coaching practice to have the jumper envision the step takeoff as purely vertical.

Jump

The final phase of the triple jump is the jump phase (figure 4.3). The goal of the jump phase is to achieve distance, conserve horizontal velocity, and position the body for an effective landing.

The jump phase is a simple bounding maneuver. As in the step phase, the secret to success in the jump phase is performing prior movements correctly so that the jumper arrives in position to execute the jump correctly.

Maintaining composure is important when executing the jump phase. The phase is very simple to execute, but frequently the simplest fundamentals of bounding are violated because of the anticipated completion of the effort. Posture and swinging mechanics are often compromised. The jumper must remain technically disciplined through this final takeoff. A frequent error in the takeoff of the jump phase is failure to block properly. Jumpers often err by continuing to lift the arms after takeoff. Proper blocking should occur prior to beginning flight mechanics.

Figure 4.3, *continued.*

During the flight of the jump phase, control of forward rotation is a concern. Some jumpers can perform a hitch-kick maneuver with the free leg, but usually flight time limits the jumper to a hang technique. The arms should be extended high overhead to effectively lengthen the body and control forward rotation. This lifting of the arms should be done only after the blocking movement at takeoff is complete.

Landing

At the peak of flight, the jumper should begin to prepare for landing (figure 4.4). Throughout the preparation for landing and the landing itself, the torso and head should remain upright. It is a common error to drop the torso toward the thighs. This effectively shortens the body's effective radius and accelerates forward rotation.

The extended arms begin a downward sweep from high overhead, and the legs are brought forward and extended in anticipation of land-ing. A common error is to begin preparing for landing too late, during the descent. This late preparation frequently results in the feet contacting the sand prematurely as they are brought forward.

At impact, the jumper should permit forward movement to continue by flexing at the hips and knees, allowing the buttocks to move forward toward the heels. It is common practice to turn the body during this flexion to ease pressure on the knees. This is an acceptable practice, but it is critical that the shoulders stay square until the jumper hits the sand. Turning prematurely results in a countering rotation of the lower body and causes one foot to land in front of the other, decreasing the measured distance.

Finally, as the buttocks reach the heels, the jumper should kick aggressively, extending the knees so that the feet leave the sand. This permits the buttocks to fall into the hole made by the feet so that distance is conserved.

Figure 4.4 The landing.

COMPETITION STRATEGY

Practice is not the only consideration in training triple-jumpers. They also need to be prepared for the complexities of competition. The triple-jumper should arrive at the competition facility at least 90 minutes prior to the competition. Upon arrival, the jumper should immediately do the following:

1. Check shoes, spikes, and any other equipment.

2. Become familiar with the facility, ascertaining the location of the jumping area, restrooms, sports medicine areas, water stations, warm-up areas, and any special check-in locations.

3. Visit the competition site to check in, if officials are present, and to place check marks.

4. Ascertain flight assignment and position in the jumping order.

5. Obtain any needed attention from sports medicine professionals.

The triple-jumper should have a plan for each competition. Although this competition plan will vary greatly depending on the nature of the competition and the athlete's unique abilities and situation, several general guidelines apply.

- Stay task oriented. Always know the key things you must do to succeed, and also be aware of your potential problems and strategies for handling them.

- Keep in mind that most successful jumpers typically hit two good jumps in the course of a competition. Use other jumps to position yourself for these.

- If you find yourself struggling, slow the back of the run and focus on the takeoff from the board.

- When you are jumping well, stay aggressive until you hit a poor jump. Then, be a bit conservative on the next one to get back into rhythm, and then be aggressive again.

- Focus on a perfect approach run on jumps 2 and 5. This will put you in a good position to hit big jumps on your third and sixth jumps.

- Consciously try to keep the drive phase of the run consistent, especially in pressure situations.

- Be aware at all times of your place in the competition and opportunities to move up. If you can't win, try to beat as many people as you can.

- If you can't beat your best mark, work hard to get a good backup jump in case of an eventual tie.

- Don't overthink, especially in major competitions, but don't be oblivious to the competition either.

PRACTICE CONSIDERATIONS

This section includes drills and activities that can be used to train triple-jumpers. Opportunities for teaching various technical points are identified and organized into teaching progressions.

Because triple jumping is a demanding activity, the number of practice sessions that involve triple jumping specifically should be limited. It is not uncommon in many good jumps programs for an athlete to have only one triple-jump session per week. Because practice time is limited, skills common to all jumping activities must be identified and addressed outside of the specific triple-jump practice. Postural conservation skills, contact skills, swinging segment usage skills, and landing skills should be taught outside of triple-jump sessions, during multijump and bounding sessions. The triple-jump practice itself should be reserved for addressing skills that are unique to the event and are not frequently performed in other training activities. These include the takeoff from the board, free-leg usage in the hop, and the hop-to-step conversion.

The triple-jump approach run and phases include both horizontal and vertical components. When teaching phase mechanics, the coach should progress from vertical to horizontal over time because postural conservation is much easier in a vertically oriented exercise. However, some remedial horizontal work must be done in the earliest stages of training. The coach should begin the training season with high volumes of vertical work and low volumes of horizontal work, and then increase the percentage of horizontal work over time.

Triple-jump skills should be taught from the simple to the complex. This is done by teaching three progressions: the horizontal progression for bounding skills, the vertical progression for bounding skills, and a specific technical training progression. The triple jump is a complex event. Yet, effective teaching results when the key tenets of the event are presented simply to the athlete. Although triple-jumpers display many stylistic differences, the coach should demand that the athletes perform the key tenets of technique correctly and consistently. This coaching approach allows triple-jumpers to develop their individual styles without compromising fundamental mechanics.

Horizontal Progression for Bounding Skills

The horizontal progression for bounding skills consists of three series of horizontal jumping exercises, each more demanding and technically complex than the previous one. During the developmental training period, the athlete patiently moves from the simplest to the most complex exercises.

The focal point of all of these exercises is proper foot contact patterns, proper free-leg swinging mechanics and positioning, and proper trajectories of takeoff. Pelvic posture is addressed by demanding correct positioning of the free leg, and complete push-off from the ground is stressed rather than cycling or recovery of the jump leg. The coach must be patient as the athlete moves through these progressions, because significant development and experience in horizontal activities must precede the use of the advanced sequences.

The simplest of these series consists of four exercises, all performed from a double-leg start.

1. Standing long jumps
2. Three consecutive double-leg hops
3. Standing triple jumps (a right-left or left-right bounding sequence)
4. Double double (a right-right-left-left or left-left-right-right bounding sequence)

The intermediate series of horizontal bounds consists of the following six exercises, all performed from a double-leg start.

1. Three rights (a right-right-right bounding sequence)
2. Three lefts (a left-left-left bounding sequence)
3. Double double (a right-right-left-left bounding sequence)
4. Double double (a left-left-right-right bounding sequence)
5. Alternates (a left-right-left-right bounding sequence)
6. Alternates (a right-left-right-left bounding sequence)

The advanced series of horizontal bounds consists of the following six exercises, all performed from a double-leg start. Unlike the previous series, which limits the number of contacts, these exercises are performed over extended distances, usually 20 to 40 meters.

1. Right-leg hops (a continuous right-leg bounding sequence)
2. Left-leg hops (a continuous left-leg bounding sequence)
3. Double singles (a continuous right-right-left bounding sequence)
4. Double singles (a continuous left-left-right bounding sequence)

5. Double doubles (a continuous left-left-right-right bounding sequence)

6. Alternates (a continuous left-right-left-right bounding sequence)

Vertical Progression for Bounding Skills

The vertical progression for bounding skills consists of four vertical jumping exercises, usually performed over distances of 15 to 20 meters. The focal point of all of these exercises is proper foot contact patterns and proper free-leg positioning and swing.

1. Right-leg hops (a continuous right-leg bounding sequence)

2. Left-leg hops (a continuous left-leg bounding sequence)

3. Double doubles (a continuous left-left-right-right bounding sequence)

4. Alternates (a continuous left-right-left-right bounding sequence)

These exercises are initially performed in a very controlled, conservative fashion. Specifically, each bound is nearly completely vertical, covering approximately half a meter only in distance. Also, the free leg is stabilized in an extended position, with the foot of the free leg placed very slightly in front of the foot of the jumping leg. This combination of position and movement makes pelvic posture very easy to achieve.

The vertical jumping exercises can be altered as the jumper progresses. Little by little, swinging movements can be introduced and increased, and at the same time the bounds can become more horizontal. If at any time the athlete becomes out of control, a return to a more vertical bound with decreased swing is called for. Eventually, these exercises resemble the horizontal extended bounds discussed earlier. Again, note that a complete push from the ground is stressed at all times, and no teaching focus is placed on the recovery of the leg. Cycling the jump leg is never addressed.

Specific Technical Training Progressions

The specific technical training progressions consist of two parts: fundamental drills and short-run jumping. These progressions are used to provide an environment to teach jump fundamentals, as well as many unique features in the event that have not specifically been addressed in other teaching progressions.

Fundamental Drill Series

The fundamental drill series consists of four exercises designed to give the jumper a controlled learning environment to perform many repetitions of basic jump skills. These exercises are typically used very early in the training season and are performed over distances of 15 to 25 meters.

1. Power skips for height (repeated skips with great vertical displacement on each takeoff)

2. Power skips for distance (repeated skips with great horizontal displacement on each takeoff)

3. Continuous takeoffs (repeated takeoffs from every other contact of the takeoff foot)

4. Hurdle jumps (galloping action over four to eight very low hurdles spaced 2 or 3 meters apart; see figure 4.5 on page 58)

Several aspects of technique are addressed throughout all of these exercises: proper foot contact patterns, proper swing-leg mechanics, and arm action. In addition, the latter two exercises mandate an extension of a free leg in flight. The hurdle jumps and continuous takeoffs require the jumper to land on the opposite leg from which takeoff was performed, inherently requiring extension of the free leg and giving the jumper experience at this maneuver.

Another key coaching point involves the free-leg action. In all of these exercises, the thigh is blocked below parallel, so that the knee is below the hip at the completion of takeoff. This develops better free-leg mechanics and permits

Figure 4.5 Hurdle jumps.

a more complete extension of the takeoff leg at the speeds these drills require.

Short-Run Jumping

In good triple-jump training programs, the majority of the jumping done in training is done from approach runs much shorter than those used in competition. This provides more repetitions and slower speeds to facilitate motor learning, and eases the pounding on the body.

Typically, short-run jumping is begun after a month or two of preparatory training. Beginning runs are 4 to 12 steps long. Over the course of the developmental training period, approach runs are gradually increased to increase velocity and intensity and to more closely resemble competition. Short-run triple jumping should be used to address technical issues specific to the event. The coach is doomed to failure if

general jump issues and bounding skills must be addressed in these sessions, because there will not be enough time available to address all of the critical factors.

A double-leg start from a staggered stance can be a valuable tool to bridge the gap between bounding and actual triple jumping for beginners. It is a good way to introduce the single-leg takeoff to novices.

SAMPLE TRIPLE-JUMP PROGRAM

The following is a sample triple-jump program designed for a full-length season. Jumpers with shorter seasons would use similar workouts but spend less time in each phase.

	September to Mid-October (General Preparation Phase)	
Monday	Warm-up jog, static and dynamic flexibility, sprint drills, acceleration development, short horizontal bounding, weight training (Olympic lifts, squats, presses), barefoot skip cool-down	Example of Tuesday workout during the general preparation phase:
Tuesday	Warm-up jog, static and dynamic flexibility, hurdle mobility, technical jump drills, general strength circuits, weight training circuit	• 800 m warm-up jog • Static flexibility • Dynamic flexibility, 10 each: Front and back eagles, splits, scissors, knee tucks, hip circles, arm circles, trunk twists, forward leg swings, lateral leg swings, donkey kicks, leg whips
Wednesday	Warm-up jog, static and dynamic flexibility, hurdle mobility, sprint drills, remedial vertical bounds, weight training (Olympic lifts only), multithrows	• Hurdle mobility, 2 × 6 hurdles each: Alternate walkovers; right-lead walkovers; left-lead walkovers; over and back, right lead; over and back, left lead; over and under, right lead; over and under, left lead
Thursday	Warm-up jog, static and dynamic flexibility, hurdle mobility, technical drills, medicine ball circuits, special strength work	• Technical drills from the fundamental drill series • General strength circuit A, each exercise 20 seconds on, 20 seconds off: Push-ups, squats, V-sits, back hypers, push-ups with clap, rocket jumps, dips, Cossack extensions, L-overs, wrestler's bridge, swimming, burpees
Friday	Warm-up jog, static and dynamic flexibility, sprint drills, acceleration development (resisted runs), in-place jump circuit, weight training (Olympic lifts, squats, presses), barefoot skip cool-down	• General strength circuit B, each exercise 20 seconds on, 20 seconds off: V-sits, back hypers, side-ups, leg tosses, toe touches, roll-ups, crunches, hypers with twist, crunches with twist, L-overs, Cossack extensions, wrestler's bridge
Saturday	Warm-up jog, static and dynamic flexibility, sprint drills, extensive tempo, weight training circuits, cool-down jog	• Weight training circuit, 3 × 10 each: Twist lunges, lateral step-ups, deadlifts, back hypers, rows, lat pulldowns, behind neck presses, Russian twists
Sunday	Rest	• 400 m jog-skip cool-down

	Mid-October to December (Specific Preparation Phase)	
Monday	Warm-up jog, static and dynamic flexibility, sprint drills, acceleration development, weight training (Olympic lifts, squats, presses)	Example of Monday workout during the specific preparation phase:
Tuesday	Warm-up jog, static and dynamic flexibility, hurdle mobility, short-run jumping, general strength circuits, weight training circuit	• Warm-up jog • Static flexibility • Dynamic flexibility, 10 each: Front and back eagles, splits, scissors, knee tucks, hip circles, arm circles, leg swings, donkey kicks
Wednesday	Warm-up jog, static and dynamic flexibility, sprint drills, runway rehearsal, bounding, weight training (Olympic lifts, single-arm and single-leg lifts)	• Sprint drills, 2 × 30 m each: A-skips, B-skips, backward skips, backward runs, side shuffles (left and right)
Thursday	Warm-up jog, static and dynamic flexibility, hurdle mobility, short-run jumps, medicine ball circuits, special strength, cool-down jog	• Acceleration development: 3 × 20 m, 3 × 30 m, 3 × 40 m from blocks
Friday	Warm-up jog, static and dynamic flexibility, sprint drills, speed development, depth jumps (boxes), weight training (Olympic lifts), barefoot skip cool-down	• Weight training: snatches (6 × 2); squats (5 × 5); incline presses (6, 5, 4, 3, 2) • 400 m jog-skip cool-down
Saturday	Warm-up jog, static and dynamic flexibility, sprint drills, intensive tempo, weight training circuits, cool-down jog	
Sunday	Rest	

(continued)

(continued)

January (Competition Phase—Indoor Season)		
Monday	Warm-up jog, static and dynamic flexibility, sprint drills, acceleration development, short horizontal bounds, weight training (Olympic lifts, ballistic lifts)	Example of Wednesday workout during the competition phase: • Warm-up jog • Static flexibility • Dynamic flexibility, 15 each: Front and back eagles, leg swings, hurdle trail leg circles • Sprint drills (2 × 30 m each): High knees, butt kicks, A-skips, B-skips • Runway rehearsal (5 or 6 repetitions) • Speed endurance: 4 × 120 m sprint-float-sprint • Multijumps: Hurdle hops (6 × 4 hurdles) • Weight training: Hang cleans (5 × 3), squat jumps (4 × 6), speed incline presses (4 × 6) • 400 m jog-skip cool-down
Tuesday	Warm-up jog, static and dynamic flexibility, short-run jumps, general strength activities, cool-down jog	
Wednesday	Warm-up jog, static and dynamic flexibility, sprint drills, runway rehearsal, speed endurance, multijumps, weight training (Olympic lifts, ballistic lifts), barefoot skip cool-down	
Thursday	Warm-up jog, static and dynamic flexibility, hurdle mobility, short-run jumps, medicine ball activities, cool-down jog	
Friday	Warm-up jog, static and dynamic flexibility, sprint drills, acceleration development, multithrows	
Saturday	Warm-up jog, static and dynamic flexibility, sprint drills, runway rehearsal, short-run jumps, competition	
Sunday	Rest	

February (Competition Phase, Peak—Indoor Season)		
Monday	Warm-up jog, static and dynamic flexibility, sprint drills, block starts, hurdle hops, weight training (Olympic lifts)	Example of Wednesday workout during the competition phase: • Warm-up jog • Static flexibility • Dynamic flexibility, 15 each: Front and back eagles, leg swings, hurdle trail leg circles • Sprint drills, 2 × 30 m each: high knees, butt kicks, A-skips, B-skips, carioca • Runway rehearsal (5 or 6 repetitions) • Speed endurance: 2 × 90 m sprint-float-sprint • Weight training: Cleans (3, 3, 2, 2, 1, 1) • 400 m jog-skip cool-down
Tuesday	Warm-up jog, static and dynamic flexibility, short-run jumps, medicine ball circuit, cool-down jog	
Wednesday	Warm-up jog, static and dynamic flexibility, sprint drills, runway rehearsal, speed endurance, weight training (Olympic lifts), barefoot skip cool-down	
Thursday	Rest	
Friday	Warm-up jog, static and dynamic flexibility, sprint drills, acceleration development, multithrows	
Saturday	Warm-up jog, static and dynamic flexibility, sprint drills, runway rehearsal, short-run jumps, competition	
Sunday	Rest	

	Early to Mid-March (Specific Preparation Phase—Following Indoor Season, Early Outdoor Season)	
Monday	Warm-up jog, static and dynamic flexibility, sprint drills, resisted runs, weight training (Olympic lifts, squats, presses)	Example of Wednesday workout during the specific preparation phase:
Tuesday	Warm-up jog, static and dynamic flexibility, hurdle mobility, technical drills, general strength circuits, weight training circuit	• Warm-up jog • Static flexibility • Dynamic flexibility, 12 each: Front and back eagles, splits, scissors, knee tucks, hurdle trail leg circles, arm circles, leg swings
Wednesday	Warm-up jog, static and dynamic flexibility, sprint drills, runway rehearsal, weight training (Olympic lifts)	• Runway rehearsal (3 or 4 repetitions) • Speed endurance: 2×150 m, 2×120 m, 2×90 m
Thursday	Warm-up jog, static and dynamic flexibility, hurdle mobility, short-run jumps, medicine ball circuits, cool-down jog	• Weight training: Olympic lifts • 400 m jog-skip cool-down
Friday	Warm-up jog, static and dynamic flexibility, sprint drills, depth jumps (boxes), weight training (Olympic lifts, ballistic lifts), barefoot skip cool-down	
Saturday	Warm-up jog, static and dynamic flexibility, sprint drills, speed endurance, hurdle mobility, cool-down jog	
Sunday	Rest	
	Mid-March to April (Competition Phase)	
Monday	Warm-up jog, static and dynamic flexibility, sprint drills, block starts, hurdle hops, weight training (Olympic lifts)	Example of Wednesday workout during the competition phase:
Tuesday	Warm-up jog, static and dynamic flexibility, short-run jumps, medicine ball circuit, cool-down jog	• Warm-up jog • Static flexibility • Dynamic flexibility, 10 each: Front and back eagles, splits, scissors, knee tucks, hurdle trail leg circles, hip circles, arm circles, leg swings
Wednesday	Warm-up jog, static and dynamic flexibility, sprint drills, runway rehearsal, speed endurance, weight training (Olympic lifts), barefoot skip cool-down	• Sprint drills, 2×30 m each: Lateral A-skips, B-skips, backward skips, straight-leg bounds, side shuffles (left and right)
Thursday	Rest	• Runway rehearsal (3 or 4 repetitions) • Speed endurance: 150 m, 2×120 m, 2×90 m ladder, with 5-minute recoveries
Friday	Warm-up jog, static and dynamic flexibility, sprint drills, acceleration development, multithrows	• Weight training: Cleans (6×4), with jerk on final repetition
Saturday	Warm-up jog, static and dynamic flexibility, sprint drills, runway rehearsal, short-run jumps, competition	• 400 m jog-skip cool-down
Sunday	Rest	

(continued)

(continued)

May to June (Competition Phase)		
Monday	Warm-up jog, static and dynamic flexibility, sprint drills, resisted runs, weight training (Olympic lifts), multithrows	Example of Wednesday workout during the competition phase: • Warm-up jog • Static flexibility • Dynamic flexibility, 15 each: Front and back eagles, leg swings, hurdle trail leg circles • Sprint drills, 2 × 30 m each: High knees, butt kicks, A-skips, B-skips, carioca • Runway rehearsal (5 or 6 repetitions) • Speed endurance: 2 × 90 m sprint-float-sprint • Weight training: Cleans (3, 3, 2, 2, 1, 1) • 400 m jog-skip cool-down
Tuesday	Warm-up jog, static and dynamic flexibility, hurdle mobility, short-run jumps, medicine ball circuit	
Wednesday	Warm-up jog, static and dynamic flexibility, sprint drills, runway rehearsal, weight training (Olympic lifts)	
Thursday	Rest	
Friday	Warm-up jog, static and dynamic flexibility, sprint drills, block starts, multithrows	
Saturday	Warm-up jog, static and dynamic flexibility, sprint drills, runway rehearsal, short-run jumps, competition	
Sunday	Rest	

Chapter 5

High Jump

Cliff Rovelto

Track and field is a beautiful sport, and the high jump is one of the most exciting and remarkable of the events in track and field. An athlete flying over a bar that is quite frequently well overhead is as impressive a feat to watch as any in sport. This chapter covers the approach, takeoff, and rotation about the bar, as well as how to teach these skills. Finally, information is included regarding specific preparation for competition, as well as issues to be addressed in competition itself. Hopefully, the contents of this chapter will be helpful to coaches and athletes at all levels of development.

WARM-UP AND COOL-DOWN

The high-jump warm-up, much like any specific event warm-up, must help the athlete transition from a resting state to a state of optimal arousal for high jumping. An effective high-jump warm-up prepares the athlete from a psychomotor standpoint and includes appropriate lead-up technical drills to prepare the athlete to run an effective approach and execute a dynamic takeoff. It should start with a general warm-up to raise the athlete's core temperature and facilitate adequate mobility to perform more complex motor skills. After that, the warm-up should include exercises specific to the athlete's individual needs to help him attain an optimal level of arousal.

When warming up, athletes should perform technical lead-up exercises specific to their own needs. Virtually all jumpers' warm-up routines will include approaches, modified jumps (including scissor jumps, short-approach jumps, or both), and full-approach jumps. Between jumps in practice, the athlete should rest at least three minutes to sufficiently recover and to restore ATP energy stores. In competition, athletes often have significantly more than three minutes between attempts. During this time, they should perform light stretching, general mobility exercises, and short acceleration runs of 10 to 20 meters.

The cool-down is a very important part of the training program. The goal is to return to a state of homeostasis, allowing for recovery for the next training session. High-jumpers often err by neglecting the cool-down. They must discipline themselves to complete the workout session, which always includes a cool-down.

APPROACH

Three variations of the high-jump approach are used today. The most common is the J approach, in which the athlete runs the initial portion of the approach straight forward and then transitions into the curved portion (see figure 5.1b on page 64). In the second variation, the flared approach, the athlete runs from a point wider than the point at which the final curve

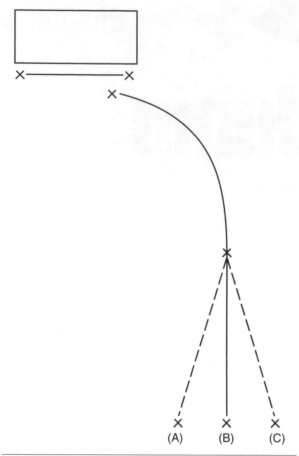

> **Figure 5.1** High-jump approaches: *(a)* hook; *(b)* J; *(c)* flared.

demonstrates this fact. At takeoff, the lean gives the athlete an increased opportunity to jump through the vertical, as viewed from the side of the apron looking down the crossbar. Viewed from the back, the elite high-jumper will actually be around 10 degrees past vertical at takeoff (Dapena, Gordon, and Meyer 2006). This lean also leads to a lowering of the athlete's center of mass. Both of these results are advantageous to the jumper and are discussed further in this chapter.

The high-jump approach, like any jumping event approach, must take four factors into account. First, the athlete must overcome inertia and accelerate in an efficient and uniform manner. High-jumpers exhibit a number of styles of starting the approach, including a standing start, walk-in start, skipping start, and bounding start, as well as combinations of these

is initiated (see figure 5.1*c*). The third variation is the hook approach: The athlete runs from a point inside the point where the final curve is initiated (see figure 5.1*a*). These three styles are each used by jumpers of all abilities and both genders. Higher-training-age athletes tend to use the flared approach more frequently, and younger-training-age athletes are more inclined to use the hook approach. All discussions and diagrams in this chapter describe a left-leg takeoff.

Regardless of which approach the athlete uses to get into the final curve, the goal of running on a curve remains the same: to create pressure against the ground, which allows the athlete to lean away from the bar. This lean is a reaction to centrifugal force, which is a force felt by an object moving in a curved path and acting outward from a center of rotation. This lean results in the athlete's center of mass actually being inside the running curve. Figure 5.2

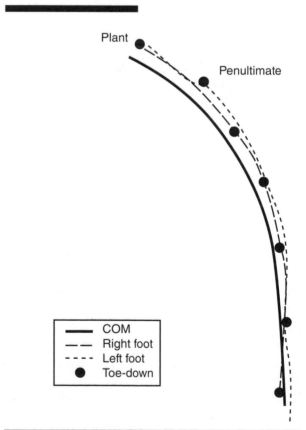

> **Figure 5.2** Illustration of the path of the center of mass (COM) relative to the path of foot contacts.

Reprinted, by permission, from S. Smith and E. Russell, 2005, "A case study: A biomechanical analysis of selected parameters measured in the approach of an elite male high jumper" (unpublished): 23.

styles. Regardless of which style the jumper uses, proper pushing mechanics must be executed. Second, the high-jumper must demonstrate proper running mechanics when transitioning into an erect running posture. Foot dorsiflexion and proper front-side running mechanics are critical to an effective approach. Third, the athlete running over the arc must demonstrate efficient curve-running postures and mechanics. The athlete must remain in an erect posture, keeping the shoulders over the hips and in the same plane as the hips. A common error is leaning forward or breaking at the waist while running over the curve. The athlete must also keep the ankles dorsiflexed while running over the curve. Athletes who plantar-flex or toe while running over the curve will experience problems with the heels sliding out, contributing to loss of pressure against the ground and the outside shoulder getting ahead of the hips. Proper curve-running mechanics will enable the athlete to apply force effectively to the ground and to stay in the curve. This means that the athlete must keep the center of mass inside the path of the arc itself (see figure 5.2). Fourth, the jumper's approach must also demonstrate a rhythm of slow to fast. The tempo of this rhythm depends on sound running mechanics, good posture, and adequate strength levels.

A number of factors need to be considered in building the jumper's approach: the number of steps in the approach, the radius of the curvature, and the angle of attack. An effective high-jump approach is the result of finding the proper mix of these three factors for each individual athlete.

Number of steps

Typically, high-jumpers use an approach of 6 to 12 steps. Younger-training-age athletes should use an approach of 6 to 10 steps. More mature jumpers will be better prepared physically to use an approach of 10 to 12 steps. An even number of steps is preferable to an odd number, which means that the first step is taken with the non-takeoff leg. A static start lends itself to a more consistent and uniform acceleration pattern than other starting styles. This is particularly critical with the younger athlete.

Radius of curvature

The radius of the curve must be athlete specific. Determining the appropriate radius is a trial-and-error process by both coach and athlete. Running mechanics, athlete strength levels, and postural positions will dictate the appropriate radius for each athlete. Consider the demands on a sprinter running 200 meters on a flat 200-meter track versus a 400-meter track. On the smaller track with a tighter radius, the athlete must be technically sound when running on the curve to maintain horizontal velocity. If the athlete is not strong enough to handle the forces, his technique will suffer. A goal of training, then, should be to develop sound running mechanics and improve strength levels. Dapena and Iiboshi (1997), in a study of the finalists of the 1991 World Championships, found that the average radius for the women was 31 feet 8¾ inches (9.65 m) and for the men was 27 feet 10 inches (8.47 m).

Angle of attack

Two items need to be addressed when laying out the approach with respect to the final two steps and their relation to the bar. The first is the path of the center of mass relative to the plane of the crossbar. Dapena (2000) observed the following data on the top nine men and top eight women analyzed in his studies over the years. The mean angle of the men's penultimate step was 51 degrees; that of the last step was 40 degrees. Data for the women are nearly identical: The mean angle for the penultimate step was 50 degrees and for the last step was 40 degrees. This information is important and must be considered to avoid an approach to the bar that is either too shallow, parallel with the bar, or too steep. These angles must be observed from overhead and are difficult to measure without the benefit of film analysis.

The second item to be considered when laying out the approach is the path of the foot contacts in the final steps. This is most readily observed in the field. The direction of the footsteps in the last step should be close to 30 degrees to the plane of the crossbar (Dapena, Gordon, and Meyer 2006).

The outline that follows describes the steps used to develop an approach according to the unique characteristics of the athlete. Steps 1 through 4 are performed on the apron *without* the standards and pit in place. Steps 5 through 7 are performed on the apron *with* the standards and pit in place.

1. The athlete runs 10 steps in a straight line at the speed she feels she can handle and executes a jump. The first step should be with the non-takeoff foot. The last step should be marked with chalk or tape, and an average should be taken of four or five trials. The athlete continues to run 10 steps in a straight line in the same manner, this time marking the fifth step. An average is taken of four or five trials (see figure 5.3).

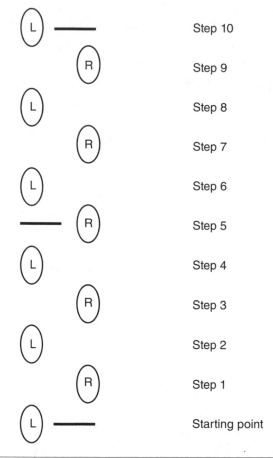

Step 10

Step 9

Step 8

Step 7

Step 6

Step 5

Step 4

Step 3

Step 2

Step 1

Starting point

▶ **Figure 5.3**   Mapping the approach: 10 steps.

2. The athlete runs a curve that feels comfortable, transitioning into the curve on the fifth and sixth steps. A takeoff point is established from an average of four or five trials (see figure 5.4).

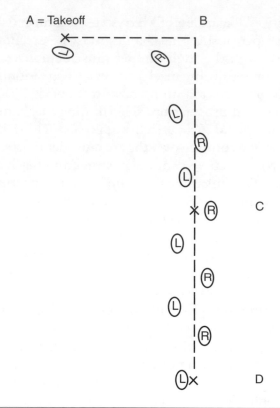

A = Takeoff   B

C

D

▶ **Figure 5.4**   Mapping the approach: establishing a takeoff point.

3. The athlete or coach measures from point A to point B in figure 5.4. This line should be parallel to the imaginary bar. Then measurements from point B to point D and from point B to point C are taken; these should be perpendicular to the imaginary bar. The athlete now has three measurements to transfer to the apron.

4. The coach and athlete determine the takeoff point on the apron and measure from that point (see figure 5.5).

5. The athlete then runs the approach on the apron with the pit and standards in place, making adjustments as needed. For example, with the standards and pit in place, the athlete may approach less aggressively and need to move her starting point forward. The coach will need to use his best judgment as to the athlete's ability to handle the curve. The tightness of the curve should depend on the athlete's strength level and run-

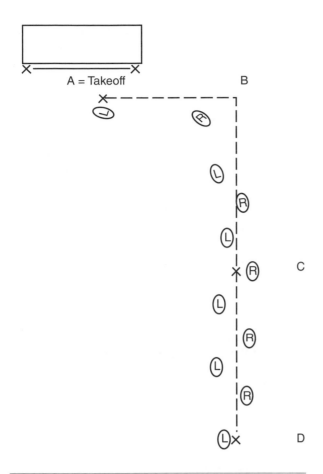

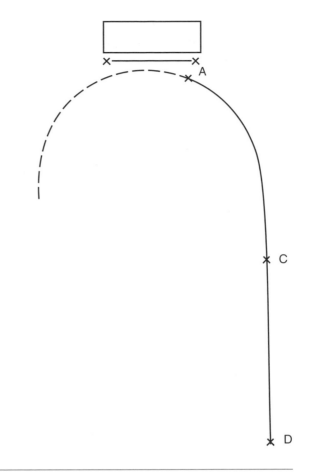

> **Figure 5.5** Mapping the approach: marking the takeoff spot on the apron.

> **Figure 5.6** Mapping the approach: athlete running by the pit.

ning mechanics. From this point on, the approach will be measured from the inside of the standard as opposed to the takeoff point.

6. When running approaches, the athlete should run by the pit, not through the pit (see figure 5.6).

The 10-step distance on the straight should be comparable to the 10-step distance with a curve—that is, the distance from the baseline to the starting point. A significant difference in these two measurements will generally indicate that the athlete (1) is failing to maintain horizontal velocity when running the arc or (2) is not running an arc (the "curve" more resembles a wide receiver running a post pattern). The midmark should be near the 5-step distance. If the first 5 steps are covering significantly less distance than the last 5 steps, this generally

indicates poor acceleration. The athlete is not pushing out of the back of the approach.

Putting the approach on paper When putting the approach on paper, I use a scale of ⅛ inch equaling 1 foot. A ruler, protractor, and compass are needed. The high-jump crossbar is 4 meters long; for the sake of the drawing, I use 13 feet. Line X passes through the takeoff point and the center of the crossbar. Line Y is perpendicular to line X. Draw an arc, using a compass, that intersects the midmark and the takeoff mark. Figure 5.7 on page 68 is provided as an example. The line represents the path of the jumper. The arc that has been drawn is *not* the path of the jumper in steps 6 and 7. However, steps 8, 9, and 10 will generally fall on this arc. This approach is used by Karol Rovelto, who has a personal best of 6 feet 5½ inches (1.97 m). Drawing the approach on paper helps the coach and athlete determine the radius of the arc the athlete is running over. They can then place this arc on the apron with chalk or tape.

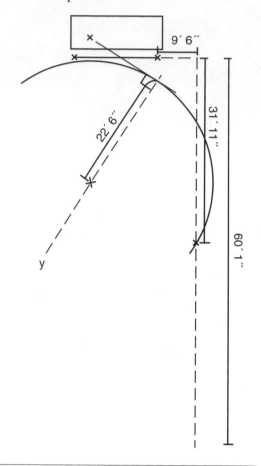

> **Figure 5.7** Mapping the approach: a filled-out example.

The penultimate step is critical in the execution of an efficient takeoff. The placement of this foot strike should fall in line with the imaginary curve that the athlete is running. The foot contact should be flat and active. The athlete's torso should be erect, and the hips and torso should be moving over the penultimate foot with as little delay as is possible. The athlete should be pushing the hips through, over the foot, and attempting to get off the penultimate foot in preparation for the placement of the takeoff foot. The heel recovery of the takeoff leg as the athlete moves over the penultimate step should be low. The takeoff leg will be actively planted with the foot dorsiflexed and making flat-footed contact with the ground.

APPROACH DRILLS

During the approach, the high-jumper should focus on three important factors: acceleration, max velocity, and curve-running mechanics. Drills involving each of these follow.

Acceleration

In the first three steps of the approach, the athlete should use pushing mechanics. Shin angles should be acute with the ground. A big arm swing, low heel recovery, and complete hip extension should be observed. Following are some acceleration drills.

>> Sticks <<

Purpose

To help the athlete learn to apply force down and back into the ground and gradually increase the stride length.

Procedure

Eight to 10 pieces of tape or sticks are placed on the ground as follows: the first stick is 50 cm from the starting line, the second stick is 65 cm farther, the third stick is 80 cm farther, and so forth. The athlete begins by putting both feet on the starting line. The athlete falls forward and steps just beyond the first stick, keeping the shin angle acute to the ground. The athlete continues in the same manner over each successive stick, gradually applying more force as the distance between the sticks increases. The ankles must remain dorsiflexed. The athlete runs over the sticks 5 to 10 times.

>> Sled Pulls <<

Purpose

To permit the athlete to feel pushing mechanics with resistance.

Procedure

The athlete begins with the takeoff foot forward, taking the first step with the non-takeoff leg. Keeping the shins acute to the ground with the ankles dorsiflexed, the athlete pushes out with the legs, pulling some form of resistance, be it a sled or similar object, for 10 to 15 meters. The resistance will enable the athlete to get complete hip extension, which is desirable when pushing out of the back to initiate the high-jump approach. The athlete repeats the drill 5 to 10 times.

>> Harness Runs <<

Purpose

To permit the athlete to feel pushing mechanics with a greater range of resistance.

Procedure

The drill is performed like sled pulls, but the resistance is now provided by a partner. As the partner provides greater resistance, slowing down the speed at which she is traveling in relationship to the jumper, the athlete develops specific strength in the muscles involved in acceleration. Resistance should be provided for 10 to 15 meters. The athlete repeats the drill 5 to 10 times.

Max Velocity

In a 10-step approach, steps 4, 5, and 6—which represent the final steps of the straight portion of the approach and the transition into the curve—should demonstrate max velocity mechanics. *Max velocity* is a bit of a misnomer because the athlete will not be running at maximal velocity. The athlete will be running at an optimal velocity depending on his ability level. Younger-training-age athletes and athletes with low strength levels will not be able to approach the bar with as much horizontal velocity as their older and stronger counterparts. Max velocity mechanics are characterized by an erect posture, foot dorsiflexion, high heel recovery, and proper front-side (step over and push down) mechanics. Shin angles are perpendicular to the ground as force is applied vertically to the ground. Following are some max velocity drills.

▶▶ Running A ◀◀

Purpose

To encourage the athlete to apply force vertically through the ground.

Procedure

The athlete runs forward, lifting the thighs until they are parallel to the ground. The athlete should run tall, keeping the torso erect. The ankles should remain dorsiflexed, and heel recovery will be higher than in the acceleration drills. The drill should be performed for 20 to 30 meters and repeated 5 to 10 times.

▶▶ Stair Running ◀◀

Purpose

To reinforce the application of vertical force.

Procedure

The stair steps should be close together so that there is not a great deal of horizontal displacement as the athlete runs up the stairs. The athlete must stay tall, taking care not to bend at the waist. The ankles should remain dorsiflexed, and the thighs should reach a point parallel with the ground. The athlete should perform 8 to 10 repetitions of 10 to 20 steps.

>> Flying Sprints <<

Purpose

To develop speed by turning a push phase into a sprint.

Procedure

The athlete sprints at maximal velocity through a zone of 10 to 30 meters with a 20- to 25-meter acceleration zone. Proper maximal velocity mechanics, as described earlier, should be emphasized. Three to five repetitions would be appropriate for the high-jumper.

>> Rhythm <<

Purpose

To develop constant acceleration and increased stride length and frequency throughout the approach.

Procedure

The rhythm of the approach should be slow to fast. Acceleration should be uniform, and the athlete should strive to run the complete approach without a noticeable deceleration at the end. With no disruption in speed, the athlete should appear to be running off the ground.

>> Rhythm Runs <<

Purpose

To encourage a slow-to-fast rhythm.

Procedure

A 10-step rhythm run emphasizing acceleration and max velocity mechanics is helpful. The athlete counts each step in the following manner: one-two-three, one-two-three, one-two-three-hit. The tempo of each set of successive three counts increases. These rhythm runs are performed in a straight line and repeated six to eight times.

Curve-Running Mechanics

Curve running teaches proper push-out of the initial steps, negotiating the corner, and maintenance of velocity over the course of the approach. The athlete runs a curve by keeping the body erect, with constant pressure toward the outside of the curve. This forces an inward lean of the body.

➤➤ Circle Runs ◄◄

Purpose

To reinforce correct curve-running mechanics.

Procedure

The athlete runs over a circle, maintaining an erect posture and keeping the shoulders in the same plane as the hips. The inside leg is pushed across slightly toward the midline of the body. Foot dorsiflexion and heel recovery should resemble max velocity running. Shin angles should be perpendicular or even slightly acute to the ground. The radius of the circle should approximate that of the athlete's approach. The athlete should perform three to five repetitions in each direction.

➤➤ Figure Eight ◄◄

Purpose

To encourage maintenance of frequency throughout the curved portion of the approach.

Procedure

The athlete runs a figure eight in which the arc at the top and the arc at the bottom of the eight approximate the arc that the athlete runs in the approach. Emphasis is on increasing frequency into and throughout the curved portion of the eight and relaxing in the straight portions. The coach should look for acute shin angles as the athlete runs over the curved portion of the eight. The athlete runs through the eight two or three times per set and performs two or three sets.

▶▶ Curve Running on a Track ◀◀

Purpose

To reinforce proper curve-running mechanics.

Procedure

The athlete runs on the curve of the track, concentrating on correct posture and using the running mechanics described in the circle runs drill. The athlete can also perform this drill with a weighted bar on his back. This forces him to stay erect and maintain proper hip and shoulder axis alignment. Repetitions of 40 to 100 meters could be performed, with three or four repetitions in each direction.

▶▶ Serpentine Runs ◀◀

Purpose

To give the athlete the opportunity to perform repeated transitions from the straightaway into the curve.

Procedure

The athlete serpentines, or performs continuous S runs, down the straightaway of the track. The emphasis is on pushing the inside leg across to the midline of the body and actively grabbing the ground while transitioning into the curve. The athlete must also concentrate on keeping the shoulders in natural alignment with the hips. Six to eight repetitions of 60 to 100 meters are suggested.

▶▶ Approach on the Apron ◀◀

Purpose

To provide repetitions of the approach without executing the jump.

Procedure

The athlete runs approaches on the apron, running by the pit rather than through it. This reinforces maintaining pressure against the ground throughout the bottom of the approach and keeping deceleration to a minimum. When the athlete is making the transition from the straight portion of the approach into the curve, the placement of the foot in the sixth step should be in line with the midline of the body. In running over the curve, the athlete should be conscious of always pushing the inside leg across to the midline of the body. Eight to 10 repetitions should be performed.

≫ Gallop ≪

Purpose

To reinforce an active movement horizontally over the penultimate foot.

Procedure

The athlete gallops—that is, pushes horizontally off the penultimate leg, placing the takeoff leg straight down into the ground. Emphasis is on pushing off the back leg and not pulling with the front leg. This drill should be performed five or six times for 20 to 30 meters.

>> Oliver <<

Purpose

To develop the strength of the penultimate leg.

Procedure

The athlete places the penultimate leg forward, beginning in a near-lunge position. Keeping the torso erect, the athlete pushes the hips forward over the penultimate foot. At the forward-most point, the shin of the penultimate leg will be nearly parallel with the ground. The athlete then pushes back into the original starting position. The hips should remain level as the athlete moves forward and backward. This drill can be performed with or without an additional load. Two or three sets of 5 to 10 repetitions should be performed.

TAKEOFF

The goal of the high-jump takeoff is to convert the horizontal velocity produced in the approach into vertical velocity. The takeoff foot is in contact with the ground for a very short time, ranging from 0.14 to 0.21 of a second for elite high-jumpers (women with personal high-jump records of 1.98 to 2.08 meters and men with personal records of 2.34 to 2.44 m; Dapena 2000). One of the leading causes of poor rotation about the bar is "landing on" the takeoff foot, resulting in a takeoff time that is too long. Athletes with this issue have a tendency to jump high but come down on top of the bar. The athlete must create as much vertical velocity as possible (resulting in increased height) in as short a time as possible. The athlete must not only create force quickly, but also create a *large* force quickly. The lean created by running over a curve has effectively lowered the athlete's center

of mass. This lowering provides the athlete with a greater range of motion through which to push against the ground.

At takeoff, the takeoff leg is actively fired into the ground. The glutes and hamstrings must be very active, pulling the takeoff leg back into the ground. The quadriceps are critical as well. They contract eccentrically on contact with the ground, stabilizing the takeoff leg and limiting the amount of flexion at the knee joint. Elite jumpers have exhibited knee flexion angles of the takeoff leg at touchdown in the 156- to 171-degree range (Greig and Yeadon 2000). The athlete actively fires the takeoff leg into the ground, catching the center of mass on the rise as opposed to landing on and having the center of mass drop as the takeoff leg contacts the ground.

The takeoff mechanism is a push-through-and-pull action. The push-through represents the hip being pushed through, over the penultimate foot. The pull action is represented by the active negative motion of the takeoff leg, resulting in the hip of the free leg being pulled through. This is the result of the stretch reflex created by the active firing of the takeoff leg.

The longitudinal axis of the takeoff foot (the line running through the center of the foot from heel to toe) should be in the general direction of the back opposite corner of the pit. The hips and shoulders should be in natural alignment with the foot. Athletes often plant with the foot directed toward the opposite standard or, even worse, parallel with the bar. This places an inordinate amount of stress on the ankle and increases the likelihood of injury.

The takeoff point will be unique to each athlete and dependent on a number of factors.

Typically, athletes who run over the curve with greater horizontal velocities will both need and want to take off farther from the bar. The path of the center of mass over the last two steps will also be a factor. The greater this angle is relative to the bar, the farther from the bar the takeoff will need to be. The takeoff foot will be planted anywhere from 2 to 3 feet (61 to 91 cm) down the bar from the standard to directly in front of the standard. Anecdotal evidence suggests that takeoff distances for females range from 18 to 36 inches (45.7 to 91.4 cm) out from the plane of the crossbar. Males tend to take off farther out; their distances range from 36 to 60 inches (91.4 to 154 cm). (These distances were observed among the athletes in NCAA Division I and postcollegiate environments.)

TAKEOFF DRILLS

≫ Continuous Pop-Off on the Straightaway ≪

Purpose

To develop a proper penultimate step, converting horizontal to vertical.

Procedure

This drill looks like a long-jump takeoff. The emphasis is on putting the penultimate foot down flat and moving over it. The takeoff foot is put straight down, and the athlete moves more horizontally than vertically, landing on the penultimate foot and continuing forward, executing this mechanism repetitively. Three to five repetitions of 20 to 40 meters are appropriate.

≫ Pop-Off on a Circle ≪

Purpose

To develop the ability to convert in a lateral-lean position.

Procedure

This drill combines the pop-off drill described previously with the circle runs drill described earlier in this chapter. The athlete pops off every sixth step while running continuously around the circle, two or three times in each direction. When running in the reverse direction, the athlete must pop off the opposite leg. This practice improves motor skills.

>> Pop-Off Over a Low Barrier <<

Purpose

To learn the proper mechanics of the penultimate step, developing horizontal quickness over the last two steps.

Procedure

In this drill, the pop-off culminates with the athlete passing over low barriers of 6 to 18 inches (15.2 to 45.7 cm). The barriers are placed 8 to 10 feet (2.4 to 3 m) apart for beginners. This distance can be increased as the athlete gains confidence and executes the drill with greater horizontal velocity. A flat-flat, quick-quick foot contact is encouraged. The barriers must be low enough that the athlete does not inhibit horizontal displacement. Four or five repetitions over 5 to 10 barriers are appropriate.

>> Skipping Takeoff <<

Purpose

To encourage an active takeoff.

Procedure

The athlete skips down the track, firing the takeoff leg down and back into the ground using the glute and hamstring. The heel recovery of the takeoff leg should remain low throughout the movement. The free-side hip should be allowed to go through its full range of motion. This drill can be performed with or without an additional load. The athlete should perform 5 to 10 repetitions of 20 to 40 meters.

>> Skipping Takeoff Over a Barrier <<

Purpose

To encourage impulse at takeoff.

Procedure

This drill is performed like the skipping takeoff drill described previously, although greater force is applied to the ground so the athlete can jump over a single barrier or a series of barriers spaced out down the straightaway. The athlete lands either in the sand or on a soft surface. Two to five sets of five repetitions over a single barrier, or five sets over four or five barriers, are appropriate.

≫ Scissors ≪

Purpose

To reinforce a quick-quick tempo of the final two steps of the approach.

Procedure

The athlete approaches the takeoff from a length of six steps and up to the full approach distance. The scissor action at takeoff calls for the athlete to grab the ground in the last two steps, getting off the penultimate foot quickly. The aggressive firing of the takeoff leg causes the free-side hip to "get through" quickly. The athlete scissors with his legs over the bar, maintaining an upright body position, and lands in the pit on his feet. The bar should be set at a height that enables the athlete to jump over it while maintaining correct takeoff postures. Because this is commonly used as a warm-up drill, repetitions are usually in the three-to-five range per session.

≫ Jump Off Ramp ≪

Purpose

To develop vertical impulse and create additional flight time.

Procedure

The athlete executes an actual jump off a ramp from six steps and up to the full approach. The ramp raises the surface from which the athlete takes off. The penultimate step is performed on the ground. This scenario creates a dynamic that prevents the center of mass from dropping onto the takeoff leg. Also, because the takeoff surface is raised, the jumper can execute a very dynamic takeoff even when the neuromuscular system is somewhat fatigued. The athlete increases her comfort level of seeing the bar high and has a chance to develop bar clearance timing at higher heights. Athletes should take 8 to 12 jumps per session off the ramp. For instructions on how to build this ramp, refer to Badon (1988).

≫ Takeoff With a Spotter ≪

Purpose

To develop proper takeoff postures.

Procedure

This drill is performed in front of the pit with the crossbar placed at a personal record height or higher. The athlete begins with the penultimate leg forward as in the Oliver drill. He then pushes through and fires the takeoff leg aggressively into the ground. If the athlete maintains the proper hip and shoulder relationship relative to the direction of the foot plant, he should fall backward after executing the takeoff. A spotter stands to the side of the jumper and places his hand in the middle of the jumper's back, guiding him safely back down to the ground. The athlete should perform two or three sets of 5 to 10 repetitions.

BAR ROTATION

Dapena (2000) succinctly described the bar clearance of a Fosbury flop high jump as a twisting somersault. The twisting rotation that results in the athlete rotating about the vertical axis causes the body to turn so that the back of the athlete faces the bar. The somersault rotation is the result of a forward and lateral somersaulting component. When the athlete plants the takeoff leg, checking horizontal momentum, a hinged moment is created resulting in a forward rotation. As the athlete is running on a curve and leaning away from the bar, angular momentum is produced at takeoff, which accounts for the lateral somersaulting component.

When the athlete leaves the ground, the path of his center of mass is predetermined and cannot be altered. However, body parts about the center of mass can be moved to facilitate rotation about the bar. For example, if the athlete were to extend his arms outward from his torso while above the bar, the rotation of his upper body would slow down. If the upper body's rotation is slower than the lower body's rotation, it would need to be increased for the athlete to be able to rotate about the bar. This would require shortening the radius of rotation of the lower body. This is generally accomplished by flexing the knees and keeping the knees apart, which shortens the radius of rotation of these limbs. The athlete with a lot of lateral somersaulting momentum has a greater margin of error with respect to the timing of clearing out the legs. The athlete with less lateral somersaulting momentum has to be more precise in the timing of leg rotation about the bar.

The act of arching and unarching is done to facilitate rotating the body about the bar. Coaches and athletes should be careful to view this aspect of the jump for what it is and not get caught up in making it aesthetically pleasing. The act of arching raises the hips. In unarching, by dropping the hips, the legs rise in reaction, which is timing sensitive. As the upper legs pass over the bar, the chin is brought to the chest, which drops the hips and, in reaction, raises the lower legs.

The amount of arch and the timing of unarching are specific to each athlete. The athlete's innate motor genius will figure this out. Most motor skills are reflexive and will occur naturally if not interfered with by external information. The location of the legs in space relative to the center of mass will dictate what must happen with the arms. If the legs are extended, their rotation about the bar will be slow. This would require that the upper body's rotation be sped up to allow for the entire body to rotate about the bar. The athlete can accomplish this by bringing the arms in closer to the body.

The goal is to land safely in the high-jump pit. The execution of the flop-style high jump culminates with the athlete landing on his back. If the athlete has rotated about the bar effectively, he will land on his upper back. Beginning high-jumpers are sometimes hesitant to land high on their shoulders because they are afraid of hurting their necks. The bar rotation drills described next will help them gain confidence that they will land properly and safely.

BAR ROTATION DRILLS

As described previously, the athlete's rotation over the bar largely depends on the approach and takeoff. The percentage of time spent on specific bar rotation drills is relatively small. One of the greatest fears for the beginning high-jumper is landing high on the back. The confidence level for these athletes will be increased by performing these drills. For all athletes, the timing of unarching is critical. The timing of a full-approach jump will be different from that of a standing drill. As warm-up drills and basic exercises, these drills can also benefit the more experienced athlete.

The goal of the landing is for the athlete to land safely in the high jump pit. The execution of the flop-style high jump culminates with the athlete landing on his back. If the athlete has rotated about the bar effectively, he will land on the upper back.

>> Back-Over Standing on the High-Jump Pit <<

Purpose

To help the athlete gain a sense of body awareness while in the air.

Procedure

The athlete stands on the top of the high-jump pit and performs 5 to 10 back-over flips, landing on top of the pit on her abdomen. She should maintain an arched position throughout the back-over. She should not jump over an obstacle. Beginners should have spotters stand on the pit to spot them as they would athletes doing back-overs on the ground.

►► Back-Over Off the Ground ◄◄

Purpose

To help the athlete gain confidence in landing high on the shoulders.

Procedure

The athlete stands with his back to the bar and jumps up and back over the bar, landing on his back high on his shoulders. Upon landing, the athlete continues to roll over until he is on his knees facing the bar. The height of the crossbar should be kept low so that the athlete's comfort level remains high. The athlete should perform 5 to 10 back-overs.

➤➤ Back-Over Off a Box ◀◀

Purpose

To give the athlete increased air time as a result of jumping off an elevated surface.

Procedure

The athlete also gains confidence in falling from higher heights with increased repetitions. The athlete performs as in the back-over off the ground drill but from an elevated surface. The athlete should begin by using a box approximately 1 foot (30.5 cm) high. The height of the box can be increased as the athlete gains confidence. The height of the bar relative to the height of the athlete can also be raised as confidence increases. The athlete should perform 5 to 10 back-overs.

➤➤ Back-Over With Run-Up ◀◀

Purpose

To enable the athlete to practice bar rotation and landing with the addition of momentum.

Procedure

The athlete runs up to the bar from a short approach (five or six steps), taking a rather direct approach to the bar. At the end of the approach, the athlete executes a jump by landing on both feet simultaneously, turning her back to the bar, and jumping up and back off both legs over the bar. The height of the bar can be increased as the athlete's confidence and competence increase. The athlete should repeat this drill 5 to 10 times.

COMPETITION STRATEGY

In competition, the high-jumper faces any number of conditions that could affect performance. Wind, high or low temperatures, rain, many competitors, and an unfamiliar track surface are a few factors they could encounter. Most, if not all, of these factors could be anticipated and modeled in practice sessions. The following section addresses these potential concerns and offers suggestions on how to prepare for them in practice.

Wind In outdoor competition, the jumper may encounter winds from various directions. To learn how to effectively make adjustments for wind in competition, the jumper should practice under varying conditions. The athlete must jump into headwinds, tailwinds, and crosswinds. This will force the athlete to make adjustments and gain confidence running the approach under all conditions. For example, an athlete confronting a tailwind will probably have to lengthen the approach somewhat.

Temperature Athletes will encounter competitions in which they must cope with cold or excessive heat. Practicing under these conditions will help them learn how to adjust their warm-ups and what they must do between jumps to stay warm or cool and prepared for the next effort. Because the adjustments necessary are unique to each individual, athletes must determine for themselves what adjustments they need to make.

Rain Few high-jumpers look forward to competing in the rain. Most jumpers fear slipping when running their approach or taking off. The time will come when an important competition will take place under rainy conditions. Those who are prepared and more comfortable and confident under these conditions will prevail. Many jumpers become tentative while running their approach in the rain. They have a tendency to plantar-flex the ankle or "toe" while running the curve, which contributes to instability, increasing the likelihood of slipping. The athlete must learn to maintain proper running mechanics under wet conditions. This can be

done by practicing in the rain or by wetting down the high-jump apron prior to a jump session.

Number of competitors Jumpers will perform in competitions with both small and large fields. The small-field situation is not different from most practice sessions and so will feel comfortable to most athletes. The large-field competitions are a different story. Because jumpers may encounter long periods of time between jumps, they need to develop routines that will bring them to each attempt ready to perform. Again, this is unique to each individual, which is why it needs to be practiced.

Track surface Jumpers will encounter aprons that are hard and fast, as well as those that are relatively soft and slow. The size of the apron may also be an issue. Beginning the approach on grass or on the oval are frequent scenarios. Making an attempt to practice on a variety of surfaces, as well as duplicating anticipated logistical issues, is recommended. For example, if the athlete must begin the approach on grass, her ability to push out of the back may be compromised as compared to beginning on the track surface. In this situation, the athlete may have to shorten her approach somewhat.

A couple of other situations may also be encountered during the competitive season. The time of day of the competition may be an issue. Typically, athletes always train in the afternoon after attending classes. However, the high jump at the state high school meet or collegiate conference meet may be scheduled for the morning. To replicate this scenario, the coach should schedule training sessions at similar times as the competition. When to wake up, when and what and how much to eat, as well as neuromuscular wake-up routines should all be considered. Again, what works best for each individual will vary slightly, but waking up a minimum of three hours prior to competition, followed by some form of neuromuscular wake-up routine and a premeet meal, is recommended. Another consideration might be the period of time between a qualification round and a final round. There could be a day or a couple of days

© Human Kinetics

between rounds, or the athlete may be required to compete on back-to-back days. Whatever the schedule, this scenario should be simulated in practice. Rest, hydration, and nutrition, as well as various recovery modalities (massage, ice baths), are all important considerations in these scenarios.

The vertical jumps in the sport of track and field are unique. Focus and the ability to raise and lower arousal levels are important in all athletic endeavors, but they are particularly critical in these events. The athlete is allowed three attempts at each height, if needed. Because athletes clear bars on different attempts, competitors cannot know exactly how much time will transpire between jumps. The jumper must always be aware of where he is in the order and make the appropriate decisions regarding adjusting his focus and arousal levels.

The selection of the starting height is somewhat unique to each jumper. The starting height should be a height with which the athlete is confident. This will vary depending on the time of the season. As the season progresses, the athlete should become more comfortable with starting at higher heights. Establishing a rhythm is critical in the high jump. Therefore, the amount of time that elapses between the conclusion of the warm-up and the athlete's first attempt should also be a consideration. Competitions abound with examples of outstanding warm-up jumps followed by poor competition jumps because the athlete started at a higher bar and during the extended interim lost her rhythm. If the athlete is well conditioned, rarely is fatigue brought on by a high number of jumps a major issue. Many a personal best has been recorded between jumps 12 and 16. More often, the decision to start higher than appropriate is due to ego. This mistake is inexcusable.

As mentioned earlier, a common strategy in the high jump is passing attempts. Athletes should always strive to be successful on first attempts, but misses will occur. When an athlete falls behind as a result of misses, he may choose to pass a height. He does this because, even if he were to succeed, he would still trail his competitor because of the count-back rule. (It is important to note that this rule differs at various levels of competition.) Athletes should be familiar with the rules appropriate to their level of competition.

Careful consideration should be given as to when to pass. For example, passing with only one attempt remaining could be highly risky. If the athlete is confident of success, it may be best to make that height and then have three attempts at the next height. If the athlete is experiencing significant fatigue, he may want to conserve his energy for the one attempt at the next height that may move him up in the placings. This scenario typically occurs later in the competition. An example of passing heights earlier in competition is the athlete who recognizes the importance of staying in rhythm. She may choose a lower starting height, make that bar, and then pass the next height confident that her approach is "dialed in."

PRACTICE CONSIDERATIONS

General training principles and the construction of an individual practice session are described in chapters 8 and 9. Because the jumps are speed–power events, practice constructs will be very similar. This section addresses considerations specific and perhaps unique to the high jump.

Successful training programs address macro, or big-picture, factors with as much attention to detail as they do the micro, or more immediate, concerns. In the high jump, perhaps the greatest deterrent to realizing one's potential is injury to the foot, ankle, or knee of the takeoff leg. Many athletes and coaches do a wonderful job of addressing the immediate concern of improving the athlete's ability to produce great force at takeoff. However, they should not forget that the force the body produces is not necessarily applied efficiently. In the high jump, frequently the takeoff foot is planted with the longitudinal axis parallel to the plane of the crossbar.

The path of the center of mass, as discussed earlier, will be around 40 degrees relative to the crossbar. This combination places the foot and ankle under considerable stress, and the medial malleolus nearly touches the ground as the foot is supinated. The musculature and connective tissue of the lower leg must be sound and strong to withstand these stresses and prevent injury. The development of the musculoskeletal system is a big-picture issue that cannot be neglected.

Another big-picture concern is improving the athlete's proprioceptive abilities. This chapter has addressed bar rotation at some length. Many actions in bar clearance are reflexive. As the athlete senses the hips passing over the bar, she brings the chin to the chest, which then drops the hips and lifts the lower legs. The timing of these movements is critical and would be impossible without the proprioceptive system.

In the high jump, developing the ability to perform several jumps during the competition is important. Although an important goal is to improve the athlete's work capacity, it should not be done at the expense of the nervous system. Stamina, or work capacity, is addressed by looking at the big picture, or the cumulative effect of all the work performed.

Athletes and coaches want to measure progress and be able to evaluate the effectiveness of the training program. Numerous measures of speed–power capabilities are available. One method has been found to be an effective measure of high-jump potential as well as a valid and reliable measure of a high-jump training program. The athlete performs two tests. The first is a standing vertical jump off both legs; the second is a three-step vertical jump in which the athlete takes off with the high-jump takeoff leg. The difference between these two measures is a telltale sign of high-jump potential. A differential of 6 or more inches (15.2 or more cm) is indicative of significant high-jump ability. Differentials of 10 or more inches (25.4 or more cm) are observed with elite high-jumpers. There does not appear to be a significant correlation between the standing vertical jump and high-jump ability.

Another practice consideration is how athletes learn complex motor skills. Typically, complex skills such as the high jump are introduced using a whole–part–whole format. High-jump programs that place an inordinate emphasis on short-approach jumping do little to stabilize the skill of full-approach high jumping. The pressure (and therefore the lean) produced in the curve in short-approach jumping is significantly different from that of the full approach. It would follow, then, that significant repetitions of full approaches and full-approach jumps must be executed in practice.

Coaches should have a plan for what to emphasize in practice jump sessions. In sessions focused on a single aspect of technique, the bar should be kept relatively low, 6 to 8 inches (15.2 to 20.3 cm) below the athlete's personal best.

In sessions that emphasize developing jumping stamina (physical as well as mental), athletes may execute as many as 12 to 16 jumps. The athlete may begin such a session jumping at a bar that is approximately 8 inches (20.3 cm) below his personal best. Following each successful attempt, the bar is raised 2 inches (5 cm). When the athlete has two consecutive misses, the bar is lowered 1 inch (2.5 cm). This type of protocol will keep the athlete focused.

The third type of jump session would be a competitive modeling session. The jumper begins the session at a bar approximating the starting height for the upcoming competition. The session is conducted as a competition. With a successful clearance, the bar is raised. Upon three consecutive misses, the session is concluded. The athlete should be limited to a predetermined number of jumps in the range of 8 to 12. When this number is reached, the session is concluded.

A common characteristic of nearly all elite jumpers is that they are capable of jumping high heights in practice. When the athlete is sufficiently prepared physically as well as technically, jumping over high bars should be encouraged when appropriate. Athletes may also decide to pass on attempts in competition. This could mean that the next bar is 6 to 10 centimeters (approximately 2 to 4 in.) higher than the preceding bar. Raising the bar in large increments in practice will help prepare the athlete for this scenario in competition.

SAMPLE HIGH-JUMP PROGRAM

September to November (General Preparation Phase)		
Monday	AM: Strength training. Pull variation, 5 × 5; pressing movement, 4 × 5; hamstring exercise, 3 × 10 PM: Multiple throws, acceleration technique, multiple jumps in sand	Example of Tuesday workout during the general preparation phase: • Warm-up • 6 × 200 m at 75% (2-minute rest intervals) • Hurdle mobility routine, 5 exercises over 10 hurdles • Core strength routine, 8 to 10 exercises of 10 to 15 reps • Cool-down
Tuesday	AM: Strength training. Lunging movement, 4 × 12; core strength circuit, 2 × 10 PM: Extensive tempo (1,200-1,600 m), hurdle mobility, core strength routine	
Wednesday	Rest	
Thursday	AM: Strength training. Squat variation, 4 × 6; box jumps, 4 × 5; calf raises, 4 × 15 PM: Multiple throws, multiple jumps in place	
Friday	AM: Strength training. General strength work in circuit fashion PM: Core strength routine, stadium steps, accelerations	
Saturday	Rest	
Sunday	Rest	
December to January (Specific Preparation Phase)		
Monday	AM: Strength training. Back squats, 6 × 3; box jumps, 4 × 3; pull-ups, 3 × 10 PM: Multiple throws, approach work, speed development (300 m), core strength	Example of Monday workout during the specific preparation phase: • High-jump-specific warm-up routine • Multiple throws, 5 exercises of 3 repetitions • Approaches • Jump session, 8 to 10 jumps • 4 × 75 m ins and outs (4-minute rest intervals) • Cool-down
Tuesday	AM: Strength training. Bench, 6 × 3; multihip and leg presses, 2 × 6 each leg; lunges, 3 × 30 seconds PM: High-jump technique, multiple throws, hurdle mobility	
Wednesday	Core strength	
Thursday	AM: Strength training. Power cleans, 6 × 3; standing or seated calf raises, 2 × 20 PM: Multiple throws, high-jump technique, speed development (300 m)	
Friday	AM: Strength training. Snatch pulls, 5 × 5; hamstring curls, 3 × 12 PM: Special strength circuit	
Saturday	Extensive tempo (1,200-1,600 m), core strength routine	
Sunday	Rest	

February (Competition Phase—Indoor Season)		
Monday	AM: Strength training. Clean pulls, 3 × 4; snatches, 3 × 4; jump squats, 3 × 10 PM: High-jump technique	Example of Thursday workout during the competition phase: • Premeet warm-up • Multiple throws, 3 × 3 • Hurdle hops, 3 × 3 • Mobility routine
Tuesday	Extensive tempo (800-1,000 m), hurdle mobility	
Wednesday	AM: Strength training. Clean pulls, 2 × 4; snatches, 4 × 2; push jerks, 2 × 4; jump squats, 3 × 10 PM: Rest	
Thursday	Warm-up, low-volume neuromuscular stimulus	
Friday	Competition	
Saturday	Strength training: Flat bench presses , 3-2-1; back hypers, 3 × 12; special-strength high jump; drills for takeoff and penultimate; extensive tempo (1,200-1,600 m); hurdle mobility	
Sunday	Rest	
End of February to Mid-March (Competition Phase)		
Monday	AM: Strength training. Cleans, 6 × 2 PM: Multiple throws, high-jump technique	Example of Monday workout during the competition phase: • AM: Strength training • PM: Warm-up. Test: Overback and underforward shot throw • High-jump technique, approaches and jump session of 4 to 6 jumps • Cool-down
Tuesday	Core strength, hurdle mobility	
Wednesday	AM: Strength training. Snatches, 3 × 3 PM: High-jump technique	
Thursday	Rest	
Friday	Premeet warm-up, low-volume neuromuscular stimulus	
Saturday	Competition	
Sunday	Rest	

(continued)

(continued)

Mid-March to April (Specific Preparation Phase—Following Indoor Season, Early Outdoor Season)		
Monday	AM: Strength training. Power cleans, 6 × 4; bench press, 6 × 4; glutes/hamstrings, 3 × 6 PM: Multiple throws, high-jump technique, core strength	Example of Thursday workout during the specific preparation phase: • Jump-specific warm-up • Figure eight drill, 4 × 2 • Oliver drill, 2 × 5 • 4 × 60 m on curve (4-minute rest intervals), 2 in each direction • Cool-down
Tuesday	AM: Strength training. Chin-ups, 3 × 10; balance drills PM: Extensive tempo (1,500 m), hurdle mobility	
Wednesday	General strength circuit (2 circuits, 10 exercises, 10 reps)	
Thursday	AM: Strength training. Back squat superset with squat jumps, 6 × 4; hanging leg raises, 3 × 12; reverse crunches, 3 × 12 PM: High-jump technique, speed development (240 m)	
Friday	AM: Travel PM: Premeet warm-up, light neuromuscular stimulus	
Saturday	Competition	
Sunday	Travel, rest	

May (Competition Phase—Outdoor Season)		
Monday	AM: Strength training. Hang cleans, 8 × 2; dumbbell flat benches, 6 × 3 PM: High-jump technique, speed development	Example of Saturday workout during the competition phase: • General warm-up routine • Core strength circuit × 2 • 3 × 3 × 100 m at 75% (1-minute and 3-minute rest intervals) • Hurdle mobility routine • Cool-down
Tuesday	AM: Strength training. Glutes/hamstrings, 3 × 10; pull-ups, 3 × 8; V-sits, 4 × 10 PM: Intensive tempo (800 m), hurdle mobility	
Wednesday	Rest	
Thursday	AM: Strength training. Snatch high hangs, 5 × 5; lunge jumps, 4 × 5 PM: Multiple throws, high-jump approaches, jump session, core strength	
Friday	AM: Strength training. Balance, dynamic pedestal routine PM: Intensive tempo (600 m), core strength	
Saturday	Core strength, extensive tempo (900 m), hurdle mobility	
Sunday	Pool workout	

June (Competition Phase)		Example of Monday workout during the competition phase:
Monday	Testing, approaches, ice bath	• Warm-up routine
Tuesday	Rest, massage	• Test: Overback and underforward shot throw, standing long jump
Wednesday	Premeet warm-up, low-volume stimulus workout	• High-jump approaches
Thursday	Competition, qualifying round; ice bath; massage	• Cool-down
Friday	Premeet warm-up, low-volume stimulus workout, mobility routine	• Ice bath
Saturday	Competition, finals; ice bath	
Sunday	Travel, rest	

Chapter 6

Pole Vault

Greg Hull

The pole vault has always had tremendous appeal to athletes, coaches, and spectators. It combines athleticism, technology, and the excitement of seeing athletes soar close to 20 feet (6 m) above the ground. The vault tends to attract athletes with a bit of daredevil in them, an attitude that fits comfortably into our current sport culture of constantly pushing the limits of athletic ability. The challenge for all coaches and athletes is to harness this spirit and combine it with sound technical knowledge for safe, yet successful, results. Many ideas are currently floating around about vault technique. The goal of this chapter is to simplify this information into a sound, basic structure that will aid the reader in understanding the true nature of this event.

WARM-UP AND COOL-DOWN

Warm-ups and cool-downs are generally individual to the athlete. Some coaches conduct structured warm-ups and cool-downs, and others leave them up to the athlete. Vaulters need to address two critical areas during the warm-up: getting familiar with the approach run and warming up the shoulder girdle and back. The athlete should run down the runway to get a visual feel for the facility and a tactile feel of the runway surface. The shoulder girdle and back can be warmed up by doing short-approach drills and vaults with lower grip heights. This will allow these muscle groups to warm up to the demands placed on them by vaulting.

Young athletes should do full-speed running prior to jumping. If they avoid this for fear of overdoing it, they will fail to stimulate the correct firing responses prior to competition. At least three 30- to 40-meter sprints are ideal, along with sprint drills and short-approach pole drills.

Most vaulters do little in the way of a cool-down, perhaps because of the length and nature of vault competitions. Once again, this seems to be an individual decision on the part of the athlete.

POLE VAULT BASICS

The fundamental technical concepts that apply to most of the jumps certainly apply to the vault. The direction of movement changes from horizontal to vertical. The athlete must increase the speed of movement during the run-up phase and transfer this energy to the implement (the pole) upon completion of ground contact. Conservation of energy and the correct application of force as well as posture, balance, and rhythm are crucial to success. The overall goal for the coach and athlete should be the consistent

Stu Forster/Getty Images

stand the following basic principles of vaulting. The vaulter and the pole are connected as a system and must be correctly timed. Each of the following principles are covered in depth in this chapter.

1. *All actions of the vaulter must be directed above and beyond the crossbar.* This simple statement contains the key ingredients that control all of the vaulter's movements. The great Polish coach Andrei Krezinski used the analogy of shooting the vaulter's body through an imaginary hoop suspended above and slightly behind the crossbar. A vaulter adhering to this principle will run, plant, take off, and rotate around the pole all while maintaining correct posture, head position, eye focus, and direction of force.

2. *The approach run must be rhythmic and consistent.* As in any athletic movement, the completion is predicated on the beginning. The vault approach run must be a controlled, consistent, and cyclical movement that allows the vaulter to set up an aggressive takeoff. Energy management on the runway is crucial to success. The vaulter must have a strong opening movement (many coaches call this *getting out of the back correctly*) but not expend all of his energy in the first half of the run. A consistent stride pattern (the distance between each foot strike) with a rhythm that increases in tempo will build confidence and allow the athlete to focus on the delivery of the pole and the takeoff.

3. *The pole must move from its initial plant position to a vertical position.* The movement of the pole is the foundation of the vault. When done correctly, it allows for the greatest opportunity for safe and successful vaults. The key to this movement is the speed with which the pole moves through this action (commonly called *pole speed*). When the correct pole speed is coordinated with the correct movement speed of the vaulter's rotation around the pole, the greatest opportunity for success exists.

4. *The pole must be kept moving at all times.* If the pole is moving, the athlete can continue to do work around it; once the pole has stopped moving, however, the athlete is forced to release from the pole and complete the vault. An under-

completion of jumps that allow the vaulter to maintain spatial awareness and achieve a safe landing in the pit. This approach, when combined with a solid physical training program and adherence to basic vault fundamentals, will, with patience, lead to success.

The technical side of the vault relies heavily on the laws of physics, with a primary emphasis on a controlled, maximal velocity takeoff and the highest effective angle of attack at takeoff. This must be executed while still effectively transferring energy into the pole and conserving that energy through all phases of the jump. It is vital that both coach and athlete understanding of what keeps a pole moving is critical. If the vaulter and coach have achieved the right combination of grip height and pole stiffness, then the basic laws of physics and the vaulter's continued actions will keep the pole moving.

The vault is frequently broken down into four or five phases. It is important to remember, however, that the vault is actually a continuous, flowing movement. The vaulter can easily be compared to the gymnast; specifically, the movements of a vaulter are similar to those of a gymnast performing a giant swing on a high bar or shooting to a handstand on the rings. Although no style points are given in pole vaulting, when done correctly, it has a symmetry that is similar to that of gymnastics.

Despite the fact that the vault includes components of gymnastics, it is foremost a jumping event. An understanding of the basic movements inherent in pole vaulting can come from looking at it from a historical perspective. Many concepts of stiff pole vaulting are applicable to competing with a highly flexible pole. Regardless of the type of pole they use, all vaulters need to move the pole from the initial position at takeoff to a vertical position on release. Also, the speed of movement of the pole and the vaulter must be coordinated so they match up at the point of release from the pole. This timing is often referred to as a double pendulum effect, in which the vaulter is a pendulum moving through a point: The top hand grips the pole, and the pole is a pendulum moving about the tip of the pole in the planting box.

When vaulting on stiff poles, athletes slide the bottom hand up during the takeoff to meet the top hand. This action allows the hands to press upward and the hips to keep moving forward. This is the same action today's vaulters are using with flexible poles, but without sliding the bottom hand. Instead, they try to press both hands upward during the plant and takeoff.

All coaches and athletes need to understand the historical connection of straight pole vaulting to flexible pole vaulting. Thinking that a flexible pole changes these fundamentals will lead to decreased performance and possibly dangerous vaults.

To understand the harmonious movement of the vaulter and the pole, consider a metronome used for musical rhythm. The sliding weight that moves up and down the steel shaft represents the vaulter, and the steel shaft represents the pole. As the weight slides up the shaft, the shaft moves slower in its movement from side to side; conversely, as the weight is lowered on the shaft, the movement speeds up. This shows the correlation between the vaulter's grip height on the pole and the pole's movement; the higher the vaulter's grip is, the slower the movement of the pole to the vertical position will be.

A vaulter must also avoid the tendency to roll onto her back when using a highly flexible pole. This movement places all of the vaulter's body weight on the top of the pole and drastically slows the pole's movement to the vertical. When vaulting on a stiff pole, the vaulter knows instinctively that this movement is wrong; the central nervous system sends a message not to do this. Instead, the vaulter stays upright, which keeps her body weight down on the pole and increases the speed of movement to the vertical. In this case, the highly flexible poles of today allow athletes to make a fundamental technical error, yet still clear the crossbar.

APPROACH AND POLE CARRY

The key terms that define an effective run and pole carry are *balance, rhythm, tempo,* and *consistency.* Most elite vaulters have a powerful, relaxed style that begins with a slight forward lean and aggressive high knee action. Correct posture and balance are the keys to developing an effective vault approach run. The hips are in correct alignment, and the foot strike is directly under the line of the hips, creating a powerful pushing action with each step. Overstriding and reaching out with the lower leg will result in a pulling action down the runway, leading to decreased speed, a poor takeoff position, and a potential for chronic hamstring problems. Most vaulters use both short and long approach runs to vary practice intensity. A short run is usually

> **Figure 6.1**   Pole position during the approach and plant.

defined as three to five takeoff strides (30 to 60 ft, or 9 to 18 m) and a long run as five to nine strides (60 to 130 ft, or 18 to 40 m) depending on the vaulter's stride pattern.

The pole should be balanced comfortably close to the body, with the majority of its weight on the skeletal system to allow the athlete to relax and focus on a smooth acceleration into the takeoff. The elbows should be kept close to the body with the wrists aligned underneath the line of the elbows. The pole is usually held at close to a 90-degree angle to the runway to start the run-up and then lowered to a 60- to 70-degree angle after the first few steps. The athlete brings it to a 45-degree angle for the planting action (figure 6.1). The hands should be relaxed, with the bottom hand palm down and the top hand palm up. The distance of separation on the pole between the vaulter's hands should equal the vaulter's shoulder width.

The spacing of the hands on the pole is not an exact science, but the general rule is that a grip that is too wide will make it easy to carry the pole but hard to complete the gymnastics movements on the top end of the vault. A grip that is too narrow will have the opposite effect. The grip spread should be as narrow as possible

without sacrificing the ability to carry and plant the pole.

The pole should fall gradually during the run, allowing the vaulter to use its drop as a natural acceleration aid (but making sure it does not drift too far from the midline of the body). The vaulter should have the pole lowered to a parallel position when he is three strides out from the box. Dropping the pole sooner than this will cause unnecessary deceleration. Dropping it too late will set up an awkward takeoff angle and a blocking action for the vaulter.

In all jump approach runs, the athlete uses a natural adjustment system commonly called *steering* (see chapter 1). This steering mechanism allows the athlete to make minor (or sometimes major) adjustments to arrive at the correct take-off position. Although it is an inevitable part of the approach run, steering causes the athlete to lose speed and tempo. For this reason, the coach and athlete should work to minimize its effect. The most common method for improving approach runs is the use of check marks. The coach and athlete can use the check mark system to ensure that the athlete is maintaining a consistent stride pattern during the run and not ending up having to make large adjustments in the planting phase. In addition to helping with consistency, these marks also build confidence.

Many coaches use a three check–mark system. The beginning mark, for the athlete's reference, is the starting point of the run-up. The second mark, or coach's mark, is used by the coach to gauge the effectiveness of the first half of the approach run. The third, or takeoff, mark is often used by a meet official or a coach to judge the second half of the approach run. Coaches and athletes should be consistent in their use of check marks, but remember that they are mostly coaching tools; the athlete should not be focusing on these marks.

Another common coaching tool is counting steps during the approach run. Once again, this method has many variations; which one to choose is a very individual decision. Some coaches count only the takeoff stride (the foot on which the vaulter leaves the ground), whereas others count both strides. Some coaches count upward, some count downward, and many like to use descriptive terms during the counting (e.g., one-two-three-plant-step-jump). Most younger athletes learn the event from a shorter distance (three to five strides) and move back gradually as their level of competence grows. Part of the art of coaching is deciding which cues work best for both the coach and the athletes.

APPROACH DRILLS

≫ Pole Runs ≪

Purpose

To teach the correct tempo and stride pattern.

Procedure

In an area on the track, the coach or athlete measures the specific distances needed for the athlete to run a three- to nine-stride approach. They should use the check mark system to be sure the athlete is hitting the correct positions and that she is dropping the pole in the correct sequence. This drill is usually done in a set of 8 to 10 repetitions.

➤➤ Mini-Hurdles ◀◀

Purpose

To emphasize posture and foot alignment through progressive tempo and stride-length drills.

Procedure

The athlete does a series of walking, running, and running with the pole over 6-inch-high (15.2 cm) mini-hurdles. The spacing should vary according to the athlete and seasonal needs. The athlete should begin by simple walking over hurdles spaced about 18 inches (46 cm) apart, focusing on posture and correct foot alignment. The coach should increase the tempo until the athlete is running through the hurdles and then gradually increase the spacing as she becomes proficient. The pole carry can be added as both a walking and running component. Spacing will eventually be the normal stride length of the athlete, but posture and foot strike must remain consistent.

PLANT AND TAKEOFF

The plant and takeoff is the heart and soul of the vault. As in all jumping events, this is the moment when the horizontal energy of the approach must be converted to the flight phase of the jump. The vault has the added complexity of having to incorporate the correct delivery of the pole (the plant) into this action.

The vaulter's goal at this point is to raise the top of the pole as high as possible while keeping it close to the midline of the body. The action of pressing the hands slightly forward and upward causes the bottom of the pole to drop. Many vaulters press the pole too far in front of the body and force the end of the pole down into the planting box. This pressing and lowering action sets up an incorrect direction of force (too low), which usually leads to an excessive pole-bending action and an uncomfortable position for the athlete. (Remember the principle that every action of the vaulter should be above and beyond the crossbar.)

The vaulter must reach up with both hands to place the top of the pole in as high a position as possible at takeoff to reduce the distance the pole must travel to the vertical, which is complemented by the vaulter having a solid upright posture at this moment. The vaulter's grip must be placed on the pole in direct relationship to his physical and technical abilities and should be increased only in small increments (3 to 6 in., or 7.6 to 15.2 cm).

The flexible poles of today (made of fiberglass) are a wonderful technological tool for use in vaulting. The high degree of bend acts to shorten the radius of the pole, allowing athletes to hold higher than they could on nonflexible poles while applying the same forces at takeoff. The poles are also capable of storing and returning some elastic energy to vaulters who understand how to use these properties.

While delivering the pole, the athlete must also focus on setting up the correct takeoff action. The best correlation for this action in another sport is the layup in basketball. During a layup, the athlete has a natural settling action on the penultimate step. This is not an action that either the basketball player or the vaulter wants to think about. Instead, this step should be a natural prejumping movement—a flat step that the athlete runs over while concentrating on extending the body as high as possible, leading with the arms, and staying balanced with an upward eye focus and head position. As in all athletic movements, the body will follow the head. When head position and eye focus are correct, the athlete tends to stay upright during the takeoff phase (keeping the weight high on the metronome and encouraging pole speed) and have good posture and spatial awareness as well. This allows the athlete to set up the correct action for a positive drive-swing phase, which follows the takeoff. One of the most common errors in vaulting is keeping the chin down and allowing the eyes to follow the tip of the pole into the planting box.

At the plant, both hands should be pushing the pole as high as possible above the shoulders. The wrists are directly under the hands, and the palms are pressing upward. A common mistake at this point is turning the palms and wrists inward, setting up a pulling action on the pole. Although this will make it easier to bend the pole, it causes the pole to move away from the vertical and usually leads to the athlete having to pull his hips up into the pole (again, placing all the weight on the top of the pole and slowing down the metronome), restricting his ability to continue a smooth forward and upward movement. The takeoff foot should finish a full driving action off the ground, extending over the toe and executing an aggressive jumping action timed with the free-leg knee drive. All three of these things happen together: the pressing upward of the pole, the extension and push-off of the takeoff foot, and the knee drive. The vaulter must learn that this is an integrated movement and not three separate actions.

It is also critical that the athlete consistently reach the takeoff position, which is dictated by the grip height on the pole. Although there is much controversy over the position of the takeoff foot relative to the position of the hands on the pole (the takeoff foot directly under, slightly forward of, or slightly behind the top hand on the pole), the crucial element is the posture of the vaulter and the conservation of energy through this phase. (Most elite vaulters tend to position the takeoff foot slightly behind the top hand.) If the athlete is planting at a high angle and jumping off the ground with a good upright posture, an inch or two outside or inside the line between the top hand and the takeoff foot will not be critical.

PLANT DRILLS

>> Walking Plants <<

Purpose

To emphasize the correct hand and foot motions during the planting action.

Procedure

The pole is placed below eye level in a normal carry action, and then the athlete slowly walks through each correct position. The athlete increases the tempo gradually and eventually ends up with full-speed pole runs and planting into a sliding box or similar object. Emphasis is on posture, correct hand position, and the timing of the pole drop.

>> Pole Throws <<

Purpose

To emphasize the correct direction of force for the athlete to apply through the pole.

Procedure

This drill is executed by walking through a three- to five-step plant drill. As the hands come up and prepare the plant, they continue the action and throw the pole in the direction it would go in a good jump. When the drill is done correctly, the tip will hit the ground and the top of the pole will roll over and fall directly in line with the athlete. The athlete should be conservative when starting the throwing drill, keeping the grip low (3 ft, or 1 m, below a normal grip) and the footwork simple. As the athlete progresses, he can raise the grip until he can no longer get the pole to roll over. This is a great drill for athletes who tend to drop the pole with the bottom arm and for those who try to plant with an extended bottom arm action instead of raising the pole and pushing upward. Timing is crucial in this drill.

DRIVE AND SWING

If the takeoff has been executed correctly, the pole and the athlete are moving quickly through the vertical and horizontal planes at the same time. The posture of the athlete is still upright, and the position is very similar to the gymnast on the bottom part of a giant swing or a shoot to a handstand on the rings. The arms are pressed upward as high as possible, there is a long stretch action in the whole body, and the core of the body is firm. The chest must now continue its forward and upward motion while the takeoff foot is continuing the extension action. If the extension action is completed correctly, the coach should be able to stand behind the athlete and see the bottom of the foot as it pushes off the runway.

The main difference between the gymnast and the vaulter is the driving action of the free knee. This aggressive forward and upward drive of the knee is one of the key components of effectively converting the energy of the approach run into the kinetic energy that can be stored in a flexible pole. The vaulter will move the shoulders forward, creating a long and powerful stretching action of the torso followed by the takeoff leg acting as a powerful lever to accelerate the lower body forward and upward. At this point, many vaulters make the crucial mistake of thinking that their work is done and they can just ride the bending pole over the crossbar. In reality, the vaulter should be doing work as long as he is in contact with the pole.

A tricky relationship develops between the vaulter and the pole during the swing portion of the drive and swing phase. The athlete must keep pressure on the pole to keep it moving (one of the key components of the vault), but cannot apply so much pressure that he blocks the free movement of his hips around the pole. As the vaulter moves through this part of the jump, he must resist the natural tendency to pull the pole toward the body. If you watch people on a rope swing over a creek, you will see this tendency to pull oneself close to the rope. It is the same tendency seen in young vaulters. Most people react to the word *pull* with an inward action of moving their hands to their chest. Doing this on a flexible pole or in a gymnastics movement will kill all of the momentum set up by an effective takeoff. The vaulter must continuously apply enough pressure to create and maintain the space between himself and the pole at this point. This pressure is not a resistance to the pole but more of a pressing action with both hands reaching above the head. This action is a part of the very important concept that the vaulter is never waiting for anything to happen; instead he is constantly working with and around the pole

to achieve success. If the vaulter has maintained correct head position and eye focus, he will find this action much easier.

The coach must look for the pole to continue its movement and for the free flow of the vaulter's hips as he rises to a position between the hands on the pole (figure 6.2). The vaulter is not trying to drop his hips under his shoulders; he is trying to elevate the hips as high as possible and then roll his shoulders underneath him. If the vaulter is in the correct position, the relationship among the hips, hands, and pole will look very similar to that of a gymnast on a high bar. This signals the end of the drive and swing phase.

This is the moment of truth for a vaulter. He must have the awareness and the courage to allow the hips to continue to rise and roll the shoulders underneath the torso. In doing so, the vaulter has now closed the space between himself and the pole, which places him in a near-vertical alignment with the pole. Only the elite vaulters hit this position consistently. Coaches can strive for this, but they must be patient and not try to push an inexperienced vaulter too far at this point. As a vaulter gains confidence and physical maturity, this position will be easier to achieve. Many female vaulters who come from a gymnastics background have an easier time hitting this position than much stronger and athletic males do. This underscores the need for both timing and strength in the vault.

> **Figure 6.2** The swing phase.

SWING DRILLS

>> Rope <<

Purpose

To allow the athlete to swing around her shoulders without any pulling action and simulate the movement of the athlete through the horizontal and vertical planes at the same time.

Procedure

The athlete stands next to a suspended rope, usually 15 to 20 feet (4.6 to 6 m) long and securely anchored. Gripping the rope with both hands in the same manner as the pole, the athlete tries to swing her hips to a position directly between her hands on the rope. Hands should be 18 inches (46 cm) apart and reaching up as high as possible from a standing position. The coach may have to assist the athlete through the first few drills. The athlete should be sure to drive the lead knee and not pull with the top arm to swing up. It is the action of the trail leg swinging up that allows the hips to rise. As the athlete continues to improve, she can increase the speed of movement until she is taking a running three-step stride into the rope and swinging up.

>> Tower Vaults <<

Purpose

To teach an explosive jumping action off the platform and into the swing, simulating the desired action off the run. It also serves to work on head position and correct arm movement on the pole.

Procedure

In this drill, the athlete stands with a pole on an elevated platform, such as a painter's scaffold or even a picnic table, that is close to the plant box. The athlete places the pole in front of him in a normal planting position. He then takes a lead step on the platform, pushing the pole in front of him and jumping off into the pit, landing on the butt in a sitting position. As the athlete gains confidence and is better able to swing around the pole and land on his back, the height of the platform and the grip height on the pole can increase. Most elite athletes use a pole that is rated at or above their body weight, and if using a painter's scaffold that is 5 feet (1.5 m) tall, hold near the top of a 15-foot (4.6 m) pole. The first time through, the coach may want to act as a spotter and be sure the pole moves through to the pit. An athlete who pulls at any point in this drill will find very negative and scary results. The coach should proceed with caution and progress slowly in this drill, but the results can be very exciting.

TURN, EXTENSION, AND RELEASE

As in many athletic movements, the finish is a reflection of the actions that preceded it. This is often the case in the vault and especially during the last phases of the jump. It is common for young coaches and vaulters to spend an inordinate amount of time worrying about this phase of the jump, when in fact they need to focus on the approach run and takeoff. Many of the jumps of world-record holder Sergey Bubka exhibited this emphasis on good approach speed and a good takeoff. Bubka was so aggressive during the takeoff and drive and swing phase that he appeared to never complete a full turn, extension, and release. In reality, he had completed all of the work he could do on the pole (relative to his grip height and pole stiffness) and was allowing the actions he had set in place to continue. In later years, as his grip height and pole stiffness increased, he exhibited a more complete set of movements through the last part of the jump.

As noted before, many vaulters are forced to do a great deal of work during the turn, extension, and release phase because of an improper setup of the plant and takeoff. The turn, extension, and release should be a smooth, relatively effortless action, but it must be timed correctly with the double pendulum of the vaulter and pole rotation.

Many include the word *pull* in this phase, referring to it as pull, turn, extension, and release. Although it is common for experienced vaulters to pull down the shaft of the pole to accelerate the upward movement of the hips, doing so is only effective when the timing is perfect. Jim Bemiller, coach of 2004 Olympic champion Tim Mack, talked about Mack's aggressive pulling action, which he used only when he had executed all the other phases correctly and was in vertical alignment with the pole. If performed too early, a pulling action will kill all of the pole speed; if performed too late, it will thrust the vaulter's hips away from the pole toward the bar.

The turn is a simple movement that incorporates a slight rotation of the head (in the direction of the turn) and a crossing of the drive-leg foot over the swing-leg foot (left over right for a right-handed jumper). A common fault among young vaulters is beginning the turn too late and then being forced to drop the feet toward the crossbar to execute the turn instead of extending along the shaft of the pole toward the vertical while turning. Dave Nielsen, longtime coach of Olympic champion Stacy Dragila, used to say, "Complete the motion on the runway side of the crossbar," indicating the need for an early setup of the turning action.

The turn is another part of the vault in which good head position and eye focus can have a very positive effect. If the vaulter has kept the head in alignment with the torso (not thrown back too far and not having the chin buried in the chest), the hips and legs will have a chance to rise above the torso. The athlete can then see the alignment of the feet with the top of the pole and use this reference point for the turn and extension (figure 6.3). Unfortunately, many vaulters focus on the crossbar. In all athletic movements, the body will follow the head; when an athlete focuses on the crossbar, the legs tend to drop out toward the crossbar. The vaulter then flags out away from the pole, loses all vertical momentum, and most likely kicks the crossbar off.

As mentioned in the pole vault basics section beginning on page 93, all actions of the vaulter must be directed above and beyond the crossbar. The most common problems in vaulting derive from violating this principle throughout the jump. Vaulters begin by overstriding on the runway, which lowers the hips (the first movement not directed above and beyond the bar) and sets up an incorrect takeoff position and a low direction of force down into the planting box (again, away from the correct direction). On flexible poles, this results in a low and overly accented pole bend. To compensate for this movement, the athlete usually does two things: pulls down on the pole and immediately tucks the legs into the chest. This places all of the athlete's weight on top of

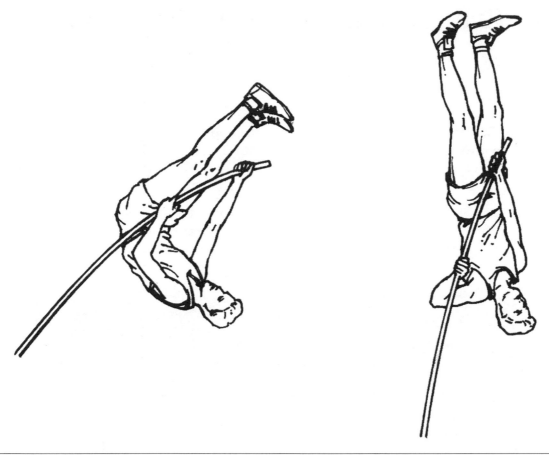

> **Figure 6.3** Using the feet as a reference point for the turn and extension.

the pole (activating the metronome concept), slowing the pole down, further emphasizing the overloading of the pole, and continuing the improper direction of force. In effect, all of the athlete's actions are now directed down and away from the crossbar.

Coaches and athletes should be careful not to react strictly to the overloading of the pole (excessive pole bend). An inexperienced coach might react to the excessive bend by suggesting that the vaulter move to a stiffer pole. The athlete, who is already making numerous bad judgments, will naturally feel he must exert more effort to load the stiffer pole, causing him to further magnify already improper actions. Both coach and athlete are now caught in a negative cycle. The coach must focus on correcting the run mechanics, takeoff actions, and

direction of force to overcome these negative actions. These items are most effectively taught with shorter approach runs, lower grip heights, and less flexible poles.

The release of the pole and subsequent crossbar clearance are the results of a correctly timed turn and extension. When this is done correctly, the athlete will release the bottom hand first and then the top hand and, keeping the hands close to the body, hollow out the chest and go over the bar. There are many examples of a poor turn and release as a result of the improper actions that preceded it; one of the most famous was the Huffman roll by Scott Huffman, a former world-class vaulter. When the turn and extension have been done correctly, it is a simple action.

TURN, EXTENSION, AND RELEASE DRILLS

▶▶ Sliding Box ◀◀

Purpose

To encourage the athlete to apply the correct pressure and direction of the pole-planting action, and time this with a proper takeoff posture. It is most often used in teaching the concept of driving through the takeoff action while continuing to apply forward and upward pressure on the pole.

Procedure

The athlete starts the drill by placing the pole in the sliding box in a normal plant position and taking two or three steps backward. Grip height should be around standing grip plus six to eight fists up. The athlete should walk forward in the planting action and initiate a full and high plant.

It is important for him to stabilize the shoulders and trunk, pushing hard with the hips and trailing leg. The athlete should maintain this high hand position as the box begins to move forward.

The actual sliding box can be purchased or constructed. Because the sliding box will move away from the athlete as this procedure takes place, it is more forgiving than the normal fixed box on the vault runway. The typical approach is to begin with a very lightweight box that will move easily for younger athletes. As they gain confidence and technical expertise, the weight of the box can be increased.

≫ Connection ≪

Purpose

To emphasize the interaction between the vaulter and the pole. When properly executed, this drill teaches the athlete to correctly set up the direction and speed of the pole movement and then connect with the pole in the proper timing sequence at the end.

Procedure

This is typically a straight pole drill, but it could also be done on a flexible pole if necessary. The athlete begins with a low grip, usually standing-grip height plus five fists up. Start with a two- or three-stride approach and the pole held below eye level in the planting position. Emphasize a driving takeoff with very high hands for the plant and an aggressive forward and upward push of the pole. Once the athlete feels that the pole is moving adequately to ensure a safe landing in the pit, she then initiates a powerful swing of the trail leg. If the athlete rotates through the shoulders with the top hand on the pole, she will soon be able to swing with enough force to drive the hips to connect with the pole (the hips should be driven to the point that the hands and hips are together touching the pole), which completes the drill.

As the athlete improves, continue to raise the grip, but do not go beyond three strides on the approach. As long as the athlete completes the connection, continue to raise the grip. More advanced athletes will try to complete the connection at the same time as the pole reaches vertical, but this can be quite unnerving for a less experienced athlete.

Another advanced level of this drill involves initiating the turn as the athlete reaches the connection point on the pole. Some coaches prefer that the athlete complete only a quarter turn and land on her side in the pit, while others have the athlete complete the full turn and land on her belly. If the coach encourages the full-turn connection drill, the athlete should be cautioned not to hyperextend her back when she lands in the pit on her front. This advanced portion of the drill is an excellent way of teaching the aspect of beginning the turn early in the vault and emphasizing that the turn is an integral part of the swing in the vault.

(continued)

SAFETY CONSIDERATIONS

To ensure the safety of the vaulter, both coach and vaulter should understand the movement sequence of the vault and the elements that lead to the correct flow of these movements. Safe and successful vaulting depends on appropriate pole selection based on an understanding of pole speed, and controlling the horizontal aspect of the vault through pole selection and standard settings.

Pole Selection

Vaulter safety has been a big concern during the past 15 years, especially in the U.S. high school system. Following a large number of catastrophic accidents in the 1990s, the U.S. National Federation of High Schools (NFHS) implemented some controversial new rules. The two most important restricted the athlete's grip height on a pole and mandated that athletes jump on poles rated at or above their body weight. The immediate effect of these rules was the minimization of the highly flexible pole and a return to the basic concepts of stiff pole vaulting. Although many questioned the rules, the obvious result was the drastic reduction of catastrophic accidents in subsequent years.

At the time of many of the accidents, the most popular pole size in the U.S. high school market was a 14-foot (4.3 m) test pole rated at 140 pounds (63 kg). Following the implementation of the rule, the most popular pole became a 13-foot (4 m) test pole rated at 160 pounds (72 kg). The conclusion was that a number of 160-pound (72 kg) athletes (girls were not jumping at this time) were jumping on poles rated 20 pounds (9 kg) under their body weight and holding 12 inches (30 cm) higher than they should (this statement is a bit simplistic, but it holds up under scrutiny).

All poles are rated by length and test weight and assigned a number commonly called a flex number. This number is an indication of how flexible the pole is relative to its length. This number is then assigned a corresponding weight rating, which states that, when used correctly, the pole will accommodate an athlete of that weight or less. The other factor that enters into pole selection is the ability of the athlete to initiate an effective takeoff and the conversion of energy into the pole. Athletes who are very effective at this and who create high velocities at takeoff need to use poles rated 10 to 20 pounds (4.5 to 9 kg) or more above their body weight.

There has been much debate about the negative effect the new NFHS rules may have on developing vaulters (especially lighter-weight girls and heavier boys), but its effectiveness in terms of safety is without question. Experienced coaches can easily work with vaulters of all sizes and ability levels and place them on poles far below their body weights without danger, but they also know to reduce approach-run speed and keep grip height low and to address all of the other factors that control pole speed.

The real culprit in the catastrophic accidents of the 1990s was pole speed. The majority of injured vaulters had excess pole speed and hit the back edges of the pit and rolled out onto hard surfaces, striking their heads. As a result, the NFHS also increased pit size and dictated that hard surfaces adjacent to the pit be padded. Some detailed and demanding work was done by 1976 Olympic bronze medalist Jan Johnson to lead to these pit dimension changes.

Although the rule changes have improved safety, coaches and athletes must still address the issue of pole speed to keep vaulting safe. As previously mentioned, a vaulting pole is a lever rotating around a fixed point (the tip of the pole in the planting box) that moves according to the forces applied to it. The fact that it is flexible or stiff does not change these laws of physics. Coaches must educate themselves in these principles and always be aware of the implications of approach-run length, grip height, pole stiffness, and takeoff dynamics. Athletes must also learn to recognize the feel of pole speed and not hesitate to abort a jump when the speed is too fast or too slow.

Very few high school–age athletes abort jumps. They seem to want to try to make the crossbar regardless of the spatial reality of their position. Coaches and parents often urge them to always finish the jump, as they would urge a distance runner to run through a pain barrier. The difference between the two sports is crucial to understand. A distance runner who is hurting and continues to run will most likely end up with a slower time, disappointment, and perhaps an upset stomach. A vaulter who ignores the warning signs of incorrect pole speed or poor spatial positioning, however, may end up on a stretcher with a broken joint, a concussion, or worse. World-class vaulters commonly abort jumps; they have probably learned from experience that pushing past obviously poor positions can have damaging results. Coaches must learn to recognize the warning signs of poor technique, be aware of weather (wind direction, cold temperatures, rain) and mental and physical issues (fatigue, personal or family issues), and make the necessary adjustments for the vaulter for that day. Perhaps he needs to jump from a shorter approach run or to lower his grip height.

Pole speed is directly related to the vaulter's grip height (defined as the distance from the tip of the pole to the top of the vaulter's top hand) and speed and efficiency at takeoff. Correct pole speed is often hard to achieve; it can be either too slow or too fast. In either case, it can be ineffective and potentially dangerous.

The preferred landing zone (PLZ) placed on landing mats and defined in the NFHS rule book is a good tool to use to evaluate the movement of the pole and the vaulter around the pole. The NFHS rule book basically states that a vaulter landing behind the PLZ is moving too fast; conversely, one who lands in front of the PLZ is moving too slow horizontally. The first step is to determine whether the run and takeoff mechanics are fairly consistent. If they are and the athlete is still landing outside the PLZ, corrections involving grip height and pole stiffness are needed. Use the following guidelines in the order listed to make these adjustments.

1. *Change grip height.* Grip height should be changed in small increments of 2 to 4 inches (5 to 10 cm). An increase in grip height will slow the pole down (again, the metronome effect), whereas a decrease will speed the pole up. These

adjustments should place the vaulter's torso in the PLZ upon landing.

2. *Change pole stiffness.* A more flexible pole will usually move faster, and a stiffer pole will usually move slower. If a coach sees a pole overbending and considers the run and takeoff to be adequate, then a move to a stiffer pole (usually in 5 lb, or 2.2 kg, increments) should have an effect similar to that of raising the grip (slower horizontal movement).

3. *Change pole length.* If both grip and stiffness have been changed with no result, then the athlete may have to switch pole length. The NFHS has a restriction on how high an athlete can grip a pole, and manufacturers recommend that grip height be restricted on poles. So when an athlete is faced with no longer being able to raise the grip on the current pole she is using, she will be forced to move to a longer pole. This is usually challenging for vaulters because longer poles tend to have different response characteristics. Coaches and athletes need to keep in mind that they still want to make small adjustments when moving from one pole length to another. Vaulters often do not have all of the pole lengths and test weights available to make these small adjustments. When this is the case, the coach must use sound judgment as to what is best.

Sometimes there are no clear-cut guidelines as to the correct pole length or grip height for an athlete. Choosing a pole can be more of an art form that years of experience help refine. The coach can offer suggestions based on careful observations of the jump. At the same time, the athlete must learn to sense the feeling of incorrect pole speed so that, when necessary, he can abort the jump. Many times both coach and athlete are so locked in to clearing the crossbar that they fail to recognize the warning signs of incorrect pole speed. Almost every severe accident in the past 15 years can be attributed to a failure to recognize incorrect pole speed. Most injured athletes were moving too fast (either the grip height was too low or the pole was too flexible), but some of the scariest moments come when grips are too high or poles are too stiff and the athlete struggles to reach the landing mat.

Standard Settings

The other recent key rule change for both high school and collegiate vaulting in the United States concerned the horizontal movement of the standards. The movement of the standards really refers to the placement of the crossbar relative to the zero line, or back edge, of the planting box. The old rule allowed the standards to be anywhere from the zero line (essentially placing the crossbar right over the back edge of the box) to 24 inches (61 cm) behind the zero line (in the direction of the pit) for high schools and 32 inches (81 cm) for colleges. This placement rule allowed an athlete to try to complete a jump without moving the pole all the way to the vertical. If he did clear the bar, the landing could be dangerously close to the unforgiving plant box. The old rule also restricted the better high school vaulters from achieving their best results because they would hit the crossbar on the way up during the swing phase of the jump. The new rule does not allow the placement of the standards any closer than 40 centimeters (15.5 in.) from the zero line and any farther back than 80 centimeters (31.5 in.); the collegiate rule is now between 45 and 80 centimeters (17.6 and 31.4 in.). The current standard placement rule not only encourages the athlete to move the pole all the way to the vertical position before release, but also allows better vaulters a chance to finish a long, powerful swing phase and obtain optimal results.

Far too often coaches use the standard placement to compensate for young vaulters' poor technique. At many competitions, the less technically sound athletes move the standards as far forward as the rule allows, whereas the better athletes move the standards as far back as possible. It is much better for the long-range development of the athlete to leave the standards as far back as possible and force the vaulter to develop the correct technique. With the standards at the maximum setting, an athlete is forced to learn the horizontal aspects of the jump, moving the pole all the way to the vertical and driving aggressively off the ground. Young athletes should be patient, keep their grip heights low, and learn to move their poles through the complete motion.

Today's equipment manufacturers have made impressive improvements in the quality and design of vaulting equipment. Poles come in almost every possible length and test weight, and they are made using modern technology so vaulters can achieve consistent and reliable performance results. Landing mats have been enlarged and reshaped to safely cushion the athlete's fall, and landing boxes are available with high-tech cushioning properties. It is now the responsibility of the coaches and athletes to pursue vaulting in a safe and responsible manner.

>> Vaulting Vocabulary and Coaching Clues <<

A unique and sometimes quirky vocabulary develops in any specialized activity; pole vaulting is no exception. The sport also has a number of valuable and innovative coaching cues. The following list includes a few of both of these.

Blow

The explosive reaction of an athlete who has timed the double pendulum effect and comes off the extension release phase with a great deal of upward energy.

Reach

The vaulter is overstriding on the last few steps to try to hit the perceived takeoff spot. This causes a low and slow takeoff action.

Get on Your Top Hand

The correct pressure point for vaulters is felt through the top hand on the pole. Many inexperienced vaulters try to put pressure on the pole with the bottom hand. This robs the vaulter of the long lever effect that moving through the top hand allows. The vaulter wants to feel this pressure early in the jump. To encourage this, coaches will often say, "Get on your top hand quicker."

Bottom Arm Thinker

Being a bottom arm thinker is the opposite of getting on the top hand. Bottom arm thinkers tend to have an overly wide grip on the pole and are so conscious of bending the pole with the bottom arm that they fail to allow the pressure and rotation to happen through the top arm. Overlooking this habit is a common shortcut for some coaches and is truly a disservice to the athlete because it is very hard to overcome.

Get Big at the Takeoff

The concept here is that the athlete wants to have very good posture and press the arms and shoulders as high as possible. It also sends a message to the vaulter to have a powerful attitude.

Chase the Pole

When an athlete has set up a correct takeoff and created space between herself and the pole at takeoff, the pole will move quickly away from her toward the vertical (a good thing). The athlete must immediately start to catch, or chase, the pole by executing the drive and swing phase to correctly time the double pendulum effect.

Swing From Zero

The swing portion of the drive and swing phase must start as soon as the takeoff foot leaves the ground. If the athlete delays this action, the timing with the pole will be very difficult to coordinate.

Be the Hammer, Not the Nail

This refers to the athlete delivering the pole in the plant phase with authority and keeping pressure on the pole through this phase. Many inexperienced vaulters allow the pole to collapse inward toward the torso and absorb the energy of the takeoff into the body instead of transferring it into the pole.

See Your Hands

This cue helps the vaulter focus on good head position and eye focus. If he can see his hands during the plant and then throughout the jump, he will have a solid reference point to work around.

Out Jump

The takeoff has been executed behind the desired takeoff point (toward the runway).

Under Jump

The takeoff has been executed inside the desired takeoff point (toward the pit).

COMPETITION STRATEGY

The pole vault offers many opportunities for various strategies during the course of a competition. The coach must evaluate the skill level, fitness level, and mental toughness of the athlete and then build the plan from there. The following are possible scenarios for various levels of athletes and varying competitive situations. In each instance, the coach must address the following basic questions:

- Is the athlete on a long-range plan or a short-range plan?
- What other events will the athlete compete in?
- Will the athlete use a short approach run or long approach run?
- What will be the starting height for the athlete during competition?
- Will there be any strategy during the competition, such as passing heights, switching poles, or changing grip heights?

High School Athlete

The typical high school pole vaulter has a short, three- to four-month season, competes in two or three events, and has a constantly changing skill level. Implementing a strategy for the high school athlete is difficult, but the following guidelines are useful.

- Starting height should be 18 inches (45.7 cm) below her seasonal best.
- An athlete competing in more than one event should use a short approach run, a lower grip, or a softer flex pole upon returning to the vault. Fatigue may be an issue. Also, the athlete may have a sense of urgency that may lead to poor decision making and unsafe vaulting conditions (especially when the athlete has run the 300 hurdles or the open 400). In the early part of the season, it may be useful to have the vaulter use a shorter approach run and a lower grip height in order to focus on the technical aspects of the vault.

- Typically, the high school athlete does not use the rule that allows for the passing of a height. It can, however, be an effective tool for the more advanced vaulter who is competing in multiple events and needs more recovery time. It is also useful in a scoring meet when the more elite athlete may choose to clear a comfortable height, thereby ensuring the team points, and then pass to higher heights for a personal challenge. It is important to note that high school rules do allow vaulters to pass a single attempt (unlike open and collegiate rules, in which athletes must pass all three attempts at that height). This can be useful for applying mental pressure on an opponent in certain situations.

Collegiate Athlete

The collegiate athlete has an entirely different set of circumstances than the high school athlete. Typically, this athlete is in a year-round program, has an indoor and outdoor season, and has a long-range plan for the season.

- Typically the vaulter would progress from a short (five-stride) approach run in the early season to a full (eight- or nine-stride) run in the latter part of the season.

- In addition to lengthening the approach run, the athlete is usually increasing grip height and pole stiffness as the season progresses.

- The collegiate vaulter typically competes only in the vault, so multiple events during a competition are not an issue. Those that do compete in multiple events should follow the guidelines listed for the high school athlete.

- Starting height for most collegiate vaulters should be 12 inches (30.5 cm) below their seasonal best. This will vary depending on the athlete. Females have a tendency to open at heights closer to 24 inches (61 cm) below their seasonal bests. The coach has the option of either encouraging a great number of vaults (10 or more) or having the vaulter's fifth through eighth jumps take place at the desired height (under the theory that the athlete is likely to achieve maximal effort during these jumps). For example, a collegiate female wants to get in as many opportunities as possible. She opens at 24 inches (61 cm) below her seasonal best in a competition in which the bar-raising increments are 6 inches (30.5 cm) up to athletes' seasonal bests and then 4 inches (10 cm) after that. The opening height for this athlete is 10 feet (3 m), which she makes on her second attempt. She then proceeds to make 10 feet 6 inches (3.2 m), 11 feet (3.4 m), and 11 feet 6 inches (3.5 m) on her first attempts. When the bar is raised to 12 feet (3.7 m), the athlete makes it on her second try. The bar is now raised to 12 feet 4 inches (3.8 m), which the athlete makes on her second try. She then makes three attempts at 12 feet 8 inches (3.9 m) and fails. The athlete has taken 13 jumps, which certainly has met the strategy of 10 or more jumps the coach laid out for the competition.

- Passing heights is very common at higher-level collegiate and open competitions. At this level, a greater emphasis is typically placed on the place the athlete is trying to attain rather than personal improvement regardless of place, which may define earlier-season or lower-level competitions. Passing heights has two purposes: to conserve an athlete's energy and to force the competition to perform. It is also a useful tool when the competitor makes a height on a first attempt and the athlete cannot win the competition by clearing that height because he is behind in the countback procedure from the previous height. For example, athlete A has made 17 feet (5.2 m) on his first attempt, and athlete B makes it on his second attempt. They are the only two competitors. When the bar is raised to 17 feet 6 inches (5.3 m), athlete A again clears on the first attempt. At this point, athlete B cannot gain any advantage by clearing that height, so he elects to pass to 17 feet 10 inches (5.4 m). Athlete A then places the pressure back on athlete B by passing 17 feet 10 inches (5.4 m), and athlete B misses all three attempts. The competition is over.

Regardless of the level of the athlete, one of the most important skills any athlete can develop is managing the time immediately prior to and during competitions. An unfortunate trend among vaulters of the current generation is a total dependence on a coach during competition. Many athletes do not complete even a basic warm-up sequence without constant feedback from the coach. They also seem incapable of making independent decisions during the competition. Most successful athletes and coaches work on these skills prior to the competition, at which time the athlete is responsible for staying in touch with the ongoing demands of the event. The athlete should learn to communicate with the officials about issues such as starting time, length of warm-up, order of jumping, and bar progressions.

Many variables lead to success in the vault, and staying on top of how the competition is unfolding can make a huge difference. Knowing when to relax, keeping track of when to become active (three or four jumpers ahead in the rotation), being aware of changing wind conditions—all of these should be the responsibility of the athlete. Coaches are invaluable in observing changes in run-up patterns, grip heights, and pole selection, but athletes must learn to take responsibility for staying aware of the constantly changing variables of the event.

PRACTICE CONSIDERATIONS

Each level of pole vaulting is unique and requires unique training programs. Athletes in high school programs in the United States have short seasons and a large number of competitions. A short seasonal plan differs greatly from a plan that extends over two or three seasons. Coaches must choose the best plan for their situation. In an address to the Reno Pole Vault Summit, the famous coach Vitaly Petrov urged the high school and collegiate coaches in the audience not to become "collectors of drills," but instead to challenge themselves to become complete coaches who are constantly learning and evolving. Chapters 8 and 9 provide direction on creating unique plans that will meet the needs of individual athletes. In addition to the concepts presented in chapters 8 and 9, the following items should be considered as part of all vault training programs.

Speed Development

As previously stated, success in the vault is predicated on the velocity of the approach run. In addition, the vaulter should not lose a great deal of velocity as a result of carrying the pole (everyone is slowed down to some extent). Therefore, the training for speed should include work with and without the pole.

Even though the approach run in the vault is less than 50 meters, both speed endurance work and pure speed work are needed. The total amount of work done in one speed session will depend on the physical maturity and makeup of the athlete. If the athlete is working on speed endurance in the early season, a reasonable total might be 1,200 meters (e.g., 6 runs of 200 m or 8 runs of 150 m). If the athlete is doing pure speed work (95 percent effort or higher), then the total might be 200 meters (e.g., 5 runs of 40 m). Pole runs should be limited to 10 or fewer in a single session and should be done for a distance similar to what the athlete will vault from.

In all speed work, correct posture, rhythm, and tempo are critical. The athlete should develop the correct mechanics first and then focus on the type and amount of work to be done. Coaches should note that correct running form may take a great deal of time to develop, more than is available in the training program. For this reason, athletes should work on running form in all warm-ups and at every possible opportunity.

Strength Training

The emphasis on core strength, balance, and agility that has been prevalent in many training programs over the past 10 years fits well in training for the vault. Traditional lifts such as the bench press, once quite popular in training programs, did not build the type of strength necessary for the vault. The fact that a female athlete 5 feet 3 inches (160 cm) tall and 100 pounds (45.2 kg) has jumped over 16 feet (4.9 m) in the vault demonstrates the true nature of the strength issues inherent in the vault. Like the gymnast, the vaulter needs a good power-to-weight ratio, which is developed with exercises such as pull-ups and bar dips.

This is not to say that weight training does not have a place in vault training; in fact, it has a crucial place. Olympic lifts such as cleans and various types of squats are part of most vault training programs. The emphasis for younger vaulters should be on developing overall natural body strength and flexibility. The medicine ball routines and abdominal circuits currently in vogue are great examples of this type of work.

As the athlete matures, traditional weight training can be added to the strength training routine. A great deal of work can be done with an overhead bar (available at many schoolyards and city parks), a medicine ball, and a bit of creativity on the part of the coach. A hanging rope is a great addition to a vault training program. It allows the athlete to move through the horizontal and vertical planes at the same time, as in the vault, while also serving as a great strength-building tool. Swings on the rope, climbing the rope in a variety of positions, and specific vault drills are all beneficial. The rope needs to be 20 feet (6 m) high, be securely suspended, and have plenty of free space around it and padding underneath.

SAMPLE POLE VAULT PROGRAM

October to November (General Preparation Phase)		
Monday	Warm-up jog, flexibility, tempo runs of 300 to 600 m (total volume of 1,200 m with 5- to 8-minute recoveries), weight training (Olympic lifts)	Example of Monday workout during the general preparation phase: • Warm-up: 800 m jog, static or dynamic flexibility, 4 × 60 m buildups • Sprint drills (barefoot on grass, if possible): A-skips, B-skips, C-skips, variations of skips, high knee work, high turnover work • Technical development: walking plants (emphasis on timing of curl or press and pushing pole away) • Medicine ball routine with partner • Weight training: Olympic lifts and squats, pressing movements • Cool-down: Jogging or skipping on grass
Tuesday	Warm-up jog, flexibility, sprint form drills (barefoot, if possible; emphasis on posture), walking plants and pole throw drills, medicine ball drills (emphasis on rotational and explosive movements)	
Wednesday	Warm-up jog, flexibility, speed endurance (150 to 200 m repeats, total volume of 1,200 meters with 3- to 5-minute recoveries), weight training (bodybuilding day)	
Thursday	General strength flexibility, circuit with body-weight exercises (total of 2 miles, or 3.2 km, covered)	
Friday	Warm-up jog, flexibility, hill runs of 100 m with 3- to 5-minute recoveries, weight training (Olympic lifts)	
Saturday	Easy tempo run of at least 3 miles (4.8 km)	
Sunday	Rest	

December to January / April to May (Specific Preparation Phase—Indoor Season / Outdoor Season)		
Monday	Warm-up jog, static or dynamic flexibility, medium-approach jumps, speed endurance (100 to 150 m, total volume of 1,000 m with 3- to 5-minute recoveries), lifts (bodybuilding)	Example of Wednesday workout during the specific preparation phase: • Warm-up: 800 m jog, 10 minutes of stretching, 4 × 60 m buildups • Technical development: Short-run jumps, emphasis on penultimate mechanics and plant action (maximum of 8 steps) • Speed development: 6 × 50 m accels to 95% with strong drive phase (5-minute recoveries) • Weight training: Olympic lifts and squats, pressing movements • Cool-down: Jogging or skipping on grass
Tuesday	Warm-up, static or dynamic flexibility, form drills and pole drills (easy day)	
Wednesday	Warm-up jog, static or dynamic flexibility, short-run jumps, speed development (50 to 70 m, 300 m total volume with 5-minute recoveries), lifts (explosive)	
Thursday	Warm-up jog, static or dynamic flexibility, gymnastics day (do not do without gymnastics coach)—focus on swinging movements at shoulders (not pulling) and trampoline work (if trained to use properly)	
Friday	Warm-up jog, static or dynamic flexibility, long-run jumps, approach work on track with pole, weight training (explosive lifts)	
Saturday	Active recovery	
Sunday	Rest	

February to March / June to July (Competitive Phase—Indoor Season / Outdoor Season)		
Monday	Warm-up jog, static or dynamic flexibility, full-approach jumps, weight training (explosive)	Example of Wednesday workout during the competitive phase:
Tuesday	Warm-up jog, static or dynamic flexibility, general strength, easy drills, film analysis of Monday	• Warm-up: 800 m jog, static or dynamic flexibility, 4 × 60 m buildups
Wednesday	Warm-up jog, static or dynamic flexibility, pole drills, short-run jumps, speed development (20 to 40 m at 95% with total volume of 150 m, full recovery), weight training (explosive)	• Technical development: walking plants, single-arm plants, penultimate work from 6 steps
Thursday	Warm-up jog, static or dynamic flexibility, gymnastics day (do not do without gymnastics coach), general strength	• Jumps: 8 to 10 steps maximum
Friday	Warm-up jog, static or dynamic flexibility, pre-meet preparation (travel, light warm-up)	• Speed development: 5 × 30 m at 95% with full recovery (time and record)
Saturday	Competition	• Weight training: Olympic lifts and squats, pressing movements
Sunday	Rest	• Cool-down: Jogging or skipping on grass

PART III

Shaping the Mind, Body, and Program

Chapter 7

Mental Training

Dr. Keith Henschen

Most track and field coaches spend a great deal of time teaching the biomechanics, techniques, and strategies of the jumps and the pole vault; but few invest the appropriate effort in the final piece of the performance puzzle—mental training. This is not meant to demean track coaches; rather, it is to emphasize that the mental side of performance is as important as the physical side. The final piece of the performance puzzle for jumpers and vaulters is to master the mental skills that are crucial for performing frequently "in the zone." Skills such as relaxation and activation, concentration, imagery, and appropriate self-talk are essential for high-level performances, as are having a preperformance mental routine, learning to ignore pressure, and responding appropriately to success and failure.

IMPORTANCE OF MENTAL TRAINING

When asked what percentage of an athlete's performance is psychological, most coaches and athletes involved in the jumps or vault would say anywhere from 50 to 90 percent. We adamantly disagree. The jumps and vault—in fact, all physical performances—are 95 percent physical and 5 percent mental. There is no substitute for physical ability or technique development; that is why physical practice is so crucial. It does take hours and hours of practice to perfect the jumps skills; but this is only the foundation for performance in the jump and vault events. After all of the hours of hard physical work, then the mind enters the picture.

In pressure situations, the mind actually controls, or oversees, the body. The body is a mere servant to the dictates of the mind. If our minds believe we can't jump a certain distance or vault a particular height, then we can't. Many track and field athletes spend thousands of hours physically training their bodies, but then have trouble performing in competitions. These are called "practice performers." They feel comfortable in practice, but uncomfortable in track meets—especially the big meets. Performance is mostly a matter of being physically conditioned and ready, but then the 5 percent (mind) takes over. Great psychology cannot overcome poor physiology, but it can enhance those who have established a solid physiological foundation (Vernacchia 2003).

An important question to ask is, "How does an athlete become a great jumper or vaulter?" There are only two ways to reach athletic potential: Cut off your head, or become so good mentally that you don't interfere with yourself.

Someone jumping or vaulting without a head attached is a pretty vivid image. At first glance, this notion may seem simplistic, humorous, or even stupid. Yet the idea is accurate. In competition, the athlete's mind should be on automatic pilot and not thinking about or analyzing what is happening. Good athletes learn to trust their training and, in essence, take their minds out of the performance realm. Because the mind is trained to focus on strategy instead of technique, less cognitive athletes are frequently more effective than thinking athletes in competition. Rather than thinking, they are free to just react to the situation. Thinking causes emotional reactions, and emotional reactions are detrimental to effective performances. Once emotional reactions enter the picture, the ability to perform is compromised.

Consider a jumper or vaulter who misses a height or fouls and is thinking about the unsuccessful attempt and subsequently becomes frustrated. The athlete must overcome this emotion to return to effective performance. Both negative and positive emotions have a tendency to help the athlete focus on previous attempts (especially the technique), which will interfere with the next attempt. Anger, despair, elation, anxiety, pleasure, pride, and fear are emotions that manifest (and need to be eliminated) during competitions. Having these emotions at the conclusion of a competition is acceptable, but not during it.

Many athletes experience tremendous performances when they feel slightly sick. This happens because they are focusing on their physical feelings instead of thinking about the actual execution of the jump or vault. They just want to finish the event and thus do not interfere with their bodies. Their minds are on automatic pilot.

Becoming so good mentally that you don't interfere with yourself is actually easier than cutting off the head, but it takes longer. Not interfering with oneself involves implementing a mental skills training program. Learning the appropriate mental skills helps athletes move from a thinking state to a state of automatic response during performances. The athletes who ultimately become the best, and most consistent, are the ones who have mastered the mental skills of performing and thus quiet the active mind (do not overthink).

MENTAL TECHNIQUES FOR IMPROVING PERFORMANCE

The mental skills in this section are presented in a hierarchical order because they build on each other; this order is most effective for improving performance. Once athletes have learned how to use relaxation and activation, concentration, imagery, and self-talk (in that order), they are ready to create preperformance mental routines. In addition to improving athletes' performances, these psychological skills help them respond effectively to pressure, success, and failure (Henschen 2005).

Relaxation and Activation

Relaxation and activation, or tension, are opposites; they cannot occur simultaneously in the body. As the performer masters the skill of relaxation, he can control the amount of activation in every muscle group of the body (Benson 1975). This requires that he be aware of how activation feels at many levels. This is not easy and takes practice. Initially, these levels will be difficult for the athlete to recognize; but the more he practices, the easier they become to recognize and control. Eventually, the athlete learns to create the appropriate levels needed to perform optimally in many situations. He learns to be intense, but not tense. When that happens, he is able to reach his ideal performance level whenever he desires (Gould and Udry 1994).

Relaxation training is not new to the world of performance. In fact, this skill enjoys a rather long and distinguished history. A number of relaxation techniques are currently available. This is good because each athlete is unique and will benefit more from one technique than from the others. Athletes should investigate all of the methods and then use the one that best suits them.

© Human Kinetics

Being relaxed is a precursor to concentration. As anxiety increases, the ability to concentrate decreases. As arousal increases, the ability to focus narrows. Relaxation and concentration are necessary for effective imagery, and imagery is necessary for effective self-talk. These four mental skills are the integral components of preperformance mental routines. Following are examples of some relaxation techniques.

Breathing Awareness

Traditionally, breathing awareness has been used to reduce high levels of anxiety and stress that have negative effects on performance. Breathing awareness frequently lowers precompetition apprehension and performance anxiety. It offers one other crucial benefit as well: It helps train the mind to communicate with the feelings of the body. Breathing awareness helps the mind and body listen to each other's signals.

Breathing awareness is a good start to learning the relaxation response. Following are some simple instructions:

1. Lie on your back with your legs straight and slightly apart; keep your arms at your sides, your palms up, and close your eyes.

2. Focus on your breathing. Do not attempt to control your breathing by speeding it up or slowing it down. Just passively be aware of it. Place one of your hands on the area where you feel the most movement. This should be on your abdomen, not your chest. Breathing into the abdomen (diaphragm) is more relaxing than breathing into the chest.

3. Begin to concentrate on the removal of tension with every exhalation. If it is helpful, you may want to say to yourself "exhale" or "relax" on each exhalation. With each exhalation you will find yourself becoming more and more relaxed.

4. You are now ready to scan your body for tension and to control that tension. Start with your feet. Passively become aware of the tension there and feel it reduce with each exhalation until your feet are relaxed. Again, you may want to say to yourself "relax" as you exhale. Next, move up your body to each large-muscle group and repeat the process: lower legs, upper legs (front), upper legs (back), buttocks, abdomen, chest, lower arms and hands, upper arms, neck, and face.

5. You are now ready to scan again and return to any areas where you still sense an uncomfortable level of tension. At each of these places, reduce the tension level to one that is comfortable through passive awareness and exhalation. Do this by imagining the exhaled air leaving through the part of your body that has tension.

6. Soon your body will be comfortable. You can now experiment with the exercise to reduce or increase activation levels. Prior to performances or practices, before going to sleep, waiting for a class to begin, and waking up require different activation levels. Practice your breathing awareness by raising and lowering your activation levels during these times. The more you practice, the easier and more efficient your control will become.

You can also experiment with various positions such as standing and sitting. Eventually, you will be able to reduce high anxiety or arousal with your eyes open and manipulate activation levels in a very short period of time, no matter where you are. Do this exercise for two weeks, two to five times daily, and at different times. Once you have mastered breathing awareness, it will be easier to move on to the other relaxation methods.

Progressive Relaxation

Progressive relaxation is considered a muscle-to-mind technique. The objective of progressive relaxation (Jacobsen 1930) is to contrast, as opposites, relaxation and tension. This is accomplished by tensing and then relaxing muscle groups one at a time. By becoming aware of tension levels, performers can learn to modify tension levels to accommodate the needed activation for the task. The following is an exercise in progressive relaxation. Although this technique is easy to learn, athletes may want to consider recording these instructions and playing them while they follow along. This will allow athletes to be more passively involved and thus more relaxed.

1. Lie down in a comfortable position with your arms at your sides and your legs straight and slightly apart. Close your eyes and focus on your breathing. As in breathing awareness, do not try to control the speed of your breathing; just let it happen.

2. Beginning with your feet, press your heels into the floor as you tighten all the muscles in both feet (tighten only the feet, not any other part of the leg). Hold for a count of 10 as tightly as you can without hurting yourself, and then release and wait for 10 to 15 seconds. Notice the difference between being tight and being relaxed. Next, move to your calves and tighten both of them for a count of 10, and then release. Again, notice the difference. Next, tighten your quadriceps for a count of 10 and then release. Next, tighten the hamstrings and buttocks for a count of 10, and then release. Then, tighten and release every muscle in the lower body at the same time.

3. Do the same thing with your abdomen and then move to the chest muscles. Next, clench your hands into fists and tighten your fists and forearms, and then release. Do the same to your upper arms (biceps and triceps). Next, tighten and release your neck muscles. Then move to your facial muscles and tighten until you have a "bitter beer face," and then release. The facial tensing should be fun because you want the face to resemble a prune. Now,

have all the muscles in the upper body tighten for 10 seconds and release, feeling the tension leave each muscle group as you relax.

4. The final exercise is tensing and releasing every muscle of the body at the same time (making your body like a bar of iron).

5. Now, as you are lying in a relaxed state, scan your muscle groups from head to toe for any areas that may still be a little tense or sore, and once again repeat the tightening and relaxing there.

6. Finally, after tightening all the muscles at once and then releasing, you should feel very comfortable and relaxed.

Progressive relaxation sessions can be long or short depending on the situation; after practice, for instance, a short session would be appropriate. This technique should *not* be used immediately before a performance, but it is ideal to use the night before. Both breathing awareness and progressive relaxation are ideal to use after demanding physical practice. They have been shown to aid in recovery from fatigue. Progressive relaxation should be done for at least two weeks, two or three times daily and in situations that require varying tension levels. As athletes become more experienced with relaxation, they can focus on raising and lowering their activation levels to affect their performance.

Autogenic Training

Autogenic training is the opposite of progressive relaxation in that it is considered a mind-to-muscle relaxation technique. Basically, this method of relaxation involves repeating a series of formulas, while controlling one's breathing from the diaphragm. The autogenic visualizations are as follows:

Comfortably warm

Comfortably heavy

Heartbeat calm and regular

Breathing, it breathes me (focusing on what each deep breath feels like)

Solar plexus comfortably warm

Forehead pleasantly cool

Each formula is practiced twice, three times a day, for one week. They are practiced in the suggested order because they are progressively challenging. The total autogenic training method requires six weeks to complete.

With the first formula (comfortably warm), for example, the athlete is attempting to raise the temperature in various parts of the body: first the right arm, then the left arm, both arms, the right leg, the left leg, both legs, and both arms and legs. The athlete goes through this process twice, three times a day. The purpose of autogenic training is to teach the body to listen to the commands the mind is sending (Krenz 1983). Each formula gives the body parts a different sensation. Autogenic training is easier to master once the athlete has learned to control anxiety and arousal levels through using other relaxation techniques.

Concentration

When discussing mental preparation for performance, athletes inevitably utter words such as *concentration, attention,* and *focus.* All jumpers and vaulters learn very quickly that without appropriate concentration, their performances are erratic, inconsistent, and less than optimal. So just what does *concentration* mean? Concentration is a skill that must be learned, just like any other skill. Good athletes have it, and not-so-good athletes wish they did!

In physical performance, *concentration* can be defined as the ability to focus on the appropriate cues in a given situation and to control one's responses to these cues for the execution of a specific performance. Concentration also includes the ability to let go of factors over which one has no control. The desired level of control in jumping and vaulting is almost a passive control. Intensifying efforts to consciously control a situation frequently results in a loss of concentration. To be successful, athletes must learn to intensify their concentration when situations require it and to lower the intensity when appropriate (Henschen 1995).

There are several types of concentration, or attentional styles, and each type of performance or situation requires a specific one. For example, a pole vaulter needs different concentration skills than a long-jumper or a high-jumper. In other words, the skills of concentration are many and vary depending on the situation. To negotiate the ever-changing demands of the sport, a jumper or vaulter must master five attentional styles:

1. *Broad external.* Total awareness of the situation. Example: A triple-jumper going down the runway being aware of the weather conditions, her steps or markers, and approaching the board.

2. *Broad internal.* An awareness of a lot of information that is simultaneously occurring in the body and the mind. Example: A high-jumper feeling the proper energy for the takeoff.

3. *Narrow external.* A narrow focus on an external object or task. Example: A vaulter focusing on the pole plant.

4. *Narrow internal.* A narrow focus on an internal object or task. Example: A high-jumper focused on his breathing for the penultimate step.

5. *Shifting.* Moving from one attentional style to another very quickly. Example: A triple-jumper changing focus during her attempt.

Jumpers and vaulters must master each type of attentional style and recognize when to use each. The following exercises can help athletes master these attentional styles. Practicing these exercises daily for a couple of weeks (about 10 minutes per day) will help athletes handle distractions automatically and stay in appropriate focus.

Be aware This helps the broad external attentional style. Lie down with your eyes closed and just listen to all the sounds around you. Do not focus on any one sound, but see how many you can detect (3 minutes).

Listen to the sounds of your body This helps the broad internal attentional style. Lie down with your eyes closed and your fingers in your ears. Concentrate on all the sounds your body is making—creaking, growling, breathing, heartbeat (2 minutes).

Pick a problem This is a narrow external attentional style–enhancing exercise. Intentionally think of a problem that has been bothering you and ask your mind to supply you with as many solutions as possible (this is internal brainstorming). As the mind provides a solution, place it into a bubble and allow it to just float away. Wait for the next solution to appear. This exercise should be done in a nonjudgmental atmosphere (5 minutes).

Study an object This is also a narrow external attentional style–enhancing exercise. Take a small object that you can easily hold in your hand (ring, coin, earring, paper clip) and focus intently on this object. If the mind becomes bored and starts to wander (which it will), refocus on the object. Use a different object each time you do this exercise (5 minutes).

Let your thoughts flow This exercise helps develop the narrow internal attentional style. While resting comfortably with your eyes closed, concentrate passively on the ideas or thoughts that your mind wants to feed you. This should be done nonjudgmentally. Passively recognize the thoughts and allow them to come into and leave the mind at their own pace (3 minutes).

Listen to your heartbeat This is a narrow internal exercise. Close your eyes and get into a comfortable position and listen to your heartbeat. Try to hear nothing but the heart beating (3 minutes).

Clear your mind This is another narrow internal exercise. Think of nothing but blackness. Control your mind so that it cannot feed you any thoughts (1 minute).

Allow your mind to shift quickly from one thought to another This is a transitional three-week exercise. Find an interesting book to read with no pictures. The book should hold your interest and be fairly easy reading. During the first week, read each night for 10 minutes for comprehension, and then tell someone exactly what you read. During the second week, read the book and listen to the radio at the same time for 10 minutes; then, tell someone what you read and heard. During the third week, read the book, listen to the radio, and watch television simultaneously for 10 minutes. This is an enjoyable exercise, but it also forces people to learn to shift their attention quickly from one object to another.

The skills of concentration are probably the most important of all the psychological skills to actual performance. Concentration, anxiety, arousal, and self-confidence are intricately interwoven; each greatly influences the others. Athletes must become so effective in all the concentration skills that they can deploy them automatically. This will occur only after many hours of practice. No one can give athletes concentration skills; they must earn them. It is also important to remember that concentration and self-talk are highly correlated. Negative self-talk disrupts concentration; but positive, process-oriented self-talk refocuses concentration (Moran 2003).

Imagery

The skills of relaxation and concentration enhance athletes' imaging abilities. "Because imagery allows a focus on important visual cues and physical skills as they unfold in the moment, it functions like a language for action" (Heil 1995, p. 183).

Unless an athlete is born with a neurological impairment, he can image. The human animal is wired in the nervous system to image. Imagery can be intentional (such as thinking about a particular aspect of a performance), or it can be unintentional (dreaming while asleep or daydreaming while awake). Think of imagery as the ability to create or recreate an experience in the mind by using all of the senses. It is trainable through practice and can be perfected with continual use. Imagery should be a multisensory experience—visual, auditory, tactile, olfactory, and kinesthetic.

Most people think of imagery as visualization. This is probably because visualization is the type of imagery we first experienced as small children. This type of imagery is vision based and relies on pictures generated in the mind. A second type of imagery, which normally appears after puberty, is kinesthetic imagery (feeling). In physical performance situations, kinesthetic imagery is more dominant than visualization. Most performers are capable of both types of imagery, but to perform well (have peak performances), they need kinesthetic imagery (Heil 1995). Regardless of the type of imagery an athlete masters, it is a powerful procedure that is beneficial to performance.

Many jumpers and vaulters use imagery in a variety of ways to enhance their ability to perform. Following are the top 10 benefits of imagery (Heil 1995):

1. To picture success
2. To perfect skills
3. To familiarize oneself with situations
4. To motivate
5. To set the stage for the actual performance
6. To refocus
7. To substitute imagery (mental practice) for physical practice when limited practice time is available, when burnout or overtraining demands less physical training, or during an injury or rehabilitation
8. To conquer performance anxiety, negative self-talk, or various stresses
9. To cope with a situation in the mind prior to being exposed to it in the real world
10. To create a positive and confident feeling about the impending performance

Following are some guidelines to follow to ensure the effectiveness of imagery:

- Choose the imagery program most effective for you. Every performer is unique.
- Be confident that the imagery will enhance your performance.
- Begin the imagery program in nonstressful situations and then move on to more pressure-packed circumstances.

- Start with easy, familiar visual scenes and then progressively upgrade by adding other sensory perceptions.

The following exercise, called Happiness Room, will aid in preparing for competition. Close your eyes and get yourself in a very comfortable position. Take a few deep breaths and relax. In your mind, see yourself at the bottom of a set of stairs (about 15 steps). As you look up, you see a large door at the top of the stairs. Now, walk up these stairs, and when you get to the top, open the door. When it opens, you will see a huge room with nothing in it. It is completely bare! Your job for the next two minutes is to decorate this room any way you like. Money is no object. You can put anything or anybody in this room. The only stipulation is that whatever you place in the room *must* make you happy. This is the only room in the world like this. It is yours; it is your happiness room.

Keep your eyes closed and stay in your room. Go to a comfortable chair in your room and recline in it. Face a wall, and imagine a big-screen television on the wall. Now take your remote control and turn on the television. See yourself performing perfectly on the TV screen. Watch and enjoy how well you are performing. See how excellent you really are and how good that makes you feel. Watch yourself for a couple of minutes. Now turn off the television. Get up and walk over to the door, open it, and look back at your room. See how good it makes you feel! Close the door and walk down the stairs. Open your eyes when you reach the bottom of the stairs. As an athlete, you should visit your happiness room every night. Redecorate it! Remember that money is no object and the room is only for you. You can go to this room, turn off the TV, and practice (perfectly) difficult parts of your performance over and over in a comfortable environment.

Athletes should start with simple imagery and build to more complex imagery. Initially, they should focus on having vivid and controlled images. The images need to be comparable to real-life experiences. The skills, routines, or sequences of the performances should

be imagined exactly as they would expect to perform them.

Imagery is a skill that takes time to learn. Practice sessions should be frequent but brief (around 8 to 10 minutes long). Athletes need to remember, though, that imagery is not a substitute for physical practice; rather, it is a supplement to it. The ultimate test of imagery effectiveness is how well it serves the person in actual competition. It should be generalized from a mental skill to a performance skill. Eventually, imagery will become automatic or second nature, occurring when needed (Heil 1995).

Self-Talk

Athletes should learn self-talk only after they have learned to be calm and composed (relaxation), to focus appropriately (concentration), and to see and feel desired actions in their minds (imagery). Without practicing relaxation, concentration, and imagery techniques, athletes are prone to negative self-talk because the mind is primarily exposed to negativity.

Self-talk, positive or negative, affects our minds, behaviors, and physical states. Negative self-talk lessens the control we have over ourselves and therefore impairs performance. Society is often very negative in the reinforcement it provides to individuals. Generally, people tend to focus on what athletes are doing wrong instead of what they are doing right. Even coaches fall into this trap because they are error-correction specialists. Most of what has been modeled to us is negative, so we rapidly learn to be the same way with ourselves. Consequently, athletes develop critics in their minds instead of enhancers. Reardon and Gordin (1992) postulated that around 70 percent of feedback on performances is negative.

Successful jumpers and vaulters learn to control their self-talk so that it enhances their ability to perform. Positive self-talk does not mean a lot of unrealistic positive statements; rather, it is often just a means of damage control, counteracting the mind's tendency to be negative. Positive self-talk programs the mind with ideas that help athletes manage performance situations more effectively. It is solution and process directed, not problem directed. Following are some guidelines for enhancing positive self-talk.

Concentrate on the process

Our thoughts generally focus on what needs to be done rather than on how we are doing. Athletes should focus on effect instead of the technical aspects of performing. When athletes are thinking about outcome, their self-talk creates anxiety because the outcome is uncertain until the conclusion of the performance. Outcome-oriented self-talk also detracts from the ability to focus on the here-and-now process of the performance. A jumper repeating the words *rhythm and flow* during each attempt is practicing positive self-talk and focusing on the process rather than the outcome.

Concentrate on the present moment

Many athletes are prone to thinking about past negative performances or projecting into the future and worrying about the outcome. Present moment self-talk is the process of immersion in the present and trusting oneself and one's abilities. A jumper telling herself to be fast on her approach instead of telling herself not to do what she did in her last attempt is concentrating on the present moment.

Focus on composure

Self-talk should be concerned with staying in control and attaining the appropriate level of arousal. Athletes should be thinking about enjoying the performance rather than reacting to distractions (internal or external). This is difficult because anxiety can decrease concentration. In addition, thinking about anxiety will increase anxiety. For this reason, athletes must focus on calmness and composure. They must believe that what they think about will happen. If they think about being relaxed and have learned the skill of relaxation, then that is the response their bodies will produce, following the directions of their minds. We are what we think. When we think *anxious,* we become anxious; when we think *composure,* we become composed. A vaulter telling himself that he is confident and controlled during each attempt is focusing on composure.

Try smarter, not harder

Many athletes have the misconception that by sheer will, as reflected in self-talk, they can force good performances. They try too hard and their self-talk is just rhetoric and not genuine. Self-talk that is oriented toward an effortless state of mind, however, is effective in enhancing performance. An old Eastern philosophy states, "You must lose yourself to find yourself." This means getting off your own back and letting yourself perform. Self-talk that frees the athlete to just perform results in seemingly less effort expended but more energy expended.

Use different self-talk in practice than in performance

Most athletes have trouble recognizing the difference between self-talk that is helpful in improving skills in practice and self-talk that is beneficial in competition. The purpose of practice is to improve, explore, and identify areas needing additional attention in order to enhance performance. Practice self-talk usually involves questioning, introspection, and considering possible areas of change. Competition self-talk is a completely different animal. Self-talk during performance needs to be enabling, encouraging, minimal, and positive and must contain elements of affirmation, trust, and enjoyment. Competition self-talk should reflect confidence, determination, and action with the desired outcome of reducing doubt (Reardon and Gordin 1992). An example of practice self-talk would be focusing on what it feels like to do a jump correctly. Competition self-talk would be powerful words repeated over and over (e.g., *strong and high, strong and high*).

The following are exercises for developing appropriate self-talk. The first exercise demonstrates how self-talk determines the distribution of energy in the body. The second exercise illustrates how occupying the mind with positive self-talk allows the body to perform without interference from the mind.

Positive versus negative self-talk

Have everyone pair up and face each other. Person 1 closes his eyes and extends his arms straight out to each side (like a cross). Person 2 stands in front of person 1 and grasps the wrist of person 1.

Person 2 instructs person 1 to think of something that makes him sad and depressed. When person 1 gets this thought in his head, he nods his head. Person 2 then pulls person 1's arms down, while person 1 attempts to keep his arms up. After the arms are pulled down, the two people change places and repeat the exercise (again with a sad or depressing thought).

After both people have completed this exercise with a sad thought, they both do the exercise with a positive, happy, and energizing thought. Normally, people are much stronger (their partners can't move their arms down) when thinking positive thoughts. This exercise illustrates that thoughts affect the energy level of the body and thus overall performance.

Trigger or cue words To perform well, athletes sometimes have to fool their minds. In other words, instead of allowing their minds to think about performing, they focus them on something else—a trigger word. In essence, a trigger word is a positive affirmation that the mind repeats over and over while the body is performing. By staying focused on the trigger, the mind cannot analyze the performance and interfere with it (because the mind can think of only one thing at a time and the trigger word already has it occupied). The following is an example of this principle:

The USA Track & Field team was practicing at a training camp in northern Australia just prior to the 2000 Olympic Games. During this training camp (about three weeks before the Games), one of the team's sport psychology consultants was approached by two 400-meter runners. They complained that they were thinking too much about the pain during the last 100 meters and consequently "tying up" at the end of the race. Of course, their times were getting worse rather than better. The sport psychology consultant told them both to see him the next day and have two power words to give him. These words were to be positive and energizing to them. The next day the runners were told to repeat their two power words, over and over, during the last 100 meters of the race. This would keep their

minds from focusing on the pain. In the next few weeks there were two practice meets, and each time both runners improved their times in the 400 meters. During the Olympic Games, one of the runners performed a personal best and won the silver medal, and both won gold medals as members of a relay team.

Like any skill, self-talk must be practiced. Habits of positive self-talk can become integrated and automatic for performers.

PREPERFORMANCE MENTAL ROUTINE

The ultimate goal of learning psychological skills is to enhance performance. Athletes who just show up and hope to perform well are likely to be inconsistent and fail to demonstrate their expertise. Because all athletes are unique, they have varying ways of preparing to perform. A consistent, orderly pattern of preparing to perform involves both mental and physical aspects. Physical preparation is usually accomplished through warm-up exercises plus some technique drills to ensure that the body is ready to move. The mental or psychological warm-up normally consists of a series of mental activities involving imagery, relaxation, positive self-talk, and, finally, some arousal, or activation. These skills should be placed in a well-established pattern that helps the athlete feel normal and comfortable. The preperformance mental routine allows the athlete to approach each performance the same way and become somewhat immune to the stresses and pressures of big performances.

The preperformance mental routine should be individualized for each athlete. A good way to determine what to include in this routine is to think back to a previous great performance and try to remember what was being done at that time. Frequently, athletes remember that they executed a number of similar procedures before the excellent performances. These specific procedures should be included in the preperformance mental routine.

Athletes should be careful not to confuse a routine with a ritual. A routine is a mindful way to get the athlete into an ideal psychological and physiological position to deliver a best effort on that day. A ritual is a mindless activity that is repeated to make sure luck is on the athlete's side. If the routine becomes a ritual, the athlete should develop a new routine (Lidor and Singer 2003).

Following are some guidelines for preperformance mental routines:

- The routine should be relatively short (three to five minutes).
- The routine should be done immediately prior to the performance.
- The routine should include two or three things that work for the athlete (e.g., a cleansing breath).
- The athlete should be alone while going through the routine. (Physical isolation is ideal because this limits possible distractions, but mental isolation can happen even in a crowd.)
- Part of the routine should deal with kinesthetic imagery.
- The routine should end with some type of activation technique.

Consider the preperformance mental routine of Josh, a successful vaulter. A couple of minutes before every attempt, Josh goes off to the side of the pole vault area with his pole in his hands. He talks to himself intently (inside his head) as he visibly goes through the physical motions of his approach, pole plant, and takeoff, and the body position he will use to clear the bar. He is relaxed as he begins the mental routine, but he is more aroused as he mentally simulates his approach. He then imagines (both visually and kinesthetically) planting the pole and changing his body position while in the air. He sees himself clear the bar, land in the pit, and address the cheering crowd that is acknowledging his successful attempt.

RESPONDING TO PRESSURE

Many jumpers and vaulters have trouble handling pressure in the big meets. Any time a title is placed on a competition (e.g., conference championship, state meet, world championship, Olympics), some athletes have difficulty performing up to their abilities. Why is this? Quite simply, they are having trouble responding to pressure. Mastering the previously discussed mental skills will help athletes control their responses to pressure. In essence, athletes deal with pressure in three ways—two are unhelpful and one is helpful. We will address the unhelpful ways first and then present the helpful way.

Divided attention When feeling pressure, many athletes try to take in more information than they are normally accustomed to taking in. The result is divided attention, which causes distractions. The mind is taking in more information than it can handle, and it becomes confused. Errors occur and frustration builds, which causes more errors.

Self-theory Some athletes become more exact or precise and focus on technique when they perceive pressure. By focusing on a technique that is already established as an automatic response, they change the rhythm of the response and thus slow it down. An old term describes this perfectly—paralysis through analysis.

Challenge A helpful way to handle pressure is to consider it a challenge that is fun to confront. Instead of being afraid or hesitant when faced with pressure, athletes should tell themselves how much fun it will be to perform in these circumstances. They should remember that pressure comes from within and so must be mastered from within. In essence, to overcome pressure, athletes should try to have fun and try less on the most important days of their lives. The mental skills provide a way to feel in control of the environment and allow athletes to trust their training and perform to the best of their abilities. Having fun is a great antidote to pressure.

RESPONDING TO SUCCESS AND FAILURE

Every great athlete must learn how to handle both good and poor performances appropriately. Great performers do one thing different from other performers: They "play forward" regardless of the results. They do not get overly elated over successes, and they do not get too frustrated or depressed over less-than-stellar performances. They realize that the competition is over and that there are no redos. They analyze their performance for a short time (30 minutes), learn from their successes and mistakes, and then start to prepare for the next competition. Fame is short-lived, and so should be the emotions associated with failure.

Three emotions frequently manifest after a competition—euphoria, depression, and aggression. Euphoria is normally felt after successful performances. This is an acceptable emotion if it does not last longer than a day. If euphoria persists, it interferes with getting back to a daily routine and focusing on the next meet. When jumpers and vaulters qualify for the U.S. Olympic team, they get excessive media attention, publicity in their hometowns, and notoriety beyond what they ever envisioned. This instant fame has ruined many promising Olympic medalists. Instead of immediately refocusing on improving their technique and strategy, they fall into the trap of thinking they have arrived and embark on the banquet circuit, putting the necessary training on the back burner. This is dangerous because it delays the training necessary for remaining at the world-class level.

Depression and aggression are the emotions frequently experienced after a poor performance. Both of these are devastating to future performances because they are so hard to get over. Because these are powerful emotions, they require time to mitigate. Coaches need to be aware of the types of emotions their athletes are prone to manifest and work with them to refocus as soon as possible on training and the next competition.

The bottom line is that success and failure are part of every track meet. Coaches must help their athletes handle these emotions appropriately and effectively. If coaches are manipulating emotions prior to competition (e.g., arousal and anxiety), then they must help their athletes deal with their emotions after successes and failures (e.g., euphoria, depression, aggression).

Chapter 8

Performance Training

Dr. Will Freeman

The talented jumper is often one of the best athletes on the team, and for good reason. The requirements to jump well include great speed, great strength, and great coordination. All of these must be trained to a high level for success to occur. Add the elements of endurance and flexibility, and you have the five biomotor elements the jumper must train: speed, strength, endurance, flexibility, and coordination.

This chapter describes how to train these biomotor elements and how to test the athlete. Testing provides a mechanism for both identifying talent and gauging the success of the training process. It is important to note that because the five biomotor elements interact significantly, they are not trained independently. The jumper working on approach training (coordination) is also training speed. Likewise, any speed training also develops elastic strength. An understanding of how to train the biomotor elements will give the coach the tools to create effective jump training programs.

WARM-UP AND COOL-DOWN

Athletes must prepare both physiologically and psychologically for training and competition. Both forms of preparation can be addressed in the warm-up and cool-down. Although research is inconclusive regarding the value of the warm-up, anecdotal evidence strongly suggests that it both acclimates the body to physical demands significantly above normal resting levels and reduces the risk of injury.

Warm-ups should meet the demands of the training loads to follow. A high-demand training day should include a more dynamic warm-up, whereas a recovery day can include a more extended and lower-demand warm-up, also called a static warm-up. The cool-down can follow the same design. On high-demand days the athlete might cool down with a progression of skipping and running that gets progressively less demanding, perhaps ending with walking. Postcompetition or postworkout, however, is a good time to use a cool-down that slowly brings the athlete back to normal operating levels. Performing cool-down elements that are progressively less dynamic and ending with static stretching is a productive way for the athlete to return to basal levels.

Static Routine

Figure four (page 174)

Static butterfly (page 174)

Hamstring stretch, seated (page 175)

Lunge stretch (page 175)

Prisoner stretch (page 176)

Single-leg quad stretch (page 176)

The following dynamic routine can be repeated for a greater load. It can also be used in an extended format with general strength exercises added as a good recovery day modality.

Dynamic Routine

30 m jog down and back (two or three times)

30 m backward run, then forward run back to start

30 m ankling walk

30 m ankling skip

30 m ankling skip with windmill arms forward, 30 m with arms backward

Jog-jog-jog-quickstep (30 m right only, then 30 m left only) (page 170)

Jog-jog-jog-quickstep-quickstep (repeat each side for 30 m) (page 170)

30 m walk with arm circles forward, 30 m walk with arm circles backward

30 m jog

30 m A-skip (page 168)

30 m jog

30 m carioca right, 30 m carioca left (ball of foot, light on feet) (page 168)

30 m straight-leg bounding (page 169)

30 m walk

30 m easy acceleration

30 m acceleration from three-point stance

30 m acceleration from start position

The cool-down will reflect the type of training day. For more demanding nervous system work, such as a high-quality jump session, the athlete might do a progressive cool-down. The athlete will begin with variations of skipping, then jogging, then walking to progressively return to a resting state.

TESTING

The first step in training is to assess the current state of the athlete. Coaches often rely on guesswork, estimations of talent, and other imperfect methods to determine a starting point for training. For optimal training to occur, the coach must determine the athlete's training age, fitness levels, biomotor strengths and weaknesses, and technical expertise. There is no place for guesswork in this process. Testing is an appropriate method of gaining much of the needed information. Testing on a regular basis is also an excellent way to monitor the effect of training during the training year.

For results to be reliable and valid, testing must be a controlled protocol and thus comparable from test to test. The protocol must be followed precisely each time the tests are administered. Following are ways to control testing:

- Test on the same day of the week in the same week of a restoration microcycle (every four to six weeks).
- Test using the same conditions and on the same facility (whether an indoor or outdoor track).
- Do the tests in the same order and with the same amount of recovery between tests.

The following tests are useful for two reasons: They provide the coach with indicators of potential talent, and they provide the coach (and athlete) with concrete measures of whether the training is working for the athlete.

- *Standing long jump (coordination and power).* A standing long jump from a squat position into a sand pit.
- *Standing triple jump (coordination and power).* A standing triple jump from the runway into a sand pit. The athlete stands as if he were beginning the standing triple jump. He jumps off both feet, then lands on only one foot (hop), then steps to the other foot, and then jumps into the pit.
- *Standing 30-meter sprint (speed).* The athlete runs from a standing start. The clock begins when the foot leaves the ground.

- *Overhead back throw with shot (power)*. An overhead back toss with shot off the toe board: 7 kilograms for men, 4 kilograms for women.
- *Underhand forward throw with shot (power)*. An underhand forward throw with shot off the toe board: 7 kilograms for men, 4 kilograms for women.
- *Standing vertical jump (power)*. The athlete stands at a tape measure on a wall and reaches to the highest point she can. This point is marked. She then jumps, and that point is also marked. The difference between the two marks is the measurement of the vertical jump.
- *150 m and 600 m runs (speed, muscular and aerobic endurance)*. One maximal effort for both 150 m and 600 m trials on the track.
- *Pull-ups (muscular endurance)*. The athlete hangs from the pull-up bar with palms facing away. He must pull himself up with his arms and touch the bar with his chin each time for it to count as a legitimate effort.

The athlete is given two attempts in all tests except the 150-meter run, the 600-meter run, and pull-ups, in which there is only one attempt (pull-ups are done to exhaustion). The best mark is recorded, and a point value is given. Total points are added, and a final score is given. Athletes should improve 2 to 3 percent or more in each test when done once per mesocycle (monthly). Any less of an improvement should prompt the coach to ask why the athlete is progressing more slowly than expected.

Coaches should note that testing requires maximal effort; appropriate rest on the days both before and after is necessary for the athlete to do well and recover. Recoveries are as needed between trials. The athlete should get a 20-minute recovery between the 150-meter and the 600-meter runs. See the appendix on page 195 for scoring tables for biomotor tests. The 600-meter, 150-meter, and 30-meter runs are all timed. All other tests are measured metrically.

BIOMOTOR TRAINING ELEMENTS

The five biomotor elements to be trained are speed, strength, coordination, endurance, and flexibility. The following sections cover each element in depth and provide drills the athlete can use to improve performance in that specific area.

Training for younger jumpers must address the five biomotor elements in a balanced way. Because these elements are interdependent, not addressing all of them invites imbalance, poor performance, and potential injury. The younger the jumper, the more balanced the training among the biomotor elements should be. As the jumper develops to a more advanced, elite level, a more specific emphasis can be placed on the technical elements of the jump. At the highest level of performance, the athlete still is training all biomotor elements early in the training year, but shifts to a greater emphasis on the technical element (coordination) during the competitive period. Figure 8.1 illustrates a progression of training that begins with multilateral development and progresses to more specific training for the jumps over time.

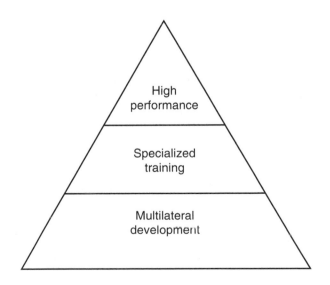

> **Figure 8.1** The progression of training begins with multilateral development and progresses to specialized training.

Reprinted, by permission, from T. Bompa, 2005, *Periodization training for sports*, 2nd ed. (Champaign, IL: Human Kinetics), 58.

Speed and Acceleration

Speed can be defined as the ability to move the system quickly. Speed is a critical requisite for jumping success and reflects a high component of elastic strength. The angle of takeoff for each of the jumps varies on a continuum from the triple jump (the lowest) to the high jump (the highest). The pole vault and long jump show nearly identical takeoff angles and lie in the middle of the continuum.

The angle of takeoff is very much related to velocity at takeoff. The higher the horizontal takeoff velocity is, the lower the takeoff angle will be. The structure of the jumper will also dictate the velocity his system will allow for at takeoff. With too much velocity, the system will amortize (give) at takeoff, setting up a domino effect of collapse and forward rotation resulting in failure, if not injury. For the horizontal jumps and the vault, velocity is critical to success; there is an almost perfect correlation between velocity on the runway and distance jumped. The high jump is a different animal. High-jumpers can be successful with both faster and slower velocities into takeoff. Speed-type jumpers create strong takeoffs with high velocity, whereas power-type jumpers do so with long application times on the ground.

It is wise to think of both acceleration and speed when training the jumper. Acceleration is the ability to move from zero velocity in a progressive, rhythmic fashion with good posture. Although the goal is to attain optimal, controlled speed at takeoff, acceleration mechanics are actually more important to the jumper than speed. Because maximal velocity does not occur until more than 50 meters from a standing start, and because jumpers do not typically run farther than 40 to 45 meters, the jumper will not be at maximal velocity at the moment of takeoff. Instead, the jumper will strive to reach a maximal, controlled velocity that is best suited to that athlete and for that jump event. The vault, long jump, and triple jump demand a higher velocity than the high jump, and thus a longer approach.

Proper postural mechanics (decreasing body lean, increasing stride length and stride rate, and decreasing ground contact times) all contribute to favorable acceleration mechanics during the approach. The approach harmonic reflects a decreasing ground contact time with each contact. Because the athlete can only effect a real change in the running mechanic when in contact with the ground, and because ground times decrease through the approach, the athlete will have a decreasing ability to change the cyclic mechanic as the approach unfolds. The point? Athletes must have it right mechanically from the first step of the approach. Before they can learn how to run at high velocity (speed), they must first know how to get to that high-velocity mechanic. The process of acceleration must be a high priority early in the teaching and training process.

Acceleration

The following acceleration drills are progressively difficult. Drill choice should reflect the time of the season and the fitness of the jumper. (See chapter 9 for information about periodization.) The drill notation indicates the number of sets and then the number of reps. "Blocks" indicates that the athlete should begin with starting blocks; "rocker start" indicates that the athlete should rock forward from a standing position, with one foot in front of the other. The athlete should run at 95 percent effort or higher on a track, if possible (otherwise, on grass). The athlete should focus on the quality of the movement and doing things with full engagement and thought.

10-15 × Sprint Ladder Sprint ladders are available from most track companies. They consist of ropes and wood and can be laid out on the track to provide an increasing stride pattern for the runner. A sprint ladder is an excellent tool for increasing stride length. Emphasis should be on increasing velocity and stride length, changing body angles, and changing arm action. Two-minute recovery between runs.

2-5 × (5 × 20 m Blocks) Three-minute recovery reps; six-minute recovery sets (i.e., recover three minutes after every rep and six minutes after every set).

2-4 × (5 × 30 m Blocks or Rocker Start)

Three-minute recovery reps; seven-minute recovery sets.

3 × (4 × 40 m Blocks or Rocker Start)

Three-minute recovery reps; nine-minute recovery sets.

2-3 × (3 × 50 m Blocks)

These are effort runs. Timing and recording athletes' efforts may help to motivate them. Four-minute recovery reps; seven-minute recovery sets.

Speed

These drills consist of repeats of high-velocity runs of 30 to 50 meters. Athletes should undertake these drills only after they have developed and stabilized proper acceleration mechanics. Use cones for the final three drills in this section. These are done at near-maximal velocity and with recoveries of three to eight minutes. The quality of work should be very high as measured by effort and time.

2-4 × (5 × 20 m) With 15 m Acceleration Zone

The watch starts only once the athlete hits the cone after the 15 m acceleration zone. Time the 20 m segments only. Three-minute recovery reps; six-minute recovery sets.

2-5 × (5 × 35 m)

Four-minute recovery reps; eight-minute recovery sets.

2-4 × (3 × 15 Accel / 10 m Max / 15 m Float / 10 m Max / 20 m Float)

Cone 1 begins the acceleration zone. The next cone is 15 m ahead; the next is 10 m farther, then 15 m, 10 m, and 20 m. The athlete accelerates from the first cone with good mechanics, starts a maximal sprint at cone 2, "floats" between cones 3 and 4 (not slow, just relaxed and not pressed), does a maximal sprint between cones 4 and 5, and then floats to the finish, slowing to a stop. Four-minute recovery reps; eight-minute recovery sets.

2-3 × (3 × 20 Accel / 10 m Max / 15 m Float / 10 m Max / 15 m Float / 10 m Max)

Five-minute recovery reps; 10-minute recovery sets.

3 × (3 × 40 m Accel / 20 m Relax / 30 m Max)

Eight-minute recovery reps; 12-minute recovery sets.

Speed Endurance

These drills include repeats of 60 to 200 meters with two- to five-minute recovery reps and up to 10-minute recovery sets, depending on the fitness of the athlete and the length of the run. The quality of work is 90 to 95 percent of maximal current effort.

1-2 × (4 × 75) @ 90-95%

Three-minute recovery reps; six-minute recovery sets. Total volume: 300 to 600 m.

2-3 × (4 × 60 m) @ 95%

Two-minute recovery reps; four-minute recovery sets. Total volume: 720 m.

3-6 × 150 @ 90%

Five-minute recovery. Total volume: 450 to 900 m.

2 × (3 × 50 m Accel / 50 m Float / 50 m Lift-Pop or High-Knee Lift)

Five-minute recovery reps; 10-minute recovery sets. Total volume: 900 m.

2-3 × (3 × 100 m) @ 95%+

Five-minute recovery reps; 10-minute recovery sets. Total volume: 600 to 900 m.

Strength

Strength can be generally defined as the ability to apply force. The nature of the jump events demands that the athlete be strong enough to handle the great forces applied at takeoff. Great strength (postural and elastic) is also needed for sprinting well during the approach. Because strength is a prerequisite to speed, strength training is critical to the development of speed. The progression of the strength development plan will go from general to specific and from simple to complex. Power, stabilization strength, and elastic strength are all important to the jumper and must be trained in a progressive, functional manner.

General Strength

General strength refers to the ability of the body to handle work and is a general measure of total strength. Specific strength measures would be more specific to the actual demands of jumping. Pillar routines and body-weight exercises are examples of general strength exercises.

The drills in this section are very good for shoring up weaknesses, developing infrastructure, and building the jumper's capacity to handle work (work capacity). They can be used as a primary strength tool early in the training year and then as a lower-priority restoration activity for recovery days later in the year. Core, or pillar, routines can be done daily throughout the year. These exercises use body weight and gravity as the resistance. The load can be increased by increasing either the number of repetitions or the time.

➤➤ Lunge Walk ◀◀

From a standing position, the athlete raises one knee high in a knee-up, toe-up (dorsiflexed) position, then extends that leg forward and lands with it approximately 3 feet (1 m) in front of the body. Upon landing, the trunk must be vertical, with shoulders back. The lead leg bends to 90 degrees with the knee exactly over the ankle at maximal flexion. The rear leg is nearly extended, and its knee does *not* touch the ground at any time. The athlete extends the knee to raise the body and recover the rear leg. That leg then repeats the action just done by the other leg. Cues are: Stay tall, 90 degrees at front leg when at lowest point, and knee over ankle and in front of ankle. This drill can be done with the hands on the head, on the waist, or used in opposition with the legs. The athlete walks 15 to 20 meters per rep.

>> Push-Ups <<

A good mechanical push-up is actually a core exercise more than an arm exercise (triceps). When in the up position of the push-up, the athlete's arms are fully extended and the trunk and legs form a single straight line (no body sag). The athlete should maintain a straight line from the head to the heels even when the arms are flexed. The movement is to flex the arm at the elbow, draw the nose toward the ground, and extend the arms again. Sagging at the waist is a common problem. Push-ups can be done with the hands wide, directly under the shoulders, or close together, or all three. Another excellent variation is simply holding the up position. The athlete should do this for one minute and build from there.

>> Speed Skaters <<

In a standing position, the athlete hops to the left side about 2 to 3 feet (60 to 90 cm), landing only on the left foot. The right foot swings behind the left and reaches as far as possible to the left. The athlete will have to swing the arms in long, powerful opposition movements to balance the body when doing this. Once the right foot lands, the athlete pushes hard off the left to the right and lands on the right foot. The left leg then swings behind the right and reaches as far as possible to the right before landing.

>> Tuck Jumps <<

Tuck jumps are done in place; the key is to try to keep the trunk vertical. The athlete jumps off both feet together and tries to bring the knees to the chest and keep the upper body tall. The chest should not come to the knees. This is a maximal effort exercise with repetitions of no more than 10 per set.

>> Crab Walk <<

In a crab position (face up with hands and feet on the floor), the athlete moves forward, back, right, and left on command. Those working in groups should be sure to have enough space. The drill is 15 seconds to start, increasing to 45 seconds over time.

➤➤ Jump Burpees ◄◄

From a standing position, the athlete squats to the ground, places both hands on the ground, and extends the legs fully, which will resemble the up position of a push-up. The middle of the trunk should not sag while in this position. The athlete jumps back to the squat position, then aggressively jumps for height before slowly sinking into the next squat.

>> Eagles <<

Eagles are very good for hip mobility and for identifying asymmetry. The athlete starts by lying on the back with arms fully extended to the side and legs together, fully extended. Keeping the shoulders fully in contact with the ground and arms at 90 degrees to the trunk, the athlete brings the left leg up to vertical and then across the body to the right hand, which is still grounded. The athlete then reverses the movement until the leg ends up fully extended on the ground next to the other leg and repeats with the other leg. Cues are to make sure the shoulders stay in contact with the ground (press with hands to do this) and to make a strong effort to get the foot to the hand that is grounded. This exercise can then be repeated facedown, swinging the leg across the back and up to the opposite hand. Eagles (front and back) are very valuable for developing hip mobility and revealing asymmetry in the hips.

▶▶ Squat Jumps for Height ◀◀

This is a maximal double-leg vertical jump exercise. The athlete squats down and jumps aggressively up off both legs for height, using the drive and block of the arms to create a transference of momentum to add to the height achieved.

>> Crunches <<

The athlete lies on the back with knees bent and feet flat on the ground, arms crossed across the chest. The athlete contracts the abs and raises the head, neck, and upper shoulders off the floor, then returns to a lying position and repeats. The key to any type of crunch working is to first stabilize the pelvic girdle before moving the upper or lower body. The athlete should press the lower back into the ground and then begin the action. This will keep the hip flexors from pulling the pelvis forward first. The key is to make the abs do the work. It is especially useful to do abdominal work across the body (specific to the core action of the body when sprinting).

>> Cossack Extensions <<

This drill is also called Russian dancing. With hands behind the head or at the chest, the athlete squats down deeply and alternately extends each leg with the other leg underneath for support. The athlete hops from one foot to another so there are times when neither foot is touching the ground.

➤➤ Russian Twist ◀◀

This drill is done in a standing position with arms extended to the sides. The athlete twists the upper body from side to side with a weight in the hands and tries to stop the swinging of the arms each way. A strong core is needed to do this. The size of the weight will vary according to the athlete's developmental level.

➤➤ Swimming ◀◀

The athlete lies facedown with legs fully extended and arms out ahead of the body and off the floor. The action is a flutter kick with knees and shoulders off the ground. Arms move as in a crawl stroke—the athlete bends one arm at the elbow to draw the elbow back near the hip and the hand near the shoulder, and then reaches forward with that arm while drawing the other arm back.

➤➤ Yogis ◄◄

The athlete is on the knees with the hands behind the head; a partner holds the athlete's feet. The athlete leans forward as far as possible without falling and then moves back to the start position. The abs control the movement. The athlete must maintain an upright posture (straight back, shoulders held back) throughout the movement.

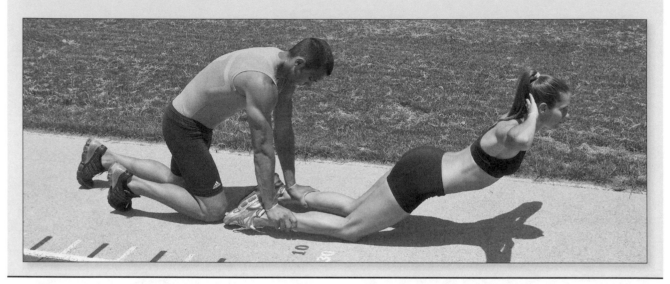

Core Strength and Stabilization

The human body is a unique structure. The skeletal system provides support and a point of origin and insertion for muscles. Yet despite its strength, the skeleton would collapse into a useless pile of bones if the muscles and connective tissues were not providing support and stability. Just standing in place requires a great deal of stability within the system. Imagine the stability needed when sprinting and then jumping!

The pelvic girdle is the critical stabilizing joint. The pelvis can rotate somewhat freely both forward and back and side to side. Without stabilization of the pelvic girdle during sprinting, the hip flexors would pull the pelvis forward, thus limiting knee lift and range of motion. This, in effect, would minimize elastic force generation, which is critical to running at high velocity.

Posture is also related to stability and has a direct bearing on movement efficiency. Both general posture and dynamic posture must be addressed on a daily basis when training elements that build stability in the system. Core, or pillar, training is a primary way to do this. The exercises in this section should be done at some level every day. They can be done at the beginning or end of the session. The load can be increased by increasing the number of repetitions or the amount of time.

➤➤ Low-Level Bikes ◀◀

Sitting on the buttocks, the athlete leans back, supported by the lower arms. The legs do a low rotation as if the athlete were riding a bicycle. The athlete extends the leg and then recovers the heel to the buttock. The feet are about 3 inches (7.6 cm) off the floor for the whole movement. The athlete should begin by performing the drill for 30 seconds and extend the time as fitness increases.

➤➤ V-Sits ◀◀

These are also called clam shells. The athlete is on the back, arms extended straight with hands overhead. The action involves tucking the chin and folding the body up with the hands and feet together at the top of the action. The athlete recovers until just short of touching the ground. It is important to maintain the contraction of the abs. If the athlete can't make the hands and feet meet, he should stretch as far as he can while maintaining the posture. This exercise is best done on a soft mat.

≫ Back Hypers ≪

The athlete lies facedown with the arms bent and elbows out to the sides. The hands are in front of the face with the palms down. The athlete lifts the hands, elbows, and upper body while lifting the legs off the ground. The upper and lower body should be raised no more than 3 inches (7.6 cm) off the ground. Only the trunk is on the ground when in the up position.

≫ Side-Ups ≪

The athlete lies on the right side with the right buttock and right lower arm supporting the upper body. The action involves raising both legs 6 inches (15.2 cm) and then lowering them slowly and under control until the right leg nearly touches the ground. The athlete then repeats on the left side.

>> Russian Leg Lifts <<

The athlete assumes a crab position (faceup with hands and feet on the floor) with toes facing straight forward. Making sure the knees are at a 90-degree angle, the athlete presses the hips as high as possible and extends one leg straight forward to 180 degrees at the knee. The athlete then repeats the action with the other leg. The key is to keep the trunk parallel to the ground (shoulders to hips) and not allow the hips to drop. The load can be increased by adding repetitions or increasing the time spent holding the hips high.

➤➤ **L-Overs** ➤➤

Lying on the back with arms straight out to the side, the athlete raises both legs until they are 90 degrees to the ground. Shoulders must stay grounded while swinging both legs together to the right. The legs lightly touch the ground (to maintain the contraction), swing up to the start position, and continue on to the left and to the ground. The athlete then returns to a vertical position.

>> Hip-Ups <<

The athlete lies on the back with knees bent and feet flat on the floor. The arms are extended out to the side. Grounding both feet, the athlete presses the hips fully up and down (without touching them to the ground).

>> Static Back Presses Into Ground <<

Lying down, faceup, the athlete contracts the abs and presses the lower back into the ground aggressively. A chin tuck is fine. Shoulders are not touching the ground, but the middle of the back is. The athlete holds for a count of five and then relaxes.

Bodybuilding

Bodybuilding exercises are for building general strength in the body, yet they use more resistance than general strength exercises. These high-quality lifts are good for jumpers and vaulters because of the high demand they place on the central nervous system. They are often done two or three times per week, with at least one recovery day between sessions.

>> Clean <<

The athlete squats down, thighs slightly higher than parallel to the floor, and grasps the barbell with an overhand grip. The feet and hands should be about shoulder-width apart. The athlete straightens the knees and hips, pulls the bar up to shoulder height, and catches it on the upper chest and shoulders.

➤➤ Snatch ◄◄

The athlete stands over a barbell placed on the floor. The legs are hip-width apart and the shins are about an inch from the bar. The athlete squats and grabs the barbell with a wide overhand grip, swings the barbell forward and up with the arms, and extends the arms straight overhead.

>> Deadlift <<

The athlete stands with feet slightly apart in front of the bar as it rests on the ground. The athlete inhales and bends forward at the waist with the chest forward and back arched. The athlete grasps the bar with an overhand and underhand grip and, keeping the arms relaxed, stands up straight by rotating the hips.

>> Squat <<

Feet are slightly wider than shoulder-width apart and flat on the floor. Barbell is high on the back, just below the neck. The athlete bends the knees, keeping the upper body tall and vertical, until the upper leg is parallel to the ground. The athlete then returns to a standing position while maintaining posture. For safety, the athlete should not lean forward. The knees must not get in front of toes as the body is lowered. Begin with lighter weight or no weight at all and progress gradually.

>> Bench Press <<

The athlete lies faceup on a horizontal bench with the feet flat on the floor. The athlete grasps the bar with an overhand grip wider than shoulder width, slowly lowers the bar to the chest in a controlled movement, and then extends the arms.

>> Pullover <<

The athlete lies on a bench with feet flat on the ground and holds a dumbbell in the palms of both hands, with the thumbs surrounding the handle and arms extended. The athlete inhales and lowers the dumbbell behind the head, bending slightly at the elbows.

>> Calf Raise <<

The athlete stands on a platform with the balls of both feet at the platform's edge. The athlete slowly raises the heels up past the platform, and slowly lowers so that the heels dip below the edge of the box.

Power and Elastic Strength

Power combines both strength and speed of movement. The impulse the jumper applies at takeoff is the perfect example of power. Power is the most critical element of strength needed for the jumper. Olympic lifts, multijumps, and multithrows are ways to train power.

Because jumping is elastic by nature, jumpers need to do elastic strength activities that have an involuntary element to them (thus eliciting the stretch reflex). Contractions that combine voluntary and involuntary contractions are more beneficial to jumpers than volitional contractions alone. Examples of exercises that provide this type of work include multijumps (plyometrics), multithrows (with shots and medicine balls), and sprinting and jumping (a very high form of elastic strength training).

Medicine Ball Exercises

Medicine ball exercises can be both general strength and elastic exercises. Stability of the core is critical when performing these exercises. The weight of the medicine ball can be any-where from two to eight kilograms depending on the ability level of the athlete. Medicine ball exercises are good for recovery days or lower-demand days of training.

➤➤ Standing Overhead Forward Toss ◀◀

Standing with feet together and arms holding a ball overhead, the athlete steps forward with the left foot and throws the ball. The cue is for the body to form a C when viewed from the left side. Blocking the stepping foot upon landing transfers momentum to the ball. This position, if the throw is done explosively, will elicit the stretch reflex. The athlete then repeats, leading with the right leg.

➤➤ Hip Catch-and-Throw ◀◀

This exercise is done in pairs. Partners face each other approximately 12 feet (4 m) apart. Holding the ball underhanded with both hands, one partner twists to the right, bringing the ball to the right hip, and tosses the ball across the body so the partner can catch it at hip level. Partners must keep both feet grounded throughout the action. The faster the ball is tossed, the more the core must stabilize.

>> Sit-Up Catch-and-Toss <<

Partners sit down with knees bent, toes touching, and feet grounded. One partner tosses the ball to the other, who catches it with extended arms and then lies down, touching the ball to the ground over the head. The athlete then contracts the abs, sits back up, and throws the ball back.

>> Partner Exchange <<

Partners stand 2 feet (60 cm) apart, facing away from each other. The athlete with the ball twists to the left (right hand on top of the ball, left hand under) and gives it to his partner. The partner has twisted to her right and takes the ball left hand on top, right hand under. That partner then twists to her left and gives the ball to the other athlete in the same manner, but shifts the right hand over when doing so. This is done quickly.

>> Prone Catch-and-Toss <<

Lying facedown and 2 feet (60 cm) from a partner (distance hand to hand), the athlete tosses the ball to the partner. Partners should keep elbows and all parts of their arms off the floor. A light medicine ball is preferable for this exercise.

>> Front Loaders <<

Grounding both feet and extending the arms out in front, the athlete holds a heavy medicine ball in an underhand position and tosses and catches it as if it were a hot potato.

>> Squat Chest Throws <<

This exercise can be done with a partner or against a wall. With elbows out, the athlete holds a ball with both hands. She then squats and jumps forward while pushing the ball for both distance and height in a shot-put action, but with both hands together. Elbows must be high, and the fingers should "flick" on the release.

>> Seated Overhead Catch-and-Toss <<

Partners sit feet to feet with knees extended fully and toss a medicine ball quickly back and forth with the arms overhead.

Multithrow Exercises

Multithrows are done with a shot or medicine ball (4-8 kg) and are very elastic, thus stimulating the central nervous system (CNS). Athletes must show good postural mechanics in these movements. Multithrows make very good testing exercises. They match up well with other elastic training units and are typically done at the end of a session.

>> Overhead Forward Throw With a Step <<

Holding a ball overhead with both hands, the athlete steps forward onto the takeoff foot and aggressively throws the ball. The takeoff foot acts as a block. The drive foot must be aggressive in the throwing action. This throw can also be done off both feet while standing on top of the toe board.

>> Overhead Back Throw From Squat Position <<

This throw can be done off level ground or off a toe board. The athlete holds a ball in an underhand position, squats down, and then drives up with full extension of the body as she throws overhead and back for height and distance.

>> Squat Chest Throw From Double-Support Squat <<

The athlete holds the ball as if she were doing a basketball pass, thumbs down and fingers around the ball. Elbows are up and to the side. The athlete squats and pushes the ball forward and up for height and distance. The key is to hold the elbows up throughout the throw.

Multijumping Exercises (Plyometrics)

This type of strength work is very elastic in nature and is critical for the jumper. The athlete should use a safe progression (both in the number of contacts and the difficulty of the exercises). These exercises are typically done on a high-demand CNS day such as a jumping or sprinting day. Doing plyometrics once a week is ample for the beginning or young jumper, and twice a week is ample for the higher-level jumper. The athlete should emphasize being light on the feet, landing on the ball of the foot, and having a short coupling (ground contact) time. The first four exercises are low-level exertion, the next seven are medium-level, and the final four are high-level.

>> Rope Skipping <<

Rope skipping is very low-level plyometric work. The athlete holds a handle of the rope in each hand and cycles the rope over the head and then under the feet, jumping over it as it passes. The athlete can jump over the rope either with one leg at a time, alternating between jumps, or with both legs at once. Jumps should be done at a leisurely pace. The athlete should begin with 30-second reps and increase the time as skill improves.

>> Line Hops <<

Line hops are simple single-leg hops from side to side across a line. From a one-legged standing position just to the left of the lane line on the track, the athlete hops across the lane line and lands on the same foot, then hops back to the start position. The athlete then repeats with the other foot.

>> 180-Degree Reversals <<

The athlete jumps and twists to the right 180 degrees so that he is facing the opposite direction upon landing. He then jumps and twists to the left so he lands in the starting position.

>> Bunny Hops <<

The athlete jumps in place, flexing only at the ankle joint. Minimal flexion occurs at the knee. This exercise can be done on one leg or both.

>> A-Skip <<

This is a skip action with the lead knee driven up aggressively as the athlete skips on the opposing foot. The knee is high with the foot directly under it and dorsiflexed. The knee stops when the thigh is parallel to the ground and the leg is then aggressively brought to the ground to skip while the other leg drives up. Repeat.

>> Carioca <<

The athlete faces to the side and runs sideways to the right, bringing the left knee across the body. When the left foot lands, the right foot is brought behind and to the right. Arms are swung in opposition to these actions. Significant trunk rotation occurs in this exercise.

➤➤ Easy Bounding ◀◀

The athlete begins by jogging forward and then moves to a bounding action, in which the knee of the forward leg is held momentarily at its highest point while the rear leg is held momentarily in its most extended position. The lead foot then is aggressively recovered to the ground to repeat the action on the opposing side. The trunk should be tall and upright throughout. The difference between this and normal bounding is that the impulse on the ground is lower (i.e., there is more ground contact time).

➤➤ Straight-Leg Bounding ◀◀

Straight-leg bounding is good for strengthening the hamstrings; this has also been called the majorette step. The athlete runs with the legs virtually straight, with only minimal flexion at the knees to prevent injury. This aggressive extension action of each leg in a near-straight position fires the hamstring group into action. The trunk must be tall and upright throughout, because posture is critical to the execution of this exercise.

➤➤ Single-Leg Hops ◀◀

Single-leg hops can be done first in place and then with displacement forward. The athlete begins with in-place, easy bunny hops, followed by in-place hops with heel recovery to the buttocks, and finally, by single-leg hops for distance (20 to 30 m maximum). The heel must recover to touch the buttocks when doing this. It is a true cyclic recovery of the hop leg. The free leg swings virtually straight as it works in opposition to the recovering hop leg.

➤➤ Jog-Jog-Jog-Quickstep ◄◄

Beginning with the right foot, jog three steps, then "pop" the ground with the left foot, driving the right foot up to the buttocks (cue: knee up, toe up). This is very explosive. Repeat.

➤➤ Jog-Jog-Jog-Quickstep-Quickstep ◄◄

Beginning with the right foot, jog three steps, then "pop" the ground with the left foot, driving the right foot up to the buttocks (cue: knee up, toe up), and immediately "pop" the ground with the right foot, driving the left foot up to the buttocks. The four steps will cause the athlete to do the quickstep with opposing legs every fourth step.

➤➤ Bounding for Distance ◄◄

Bounding is a running action that emphasizes holding the knee of the lead leg up with each stride. As the back leg drives off the ground (and the opposing knee is at its highest point), there is a momentary hold in the action before the lead leg actively recovers to the ground. Bounding for distance requires great strength. The athlete should begin by bounding for 20 meters and increase the distance as fitness improves.

➤➤ Single-Leg Hops for Distance ◄◄

The athlete drives off the ground, recovers that foot to the buttocks, and cycles that leg out in front and down to the ground. A big amplitude of the cycle is important. The drive and block of the opposing knee provide a transference of momentum to the body and help with impulse on the ground. The athlete should alternate legs after each distance executed. Because this is a very difficult exercise, the athlete and coach should watch for fatigue and postural breakdown. Either one is a signal to terminate the exercise. Because this exercise is typically done after a fair portion of the workout has already occurred, the athlete should err on being conservative with the load.

►► Depth Jumps ◄◄

Depth jumps are double-leg jumps off a series of boxes to the ground (providing a greater load on the body when landing). The critical part of this action is the response off the ground when jumping up onto the next box. The jump must be quick and explosive. Again, the key to multijumps working is in the coupling (contact) time with the ground, which must be short enough to elicit the stretch reflex. If the athlete spends too long on the ground, he misses the reflexive action. Athletes should begin with 8-inch (20 cm) boxes and progress to 24-inch (60 cm) boxes, making sure not to progress too quickly. Three or four boxes in a row is a good starting point, and eight should be the maximum.

►► Right-Right-Left-Left ◄◄

This exercise is a staple in triple-jump training. The athlete hops twice on the right leg, twice on the left leg, twice on the right leg, and so on. The athlete should begin with repeats of 20 meters and increase as fitness increases. Postural breakdown is the key to knowing when the athlete has done too many of these in a row.

Coordination

Coordination can be defined as the level of efficiency in performing a skill. Each jumping event has its own rhythm, harmonic, and firing order of the nervous system. Coordination of these firing orders, what most call *timing*, must be taught in a progressive manner as the nervous system learns what the event demands.

Training coordination and skill takes time. The process moves from general to more specific demands, and from simple to complex movements over time. The coach must ensure that the athlete is not being asked to do something technically that is not possible structurally. This is a common mistake because both coaches and athletes often want immediate gratification. The training of skill demands patience, time, and the appropriate progression.

Consider a young male high-jumper who, when doing a relatively long approach run, is continually jumping into the bar. The frustrated coach is giving the athlete the appropriate verbal technical cues, yet the athlete cannot do what the coach is asking. This athlete, lacking the strength needed to handle the velocities generated from a long approach, cannot create a high enough impulse at takeoff (great force in little time) to go up. On the ground too long, the athlete's center of mass quickly moves well ahead of the body before the takeoff. The result: Into the bar he goes. This athlete would be well served to both shorten the run and work on a strength plan that could create more power at takeoff.

All of the following coordination exercises are done at the lowest height with groups of 10 hurdles set 6 to 12 inches (15-30 cm) apart. These exercises are good for general strengthening, coordination, and mobility at the hip joints. They are often done on recovery days.

▶▶ Two-Touch Walkovers ◀◀

The athlete steps over the hurdle with the knee high and in front of the body. Upon landing, the opposing foot is lifted high and over the hurdle and lands beside the other foot between hurdles. Thus, the athlete leads with the same foot each time. She then repeats with the other foot.

▶▶ One-Touch Walkovers ◀◀

The athlete steps over the hurdle and recovers the other foot, which then immediately steps over the next hurdle without grounding between hurdles. Thus, the athlete is alternately stepping over the set of hurdles. The cue is a high knee on the step.

▶▶ Two-Touch Backward Walkovers ◀◀

The athlete steps backward over the hurdle and recovers the other foot as well so that both feet are together before initiating the next backward step over the following hurdle.

▶▶ Over Three, Back One ◀◀

The athlete begins by stepping over hurdles using the one-touch walkover movement. After three touches, he reverses the motion to a backward action for one touch and then begins again with three forward touches. He repeats until he is through the full set of hurdles.

>> Over and Unders <<

Ten hurdles are lined up end to end; every other hurdle is raised to 42 inches (107 cm), and the others are at the lowest setting. The athlete steps over the first hurdle (at the lowest setting) with the left foot. As the left foot lands between hurdles, the athlete steps under the next hurdle (on a higher setting) with the right foot, squatting fully to go under it in a single support action. The left foot then steps over the next hurdle, and the action repeats to the end. For the next flight, the athlete leads with the right foot.

Flexibility

Flexibility is defined as range of motion at the joints. Both stride length and stride rate increase as velocity increases through the approach run. The jumper begins the approach in a highly volitional manner with a strong drive phase. As velocity increases, the cyclic motion of the stride becomes increasingly nonvolitional (driven by the stretch reflex and not so much by conscious thought processes). Optimal high-velocity mechanics require large amplitudes in the stride (a large range of motion). Stretch reflex processes in the glutes (at the highest point of knee lift) and in the hip flexors (after toe-off) are what "drive the elastic machine." Interestingly, although these contractions are a complicated medley of well-timed events, they

work best when the athlete is allowing them to happen. Too much tension in the system will inhibit these stretch reflexes from offering their best return to the athlete. Flexibility is necessary for this process to be optimal.

Flexibility can be trained via active and passive means. Active means involve the athlete using static stretches unassisted to enhance range of motion. Passive means involve another person helping the athlete increase range of motion and stretch. Proprioceptive neuromuscular facilitation (PNF) is an example of a passive means to train flexibility. Dynamic exercises that use momentum are another method of enhancing flexibility and mobility. Variations of leg swings in multiple planes are examples of dynamic exercises.

>> Figure Four <<

The athlete lies on the back with the arms out to the sides and swings the left knee across the body, resting the ankle on the right leg above the knee. The position should be held for 30 seconds or longer before repeating the stretch on the other side.

>> Static Butterfly <<

The athlete sits on the floor with knees pointing out to the sides and the soles of the feet together. Sitting up straight with shoulders back, the athlete presses the knees out with the elbows and holds for 30 seconds or longer.

▶▶ Hamstring Stretch ◀◀

Seated with legs extended straight out in front, the athlete reaches toward the toes with back straight and shoulders held back. The athlete stretches only as far as he can while maintaining good posture and holds for 30 seconds or longer.

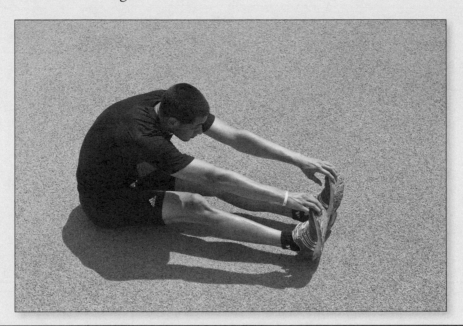

▶▶ Lunge Stretch ◀◀

Feet are staggered with the lead leg in front of the body. The athlete drops down so the lead knee is at 90 degrees and the knee is directly over the ankle. The rear leg is extended back with the foot in contact with the ground.

➤➤ Prisoner Stretch ◀◀

The athlete squats deeply with the knees pointing out slightly, the arms inside the legs, and the hands down in front of the body. The position is held for 30 seconds or longer.

➤➤ Single-Leg Quad Stretch ◀◀

The athlete reaches behind and grasps the right foot with the right hand, keeping the knees together. She presses her hips forward and holds for 30 seconds, supporting herself against a wall with the left hand if necessary, and then repeats on the other side.

Endurance

Endurance is the ability to sustain the application of forces over time. The jumps do not directly qualify as endurance events. Because the jumper runs only a maximum of 45 meters in an approach run, we are most interested in quality and not quantity of movement. We are, however, very interested in training the athlete's work capacity, which has an endurance quality to it. To succeed, the jumper must perform a great deal of repetition, which requires fitness. Also, at big meets jumpers often compete on multiple days, with a preliminary round on one day and the final on another. Jumpers, being the athletes they are, often perform in other events beyond jumping. The ability to handle high-quality work for extended periods is called *special endurance* and is developed over time through an increasing load on the system.

There really are no endurance drills. Endurance is gained by gradually increasing the load on the body. To directly address endurance with these athletes is not specific to the demands of jumping. Once reaching a general level of fitness, endurance is not necessary for a jumper. The desired goal for all jumps is that of specific endurance. This means training must be specific to the demands of the event. Specific endurance is developed by performing repetitions of the total activity of jumping. For example, sprint endurance is developed by sprinting and vault endurance is developed by vaulting.

Chapter 9

Designing Your Program

Dr. Will Freeman

The jumps begin with the cyclic action of approach runs and end with acyclic jump actions. Optimal performance requires a maximal controlled approach velocity combined with maximal force application at takeoff and optimal takeoff and flight mechanics. The goal of training for the jumper is the stabilization of technical skill at the highest possible level for that athlete. Training age, fitness levels, genetic predisposition, infrastructure development, and coaching all influence success. For the coach, developing the jumper requires intuition, experience, and science to offer the athlete the optimal performance package. It is fundamental that the jumps coach understand the concepts of overload and restoration and the variables that affect the adaptation of the athlete (training, rest, nutrition, coaching, academics, and other potential stressors). This chapter will help the coach and athlete develop training plans for the jumping events.

LOADING VARIABLES

This section discusses load and adaptation and explains why they are crucial elements in an athlete's training. Before learning about the principles involved in loads and adaptation, though, athletes and coaches should understand how load is measured. Loads are characterized by volume, intensity, and density of training.

Volume Volume is the amount of (quantity of) training. In general, training volume begins commensurate with the fitness and developmental level of the athlete and should be higher early in the training year before dropping during the competitive period. Volume is easily measurable by number of efforts, meters per second, stride frequency, total distance run in a given time, tonnage (pounds or kilograms), and, specifically regarding the jumps, height or distance jumped. The coach can determine the volume of work for a given session "according to individual abilities, the phase of training, and a correct ratio between volume and intensity" (Bompa 1999, p. 90).

Intensity Intensity is a measure of quality of training and is usually measured as a percentage of a maximal effort. In general, intensity

Table 9.1 Quantifying Volume and Intensity

Modality	How to measure volume	How to measure intensity
Acceleration/speed	Meters/reps/sets	Percentage of maximum effort (high)
Strength circuits	Length (time) of circuits	Percentage of maximum effort (varies)
Weight training	Weight/reps/sets	Percentage of maximum effort (varies)
Multijumps	Number of contacts/meters	Percentage of maximum effort (high)
Multithrows	Number of throws	Percentage of maximum effort (high)
Technical work	Number of jumps/reps	Percentage of maximum effort (high)

increases as the season progresses. Because athletes in the jumping events rely on the central nervous system (CNS), intensity will reach a high level in training and stay there. Only volume drops during the competitive period and as the athlete peaks for a target competition. The quality of work at this time, however, stays high.

The coach must have a system that quantifies the volume and intensity of training, especially with regard to speed, strength, and technical training. Table 9.1 shows how to quantify types of training in these biomotor areas. Coaches should keep records of the quantification loads for all athletes over time.

Density Density is the frequency of training, or the number of training sessions used in a given time span. The density of training will be higher for athletes who are fitter and older. Because younger, less fit athletes need more recovery time from loading than fitter, older athletes, they should train less often. Conversely, the older, fitter athlete can do more work than the younger, less fit athlete, and thus can train more often.

PROGRESSIVE TRAINING

Progressive training involves loading and adapting the jumper's system in a systematic and progressive manner. Related to progression of training is the concept of specificity—that is, training jumpers in a manner that is specific to the demands of their jump events. Both progression (overload, adaptation, and recovery) and specificity are covered in the following sections.

Overload, Adaptation, and Recovery

The process of loading and unloading (recovering) the athlete is what coaching is all about. The normal state of operation of the human system (homeostasis) is interrupted with a training load. The energy systems used result in fatigue, and lactic acid is released into the system. Upon completion of the loading (termination of the workout session), the system begins to return to homeostasis. Recovery from work and caloric intake operate together to compensate for the load that was placed on the system. When energy sources and rest are appropriate, the system can actually recover to a level above the previous homeostasis line. This is called *supercompensation* and is the root of positive adaptation to work.

The athlete's ability to adapt to work changes with her fitness level. Training load must increase as the athlete's fitness increases. A load that was optimal several weeks earlier in training will no longer have the same effect on the athlete. As adaptation occurs, the coach should increase volume and intensity; following are several ways to do this, listed in no particular order (Bompa 1999, p. 89):

To increase volume:

Increase the duration of the training session.

Increase the number of training sessions per week.

Increase the number of repetitions, jumps, drills, or technical elements within the session.

Increase the duration or distance of a drill or repetition.

To increase intensity:

Increase the velocity of the run.

Increase the load in strength training.

Decrease rest intervals between repetitions.

Increase effort in any activity.

Providing specific guidelines for when and by how much to increase load is very difficult. Both the starting level of training and the load increase will depend on the athlete's training age, fitness level, and biomotor ability, among other things. The art of coaching consists of knowing the athlete and designing the program with the best fit for him.

Volume and intensity are not mutually exclusive. Figure 9.1 shows a single periodization model in which volume and intensity work together over time. As the volume of training increases, the intensity also often increases, but to a point. Total workload is a function of both volume and intensity. At some point the athlete will run the risk of injury as a result of the total workload. This point is often in the specific preparation phase of training. As the quality of work increases, the volume of work should begin to drop until it functions simply to maintain the athlete's fitness level. At this point, the quality of training is most important.

The coach must keep records of all training increases to monitor the adaptation of the ath-lete. Early training loads will show increases in both volume and intensity. The period of highest load (i.e., highest volume and intensity) should occur late in the specific preparation phase. At this point, increasing both volume and intensity together will create the potential for overload and injury. Progressive training dictates that intensity continue to rise while the volume of training begins to drop.

Recovery is a critical part of the supercompensation model. Coaches are adept at loading athletes, but often underestimate athletes' need to be restored to homeostasis after the load is imposed. The body's response (i.e., adaptation) to training occurs during recovery. A number of factors influence recovery from training (Bompa 1999, pp. 96-97):

- *Age of the jumper.* Athletes under 18 and over 25 require longer recoveries.

- *Fitness level of the jumper.* Fitter, more experienced athletes recover faster than unfit, less experienced athletes.

- *Sex of the jumper.* Females may require more recovery than males because of endocrinological differences (particularly, less testosterone).

- *Weather.* Cold weather slows recovery.

- *Altitude.* Altitude slows recovery.

- *Nutrition.* Proper nutritional replenishment speeds recovery.

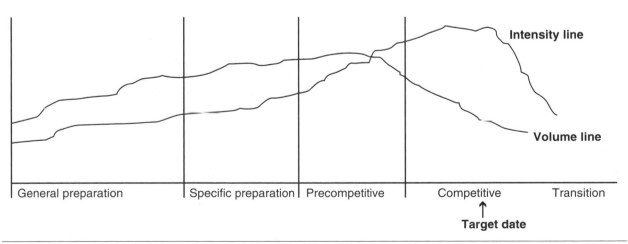

| General preparation | Specific preparation | Precompetitive | Competitive | Transition |

↑
Target date

> **Figure 9.1** Relationship of volume and intensity over the training year.

The type of work that is presented in the load will dictate the length of recovery (compensation) needed. Low-quality work such as easy aerobic runs require short recovery times (as low as 6 hours) before the next bout of exercise. High-demand work, which is common in jumping, requires longer recovery periods between bouts (12 to 36 hours depending on the load). However, following a load that places a high demand on the CNS, an athlete can return more quickly to the next workout if that workout is a recovery-type session (low intensity).

Volume also affects total load. A tough CNS-type workout of jumps, multijumps, and multithrows would no doubt have the athlete quite "flat" for a couple of days. Yet, if the athlete were to do the same type of work with less volume (i.e., fewer jumps and less effort in the multijumps and multithrows), she would recover more quickly because the total load on the system would be lighter.

Active recovery is a useful concept in the jump events. The initial response of the body to high-intensity work will be lactic acid in the system. The faster the system can rid itself of this lactic acid, the better. Low levels of work at the end of intense sessions (such as jogging and swimming) are excellent for flushing the system of lactic acid and restoring the body quickly to homeostasis and balance. The jumps coach must understand that the body does not deal well with imbalance. The training model needs to be designed to get the body back into balance as quickly as possible. Active recoveries help to accomplish this. Having a recovery microcycle in each mesocycle (every four weeks) will help the body regenerate from the training load.

When the athlete does not have enough recovery time before the next load, homeostasis is not achieved, much less supercompensation. Repeated cycles like this will result in a decline in performance, overreaching, and, eventually, overtraining. Open and functional communication with the athlete will help the coach make sure that the athlete is not overreaching or overtraining. Meyers and Whelan (1998,

p. 338) offered these signs that the athlete is overtrained:

- Apathy
- Lethargy
- Mental exhaustion
- Sleep disturbances
- Weight loss
- Muscle soreness not healing
- Gastrointestinal disturbances
- Appetite loss
- Lowered self-esteem
- Mood changes
- Substance abuse
- Emotional isolation
- Increased anxiety
- Change in values and beliefs

Any of these signs may necessitate a reduction in total workload. More than one may require a significant reduction in or a break from training altogether to allow the system to restore itself.

Specificity

The ultimate goal of training is the stabilization of (i.e., the consistent performance of) technique at the highest level. The process of training begins with an initial assessment of the athlete and progresses to infrastructure development (and the shoring up of any biomotor weaknesses). After that, the earlier stages of training for the jumper are characterized by general, simple types of training that do not resemble the jump events. As the athlete gains fitness, training becomes both more complex and more specific to the jumping events. This progression can be characterized by the statement, "Train the athlete first, the jumper second." Such a progression keeps the jumper healthy and allows for adaptation and learning to occur.

How well learning takes place is directly related to the proficiency level of athlete, the quality of instruction, environmental conditions, social issues, and facilities. A jumper who is training progressively in a functional training model and who is adapting well to that training will improve and gain confidence in himself, the coach, and the training model. "Problem athletes" are often athletes who are in dysfunctional training models that are not giving them positive cues of improvement and progress.

Coaches often get ahead of themselves regarding progression. Before being expected to show proficiency in a jumping event, an athlete must first have the requisite physical attributes and fitness level. Coaches often ask athletes to do something technically that is not possible because of structural limitations. Such a scenario results in frustration on the part of both coach and athlete. Thus, the coach must identify early any limitations that might inhibit learning. Initial testing can help illuminate the athlete's needs.

PERIODIZATION

Periodization is the process of training the athlete in specific time frames within the training year that have specific goals and themes. Because periodization involves progressive training loads, it ensures the athlete's adaptation to stresses placed on the system. Training can be broken down into several time frames: From the longest time frame to the shortest, these are periods, phases, mesocycles, microcycles, workouts, and training units.

Periods

Periods of training are the longest time frames of training. The training year is broken down into three periods: preparation, competition,

and transition (figure 9.2). The preparation period is a significant time frame (up to half or more of a training year). During this time, the jumper builds infrastructure and biomotor elements in a general way to prepare for the competitive season to follow. Once the competitive season is completed, the athlete transitions (progressively detrains) into the next season.

Phases

The preparation and competitive periods are divided into four phases of training: general preparation, specific preparation, precompetitive, and competitive (figure 9.3 on page 184). Athletes and coaches should keep in mind that training is both progressive in the load (increasing in load over time) and specific to the demand of the jump events. The jumper initially will be doing general training to get fit and then will move to more jump-specific training. Each phase of training is unique.

General preparation phase: Training to train

The general preparation phase is a chance to identify strengths and weaknesses and to shore up potential biomotor issues. It is the longest phase of training and can last from a third to half of the training year. Training in this phase is general.

Specific preparation phase: Moving to jumps   The training load progresses volumetrically in the specific preparation phase, and the athlete is also now doing more jump-specific activities. The combination of increasing volume and increasing complexity in training makes for high training loads. At this point, the coach must be cognizant of the potential for injury and understand that sufficient

Preparation						Competition				Transition	
Sept.	Oct.	Nov.	Dec.	Jan.	Feb.	Mar.	Apr.	May	June	July	Aug.

➤**Figure 9.2**   Periods of training.

recovery is necessary as part of the training process. Jump-related drills and short-run jumping begin in this phase.

Precompetitive phase: Competition begins

As the intensity of training continues to increase, the quality of training becomes the priority over the quantity. The goal during the precompetitive phase is the stabilization of technique. This is when the jumper begins to put it all together. Early-season meets begin. These meets are factored into the training model, and their importance reflects the training goals for this phase.

Competitive phase: The target approaches

The volume of training drops and intensity of training increases in the competitive phase: "Quality over quantity" is now the motto. The technical focus of the jumps is now the priority in training and is reflected in the fact that competitions now take priority over the training.

During the competitive phase, the jumper must be able to do a high quality of work and to recover quickly from that work to achieve peak performance. Without both, tapering will not occur. If the jumper has been trained to a high working capacity, the 7 to 10 days prior to the target competition should include recovery, relaxation, and the normal process of supercompensation (Bompa 1999, p. 297). The coach should stimulate the nervous system with the goal of CNS maintenance only. Volume is dropped during this period, yet intensity is maintained with high-quality, high-demand work to keep the nervous system "charged." Coaches often mistakenly overload the athlete during this period, thus creating CNS fatigue

that manifests as a decrease in performance during the target competition.

The psychology of the jumper also needs to be addressed during the competitive phase. Positive reinforcement from the coach, positive self-talk from the athlete, and mental rehearsal all can enhance performance.

Mesocycles

A mesocycle is a month of training (figure 9.4). Themes generally drive the training within a mesocycle. These themes would be reflected in all of the training the athlete does during that phase. For example, in a block of training in which speed is the main theme, speed would be reflected in all biomotor activity (speed work, jump-related activities, strength work), as shown in table 9.2.

Microcycles

A microcycle is typically a week of training (figure 9.5), but it can be as long as 14 days. Just as themes drive the training in mesocycles, they also dictate what is done each day of the shorter microcycle. Themes drive the training choices and help distinguish microcycles from mesocycles.

Coaches can teach athletes using a block style of training. For instance, mesocycle 1 of training outdoors (a four-week cycle) might have a heavy strength focus. Mesocycle 2 (the next four weeks) might have a speed theme, and the final four weeks might have a competitive theme.

Each day of a microcycle might have its own theme through the year (e.g., Monday is speed day, Tuesday is jump day, Wednesday is power/

General preparation	Specific preparation	Precompetitive	Competitive	
Preparation		Competition		Transition

Sept.	Oct.	Nov.	Dec.	Jan.	Feb.	Mar.	Apr.	May	June	July	Aug.

➤ **Figure 9.3** Phases of training.

1	2	3	4	5	6	7	8	9	10	11	12
General preparation			Specific preparation			Precompetitive		Competitive			
Preparation						Competition				Transition	

Sept.	Oct.	Nov.	Dec.	Jan.	Feb.	Mar.	Apr.	May	June	July	Aug.

>**Figure 9.4**   Mesocycles.

Table 9.2   Sample Breakdown of Training Program by Mesocycle

Mesocycle	Number of weeks	Theme
Mesocycles 1-4	16	Multilateral training
Mesocycles 5-6	8	Strength and jump drills introduction
Mesocycles 7-8	8	Acceleration, speed, and approach development
Mesocycles 9-10	8	Technical development

elastic focus day, Thursday is drill day, and Friday is rest day). The coach must pay special attention to compatibility issues from day to day—specifically, how load and recovery work together to create adaptation in the jumper. Training days that tax the CNS will demand longer recoveries. It is highly recommended that total workload (volume × intensity) be dropped for one microcycle during each mesocycle.

Workout Session

The session is the workout itself and will also have a general theme. A session with a technical theme might be a jump day that includes complementary units that reflect the high-CNS demand of jumping (such as sprints, multi-jumps, multithrows, or Olympic lifts). Likewise, a session following a hard CNS session might include lower-level restorative units such as an aerobic run and aerobic-type strength circuits. A guide to how to design a session appears later in this chapter.

Training Unit

The smallest elements of training, units, are the individual elements of the workout session. Typically, most jumper workout sessions include some form of the following: a warm-up unit, technical unit, strength unit, fitness unit, and cool-down unit. The level and amount

1	2	3	4	5	6	7	8	9	10	11	12	13	14	15	16	17	18	19	20	21	22	23	24	25	26	27	28	29	30	31	32	33	34	35	36	37	38	39	40	41	42	43	44	45	46	47	48	49	50	51	52

1	2	3	4	5	6	7	8	9	10	11	12
General preparation			Specific preparation			Precompetitive		Competitive			
Preparation						Competition				Transition	

Sept.	Oct.	Nov.	Dec.	Jan.	Feb.	Mar.	Apr.	May	June	July	Aug.

>**Figure 9.5**   Microcycles.

of work done in each unit are dictated by the athlete's training level, the time in the training year, and the themes or goals that are driving the training for that session.

The high school jumper faces different obstacles to training than the college or elite athlete does, the greatest of which is a shorter season. Cold-weather states often have only a 9- to 12-week season. Also, many high school athletes come out for track from other sports. They sometimes bring injuries from other sports and may be suffering from some level of burnout as they begin the track season. The coach must assess the starting point of each athlete, both physiologically and psychologically. The important thing for the coach to understand is that all four phases of training must be done regardless of the number of weeks the athlete has to work with. General preparation, specific preparation, and competitive phases must all be included in the plan; there are just fewer weeks to work with in each. Athletes can greatly enhance their performances if they can spend significant preseason time in the two preparation phases of training.

PRINCIPLES OF JUMP TRAINING

Principles of jump training are the laws and rules by which the coach designs the training model. Bompa (1999, pp. 27-52), Harre (1982, pp. 73-94), and Freeman (1989, pp. 9-13) all speak to the value of these principles in helping the jumps coach.

Multilateral Training

Like the foundation of a well-built house, multilateral training provides the foundation for the jumper. Multilateral training emphasizes all biomotor elements. Balance among these elements is the key concept. During the training year, the athlete will progress from multilateral training to specialized training, and then to specialized high performance and hopefully the stabilization of high-level performance.

Variety

Although repetition is important to learning, the coach must also recognize that training can become stale and jumpers can become bored. The coach should be creative in designing an inventory that offers multiple ways to accomplish the goals of training. Variety in training has both physiological and psychological value. Multiple mechanisms of testing and challenging the CNS promote positive adaptations to loads. Periodization is not just about varying the loads in a progressive, logical manner; it is also about varying the mechanisms that provide those loads.

Individualization

Every athlete reacts to training loads differently. The plan that will work best for a given jumper may not work best for another jumper. This process is dynamic for each athlete. "It will change gradually over the years as that athlete's fitness and skill level (and physical maturity) progress. The coach must consider the athlete's chronological and biological (physical maturity) age, experience in the sport, skill level, capacity for effort and performance, training and health status, training load capacity and rate of recovery, body build and nervous system type and sexual differences" (Freeman 1989, p. 10). The coach should design the general elements of the workout session (warm-up and cool-down) for a large group, but separate the athletes into small groups of similar abilities and needs for the primary load elements of the session.

Reversibility

A system that is no longer stressed will return to the lowest level of operation needed to work functionally. This is often what happens with athletes who simply stop training at the end of a season. Such an abrupt change in training is hard on the system. The trajectory looks like this:

Train → get fit → quit training → lose all conditioning → begin training for next season

Many athletes repeat this roller-coaster ride year after year, compromising any hope of long-term improvement or an increase in fitness. A progressive load over an extended period of time (e.g., four years) needs to be in place to avoid compromising fitness. Also, athletes should work to minimize the total loss of fitness during transition periods between seasons.

Compatible and Complementary Training

Compatible training combines units that complement each other. It makes sense to train energy systems or CNS demands that are similar in a given session. This is what is meant by setting themes for a workout session. Training units and subsequent days of training can be combined in the following manner (B. Myers, B. Schexnayder, D. Pfaff, G. Sefcik, R. Light, G. Winckler, and C. Rovelto, pers. comm.):

- *Neuromuscular demand.* Activities such as sprinting, jumping, Olympic lifts, multithrows, and multijumps are examples of high-CNS-demand movements and activities that fit well together in a session.
- *Metabolic, or energy system, demand.* Easier activities such as easy-tempo runs and general strength–type activities fit well together and are commonly matched up on a recovery day.
- *Duration of power output.* Highly explosive movements of the same duration match up well. Multithrows, for example, are a good match for Olympic lifts done earlier in the session.
- *Ground contact times.* Activities with similar ground contact times, such as sprinting and multijumps, match up well.
- *Technical commonality.* Activities with common technical elements, such as run-run-jumps (gallops) and continuous pop-off drills, complement each other.
- *Dynamic nature of the movement.* Jump squats and double-leg hurdle hops, both quite dynamic, fit well together in the same session.
- *Rhythmic demand.* An example of activities with similar rhythmic demands would be running curve runs on the track and approach runs on the apron for the high-jumper.

Complementary training links sessions back to back to enhance training (e.g., alternates loading for harder and easier days, alternates energy systems, uses restoration methods). When determining what to do for the next day of training, the coach has a number of options:

- *A day of rest.*
- *Restorative activities.* Examples include ice baths, sauna, and massage.
- *Restorative training session with a much lower demand on the system.* Examples include a water workout, easy-tempo running (conversational running pace), and low-level circuits.
- *Training session with the same theme but a heavier load.* For example, a jumper working on acceleration will perform underhand shot throws and falling starts with three pushes one day. The following day, the jumper will run uphill for 20 meters concentrating on full hip extension.
- *Training session with the same theme, but a lighter load.* For example, a jumper will do approach work one day and rhythm runs on the straightaway the next day. The emphasis on both days is rhythm, but the second day is less strenuous.
- *Training session with the same theme, but different drills.* For example, general strength is trained using the medicine ball one day and body weight circuits the next day. Both are training general strength and have similar recoveries.
- *Training session with a different theme and different load.* The classic example of this is a hard neuromuscular demand session followed the next day with a low-intensity session for recovery purposes.

PEDAGOGICAL ISSUES IN TRAINING

Pedagogy is the art and science of teaching or coaching. The athlete must trust the coach to determine a plan that is both progressive (adaptive) and functional for the given athlete and phase of training. The art of coaching is a combination of common sense and experience that, when added to the science of coaching, gives the coach what he needs to plan training effectively. It is critical that both coach and athlete understand that general fitness must precede jumping fitness in the training model. The following pedagogical issues address this critical point:

- *Train the athlete first, the jumper second.* The demands of jumping events require that the jumper be both athletic (having the skills to jump) and fit (in condition to train safely). The coach should aid the athlete in developing all of the biomotor elements in a general and balanced fashion first and the jump-specific elements second. Such a training progression both ensures fitness early and helps to minimize the risk of injury later. This follows the "general to specific, simple to complex" concept of progressive training espoused by Bompa (1999), Harre (1982), and others. The critical elements of speed, power, and coordination must all be developed in a functional and progressive manner that is dictated by the demand of the particular phase of training. For example, full-run jumps are counterproductive early in the process of training, but are critical to success late in the process.

- *Train rhythm before speed.* Athletes are best served by learning the rhythm of the movement without complicating the learning process with high velocities. As proficiency increases and strength levels allow, speed will increase.

- *Every jump has a unique harmonic.* The jumping events involve more than just a cyclic (approach) to acyclic (transition into take-off and the jump itself) rhythm. Each of the four jumps has an optimal harmonic to the approach and the jump itself. The high jump has the highest vertical component at takeoff, for example, and the triple jump has the lowest. The goal of the jump will define the harmonic of the approach (rhythm). Both coach and athlete must understand these big-picture harmonics before breaking them down into pieces for learning.

- *A whole–part–whole method of learning may be best for jumps.* Teach the general rhythm first and then break it down into trainable pieces. The parts can be put back together in a later stage of learning.

CREATING THE PROGRAM

Having addressed the conceptual and theoretical elements of training the jumper, we now look at the training for a given athlete. This section discusses determining appropriate training for the athlete, designing a workout session, and designing a phase.

Determining Appropriate Training

In determining the appropriate training for the jumper, the coach must first ask these questions:

- *What is the chronological age of the athlete?* Older athletes typically are more developed physiologically and thus can handle more work.

- *What is the training age of the athlete (the number of years actually spent training for the jumps)?* This will dictate the amount of specific jump-related work the athlete can do.

- *What is the athletic maturity of the athlete?* Athletes develop at different rates. We are all aware of early and late bloomers in athletics. Again, different rates of development will dictate different training expectations.

- *What are the biomotor measures for the athlete (speed, strength, endurance, coordination, flexibility)?* Biomotor testing in these areas can help identify strengths and weaknesses. It is fundamental to test the jumper often to determine both strengths and weaknesses and whether the training is working.

- *What is the time frame for training this athlete?* Each level of the sport is unique. High school jumpers often have short seasons. A shorter season simply means that the jumper spends less time in each phase of training. The percentage of time spent in each phase, however, will be the same as in a longer season.

Once the preceding questions have been answered, the coach should set a target date for achieving training goals and work backward. Attaining training goals, and not the competitive schedule, should drive training choices. Competitions will become the priority later in training as the target gets closer.

Determining what to do in training sessions begins with developing training progressions. As mentioned earlier in the chapter, themes should drive the training at any given time in the training year. Progressive themes for the three biomotor qualities that are most important to the jumper are as follows:

Speed

Strength

Technical

Once the coach understands the concept of progression within the biomotor elements of speed, strength, and technical elements, she can go to the inventory and choose appropriate units of training to use for a given time frame. A training inventory is a list of units of training to draw from when designing specific workout sessions. Coaches designing a training plan are

© Human Kinetics

interested in *what* to do, *when* to do it, and *why* they are doing it. The inventory is the *what* to do and reflects the goal of training for a given time frame. The actual training units chosen are specific to the biomotor development of the athlete as well as the specific demands imposed on the athlete by the nature of the jumping event.

Designing a Workout Session

The workout session should be designed in a logical and progressive manner with a rationale and goal to every training unit that is included. Because the athlete is freshest at the beginning of the session, nervous system work should be done before metabolic work. Thus, actual jumping (or any highly technical elements) should be done early in the session. Strength work and fitness work are done later in the session. The ordering of units is as follows:

- *Warm-up.* This is a period to prepare for the high-intensity work to follow.

- *Technical.* Jumping and other event-specific training should be done first while the system is fresh. When athletes are fatigued, technique can change dramatically (creating the potential for bad habits, postural breakdown, and even injury).

- *Speed.* If not included in the technical training, acceleration and speed work are done after technical work. Again, this is best to do when fresh. Most speed-related injuries occur when athletes are fatigued.

- *Strength.* Strength work should follow technical and speed work because it is the least affected by fatigue. The strength work that is chosen will reflect the type of technical and speed work done (compatible training units).

- *Fitness.* The term *fitness* here refers to any general fitness-type routines or pillar work.

This kind of work is general, often not specific to the jumps. Fitness work will be more prevalent earlier in the training year and also on restoration-type days of training.

- *Cool-down.* This element helps to bring the body back to homeostasis and often involves a decrease in load from previous units. A cool-down jog is a common example.

The preceding workout elements can overlap in many ways. For instance, a technical jump session in which an athlete jumps from 12 steps trains technique, speed, and strength together. The training of biomotor units almost always overlaps to some degree, an important concept to understand when determining load and recovery.

The tables on pages 191 to 193 show how to design a program, from the general preparation phase through the outdoor competition phase, using the workout elements covered in this section.

General Preparation Phase	
Activity	**Drills**
Running	30-min runs or fartlek Extensive tempo, long intervals (medium recovery or short intervals) Intensive aerobic power: 80-89% hills or flat Speed: 80 m, 90-100%
Strength	Body weight circuits Cleans: 3 × 10 High step-ups: 3 × 15 Quads: 3 × 15 Hamstring curls: 3 × 15 Incline benches: 3 × 15 Dumbbells: 3 × 25
Strength and speed	For endurance (one-half mesocycle): • Lateral bench hops: 2 × 20 s • Double-leg hops: 20-40 m/set, progress double to single • RR-LL (single, flat, and stadium stairs) • Backward hopping For power (one-half mesocycle): • Depth jumps • Hurdle hops • Longer jumps
Technical	Changes in events Short run appoaches (acceleration curve) Work last two steps Form running
Multithrows	For endurance (one-half mesocycle): • Light medicine ball For strength (one-half mesocycle): • Heavy implement throwing and drills • Heavy medicine ball work (two sessions/week)
Flexibility	Static stretching Dynamic stretching

(continued)

(continued)

Specific Preparation Phase	
Activity	**Drills**
Running	Speed (runways) Speed endurance Aerobic power: 2/week Sprint drills: 2/week Power speed (hills, stadium stairs): 1 each, 2/week
Strength	On Thursday, Sunday: • Cleans: 3 × 5, 1 × 10 @ 70% • Squats: 3 × 5, 1 × 10 @ 70% • Hamstrings: 3 × 5, 1 × 10 @ 70% • Dumbbells: 3 × 10 @ 80% • Incline benches: 3 × 5, 1 × 10 @ 70% On Tuesday: • Clean and jerks: 2 × 3 @ 80%, 2 × 2 @ 85%, 1 × 3 @ 90% • Inverted leg presses: 3 × 8 @ 80% • Hamstrings: 3 × 8 @ 80% • Snatches: 3 × 5 @ 70% • Low step-ups: 2 × 3 @ 80%, 2 × 5 @ 80%
Strength and speed	For power (one-half mesocycle): • Standing one-step, two-step jumps • Half-approach, full-approach jumping • Box jumping • Lateral bench hops • Hurdle hops • Depth jumps For endurance (one-half mesocycle): • Longer jumps: 3-4 sets
Technical	Full run approaches Event-specific drills
Multithrows	Medicine balls and varied medium-weight implements
Flexibility	Static stretching Dynamic stretching
Coordination	Event-specific drills

Indoor Competition Phase	
Activity	**Drills**
Running	Sprint hurdle drills Power-bound/power-sprint
Strength	Specific strength (one-half mesocycle); 2 sessions/week: • Snatches: 1×6 @ 80% • Squats: 1×6 @ 70%, 1×5 @ 80%, 1×4 @ 85% • Hamstrings: 1×6 @ 70%, 1×5 @ 80%, 1×4 @ 85% • Lateral bench hops: 1×20 s • Cleans: 1×6 @ 70%, 1×5 @ 80%, 1×4 @ 85% One-half mesocycle: • Max or near-max lift, 1 every 14 days or less
Strength and speed	Full-approach or skill drills: • Speed bounding • Depth jump, low variety • Short jumps Lightweight implement throwing
Technical	Event-specific drills
Flexibility	Static stretching Dynamic stretching
Outdoor Competition Phase	
Activity	**Drills**
Running	Speed
Strength	One-half mesocycle, 2 sessions/week: **Day 1:** • Snatches: 1×6 @ 70%, 1×4 @ 80% • Hamstrings: 1×6 @ 70%, 1×5 @ 80%, 1×4 @ 85% • Lateral bench hops with dumbbells: 1×12 s • Cleans: 1×6 @ 70%, 1×5 @ 80%, 1×4 @ 85% **Day 2:** • Squats: 1×6 @ 70%, 1×4 @ 85% • Low step-ups: 1×8 @ 70%, 1×6 @ 75%, 1×6 @ 80% • Hamstrings: 1×5 @ 75%, 1×4 @ 85% • Lateral bench hops: 1×15 s • Cleans: 1×6 @ 75%, 1×4 @ 85% One-half mesocycle, one session/week: • Cleans: 1×6 @ 70%, 1×5 @ 80%, 1×4 @ 85% • Squats: 1×6 @ 70%, 1×5 @ 80%, 1×4 @ 85% • Hamstrings: 1×8 @ 70%, 1×6 @ 75%, 1×6 @ 80% • Lateral bench hops: 1×12 s
Strength and speed	Jump-specific drills
Technical	Competitive analysis
Multithrows	Lightweight implement throwing
Flexibility	Static stretching Dynamic stretching

CONCLUDING GUIDELINES

To sum up the material presented in this chapter, here are some guidelines for the jumps coach to help with the planning of training:

- *Think big to small, long term to short term.* Begin with the goal in mind, thinking general to specific and long term to short term. Early-season training is more general and broad in design, with the emphasis on building the athlete first, the jumper second.

- *Have a plan and keep records.* Even a bad plan is better than no plan. At the least, it will tell you what didn't work. Monitoring a long-term training process is virtually impossible without records.

- *Be progressive.* Understand loading, especially how volume and intensity interact. Also understand the value of restoration to the training process.

- *Always build the training model backward from the target date.*

- *Increase volumes 10 to 15 percent per year.* More than that invites injury.

- *Keep a holistic focus on training.* The training elements are only part of the stressors placed on the athlete. Be aware of the impact of other variables outside of training that might affect performance and training goals.

- *Build your training based on themes.* Progressive themes for training speed, strength, and technical elements are important because they provide a general-to-specific model that parallels the adaptation of the athlete. More intensive, more complex actions are asked of jumpers as they adapt to the training.

- *Remember how important rest is to the process of training.* Recovery is important both in the short term (within the session itself) and in the long term (building in a restoration microcycle every four weeks of training). The younger athlete will require more rest and recovery than the older athlete.

How easy coaching must look to those outside the sport: Put something down on paper, be there each day with a tape measure and stopwatch in hand, and then let the athletes do their thing. Of course, coaches know that the process is far more complicated than that. Coaches are not just dealing with the Xs and Os of training. That is the easy part. To excel, coaches must read a lot, make contact with the best coaches in the field, and study films of successful athletes.

The Xs and Os can be learned easily with a little work and discipline. But understanding the physiological part of training is just a starting point. Other salient issues are beyond the coach's knowledge base and the training model that will influence performance: the personality of both coach and athlete (and related communication issues) and the environmental issues of family, social life, nutrition, academics, and work. The coach must always be cognizant of how these issues influence each other. A problem in one will likely cause fallout in the others. Balance is key to consistent and progressive training. Awareness should always be a coach's primary goal.

Appendix

30m: Standing 30-meter sprint
SLJ: Standing long jump
UHF: Underhand forward throw with shot
STJ: Standing triple jump
OHB: Overhead back toss with shot
150m: 150-meter run
600m: 600-meter run

POINTS	30m	SLJ	UHF	STJ	OHB	150m	600m
1000	3.60	3.60	22.80	10.50	17.00	16.00	01:20.0
990	3.61	3.58	22.57		16.88	16.10	01:20.7
980	3.62	3.56	22.34	10.35	16.76	16.20	01:21.4
970	3.63	3.54	22.11		16.64	16.30	01:22.1
960	3.64	3.52	21.88	10.20	16.52	16.40	01:22.8
950	3.65	3.50	21.65		16.40	16.50	01:23.5
940	3.66	3.48	21.42	10.05	16.28	16.60	01:24.2
930	3.67	3.46	21.19		16.16	16.70	01:24.9
920	3.68	3.44	20.96	9.90	16.04	16.80	01:25.6
910	3.69	3.42	20.73		15.92	16.90	01:26.3
900	3.70	3.40	20.50	9.75	15.80	17.00	01:27.0
890	3.71	3.38	20.27		15.68	17.10	01:27.7
880	3.72	3.36	20.04	9.60	15.56	17.20	01:28.4
870	3.73	3.34	19.81		15.44	17.30	01:29.1
860	3.74	3.32	19.58	9.45	15.32	17.40	01:29.8
850	3.75	3.30	19.35		15.20	17.50	01:30.5
840	3.76	3.28	19.12	9.30	15.08	17.60	01:31.2
830	3.77	3.26	18.89		14.96	17.70	01:31.9
820	3.78	3.24	18.66	9.15	14.84	17.80	01:32.6
810	3.79	3.22	18.43		14.72	17.90	01:33.3
800	3.80	3.20	18.20	9.00	14.60	18.00	01:34.0
790	3.81	3.18	17.97		14.48	18.10	01:34.7
780	3.82	3.16	17.74	8.85	14.36	18.20	01:35.4
770	3.83	3.14	17.51		14.24	18.30	01:36.1
760	3.84	3.12	17.28	8.70	14.12	18.40	01:36.8
750	3.85	3.10	17.05		14.00	18.50	01:37.5
740	3.86	3.08	16.82	8.55	13.88	18.60	01:38.2
730	3.87	3.06	16.59		13.76	18.70	01:38.9

(continued)

POINTS	30m	SLJ	UHF	STJ	OHB	150m	600m
720	3.88	3.04	16.36	8.40	13.64	18.80	01:39.6
710	3.89	3.02	16.13		13.52	18.90	01:40.3
700	3.90	3.00	15.90	8.25	13.40	19.00	01:41.0
690	3.91	2.98	15.67		13.28	19.10	01:41.7
680	3.92	2.96	15.44	8.10	13.16	19.20	01:42.4
670	3.93	2.94	15.21		13.04	19.30	01:43.1
660	3.94	2.92	14.98	7.95	12.92	19.40	01:43.8
650	3.95	2.90	14.75		12.80	19.50	01:44.5
640	3.96	2.88	14.52	7.80	12.68	19.60	01:45.2
630	3.97	2.86	14.29		12.56	19.70	01:45.9
620	3.98	2.84	14.06	7.65	12.44	19.80	01:46.6
610	3.99	2.82	13.83		12.32	19.90	01:47.3
600	4.00	2.80	13.60	7.50	12.20	20.00	01:48.0
590	4.01	2.78	13.37		12.08	20.10	01:48.7
580	4.02	2.76	13.14	7.35	11.96	20.20	01:49.4
570	4.03	2.74	12.91		11.84	20.30	01:50.1
560	4.04	2.72	12.68	7.20	11.72	20.40	01:50.8
550	4.05	2.70	12.45		11.60	20.50	01:51.5
540	4.06	2.68	12.22	7.05	11.48	20.60	01:52.2
530	4.07	2.66	11.99		11.36	20.70	01:52.9
520	4.08	2.64	11.76	6.90	11.24	20.80	01:53.6
510	4.09	2.62	11.53		11.12	20.90	01:54.3
500	4.10	2.60	11.30	6.75	11.00	21.00	01:55.0
490	4.11	2.58	11.07		10.88	21.10	01:55.7
480	4.12	2.56	10.84	6.60	10.76	21.20	01:56.4
470	4.13	2.54	10.61		10.64	21.30	01:57.1
460	4.14	2.52	10.38	6.45	10.52	21.40	01:57.8
450	4.15	2.50	10.15		10.40	21.50	01:58.5
440	4.16	2.48	9.92	6.30	10.28	21.60	01:59.2
430	4.17	2.46	9.69		10.16	21.70	01:59.9
420	4.18	2.44	9.46	6.15	10.04	21.80	02:00.6
410	4.19	2.42	9.23		9.92	21.90	02:01.3
400	4.20	2.40	9.00	6.00	9.80	22.00	02:02.0
390	4.21	2.38	8.77		9.68	22.10	02:02.7
380	4.22	2.36	8.54	5.85	9.56	22.20	02:03.4
370	4.23	2.34	8.31		9.44	22.30	02:04.1
360	4.24	2.32	8.08	5.70	9.32	22.40	02:04.8
350	4.25	2.30	7.85		9.20	22.50	02:05.5
340	4.26	2.28	7.62	5.55	9.08	22.60	02:06.2
330	4.27	2.26	7.39		8.96	22.70	02:06.9
320	4.28	2.24	7.16	5.40	8.84	22.80	02:07.6

POINTS	30m	SLJ	UHF	STJ	OHB	150m	600m
310	4.29	2.22	6.93		8.72	22.90	02:08.3
300	4.30	2.20	6.70	5.25	8.60	23.00	02:09.0
290	4.31	2.18	6.47		8.48	23.10	02:09.7
280	4.32	2.16	6.24	5.10	8.36	23.20	02:10.4
270	4.33	2.14	6.01		8.24	23.30	02:11.1
260	4.34	2.12	5.78	4.95	8.12	23.40	02:11.8
250	4.35	2.10	5.55		8.00	23.50	02:12.5
240	4.36	2.08	5.32	4.80	7.88	23.60	02:13.2
230	4.37	2.06	5.09		7.76	23.70	02:13.9
220	4.38	2.04	4.86	4.65	7.64	23.80	02:14.6
210	4.39	2.02	4.63		7.52	23.90	02:15.3
200	4.40	2.00	4.40	4.50	7.40	24.00	02:16.0
190	4.41	1.98	4.17		7.28	24.10	02:16.7
180	4.42	1.96	3.94	4.35	7.16	24.20	02:17.4
170	4.43	1.94	3.71		7.04	24.30	02:18.1
160	4.44	1.92	3.48	4.20	6.92	24.40	02:18.8
150	4.45	1.90	3.25		6.80	24.50	02:19.5
140	4.46	1.88	3.02	4.05	6.68	24.60	02:20.2
130	4.47	1.86	2.79		6.56	24.70	02:20.9
120	4.48	1.84	2.56	3.90	6.44	24.80	02:21.6
110	4.49	1.82	2.33		6.32	24.90	02:22.3
100	4.50	1.80	2.10	3.75	6.20	25.00	02:23.0
90	4.51	1.78	1.87		6.08	25.10	02:23.7
80	4.52	1.76	1.64	3.60	5.96	25.20	02:24.4
70	4.53	1.74	1.41		5.84	25.30	02:25.1
60	4.54	1.72	1.18	3.45	5.72	25.40	02:25.8
50	4.55	1.70	0.95		5.60	25.50	02:26.5
40	4.56	1.68	0.72	3.30	5.48	25.60	02:27.2
30	4.57	1.66	0.49		5.36	25.70	02:27.9
20	4.58	1.64	0.26	3.15	5.24	25.80	02:28.6
10	4.59	1.62	0.03		5.12	25.90	02:29.3

References

Chapter 1

Tellez, T. 2003. *Biomechanics of sprinting.* Unpublished.

Chapter 2

Dapena, J. 2000. The high jump. In *Biomechanics in sport,* ed. V. Zatsiorsky, pp. 284-311. Oxford, UK: Blackwell Science.

Dyson, G. 1977. *Mechanics of athletics.* New York: Holmes and Meier.

Hay, J., J.A. Miller, and R.W. Canterna. 1983. *Biomechanical analysis.* 1983 TAC Championships: Indianapolis, IN.

McGinnis, P. 2006. *Research results from top male and female pole-vaulters from 2003-2006.* USATF Elite Athlete Scientific Studies Program: Indianapolis, IN.

Miller, J.A., and J. Hay. 1985. *Biomechanical analysis.* 1985 TAC Championships: Indianapolis, IN.

Chapter 3

Ecker, T. 1996. *Basic track and field biomechanics* (2nd ed.). Mountain View, CA: Tafnews Press.

Chapter 5

Badon, T. 1988. Constructing and utilizing the "ultimate" jump ramp. *Track Technique,* 106, 3378-3380.

Dapena, J. 2000. The high jump. In *Biomechanics in sport,* ed. V. Zatsiorsky, pp. 284-311. Oxford, UK: Blackwell Science.

Dapena, J., Gordon, B., and B. Meyer. 2006. *High jump, #20 (women) report for scientific services project (USATF).* USA: Track & Field. Indianapolis, IN. 11, 22, 97.

Dapena, J., and A. Iiboshi. 1997. A closer look at the shape of the high jump run-up. *Track Coach,* 138, 4406-4411.

Greig, M., and M. Yeadon. 2000. The influence of touchdown parameters on the performance of a high jumper. *Applied Biomechanics,* 16, 367-378.

Chapter 7

Benson, H. 1975. *The relaxation response.* New York: Avon Books.

Gould, D., and E. Udry. 1994. Psychological skills for enhancing performance: Arousal regulation strategies. *Medicine and Science in Sports and Exercise,* 26, 478-485.

Heil, J. 1995. Imagery. In *Sport psychology: An analysis of athletic behavior,* eds. K. Henschen and W. Staub, 3rd ed., pp. 183-191. Longmeadow, MA: Movement Publications.

Henschen, K. 1995. Attention and concentration skills for performance. In *Sport psychology: An analysis of athletic behavior,* eds. K. Henschen and W. Staub, 3rd ed., pp. 177-182. Longmeadow, MA: Movement Publications.

Henschen, K. 2005. Mental practice—Skill oriented. In *Handbook of research in applied sport and exercise psychology: International perspectives,* eds. D. Hackfort, J.L. Duda, and R. Lidor, pp. 19-34. Morgantown, WV: Fitness Information Technology.

Jacobsen, E. 1930. *Progressive relaxation.* Chicago, IL: University of Chicago Press.

Krenz, E.W. 1983. *Modified autogenic training.* Salt Lake City, UT: I.I.P. Associates

Lidor, R., and R.N. Singer. 2003. Performance routines in self-paced tasks: Developmental and educational considerations. In *The psychology of team sports,* eds. R. Lidor and K. Henschen, pp. 69-98. Morgantown WV: Fitness Information Technology.

Moran, A. 2003. Improving concentration skills in team-sport performers: Focusing techniques for soccer players. In *The psychology of team sports,* eds. R. Lidor and K. Henschen, pp. 161-169. Morgantown, WV: Fitness Information Technology.

Reardon, J., and R. Gordin. 1992. Psychological skill development leading to a peak performance "flow state." *Track and Field Quarterly,* 92, 22-25.

Vernacchia, R.A. 2003. Working with individual team sports: The psychology of track and field. In *The psychology of team sports,* eds. R. Lidor and K. Henschen, pp. 235-263. Morgantown, WV: Fitness Information Technology.

Chapter 9

Bompa, T. 1999. *Periodization: Theory and methodology of training,* 4th ed. Champaign, IL: Human Kinetics.

Freeman, W.H. 1989. *Peak when it counts.* Los Altos, CA: Tafnews Press.

Harre, D. 1982. *Principles of sports training.* Berlin, Germany: Sportsverlag.

Meyers, A.W., and J.P. Whelan. 1998. A systemic model for understanding psychosocial influences in overtraining. In *Overtraining in sport,* eds. R. Kreider, A. Fry, and M. O'Toole, pp. 335-372. Champaign, IL: Human Kinetics.

Bibliography

Dapena, J. 2000. The high jump. In *Biomechanics in sport,* ed. V. Zatsiorsky, pp. 284-311. Oxford, UK: Blackwell Science. 284-311.

Dapena, J., and R. Vaughn. 1993. *Men's high jump #10.* Indianapolis, IN: TAC/USOC.

Dyson, G. 1977. *Mechanics of athletics.* New York: Holmes and Meier.

Gros, H., and K. Kunkel. 1988. *Biomechanical research: Olympic Games in Seoul.* Seoul, Korea: Amateur Athletic Federation.

Hay, J. 1973. The biomechanics of sports techniques. In *Athletics,* 2nd ed. Englewood Cliffs, NJ: Prentice Hall.

Hay, J., and J.W. Feuerbach. 1989. *Biomechanical analysis and technique of Carl Lewis.* Iowa City, IA: University of Iowa.

Hay, J., J.A. Miller, Jr., and R.W. Canterna. 1986. The techniques of elite male long jumpers. *Journal of Biomechanics,* 19(10), 855-866.

Jacoby, E., and B. Fraley. 1995. *The complete book of jumps.* Champaign, IL: Human Kinetics.

Light, R., C. Rovelto, G. Sefcik, and I. Schexnayder. 2003. *USATF coaching education level 2 curriculum combined events.* Unpublished. 41-42, 43, 90-92.

McGinnis, P. 2006. *Research results from top male and female pole-vaulters from 2003-2006.* USATF Elite Athlete Scientific Studies Program: Indianapolis, IN.

Miller, J.A., Jr., and J.G. Hay. 1986. Kinematics of a world record and other world class performances in the triple jump. *International Journal of Sport Biomechanics,* 2(4), 272-288.

Novacheck, T. 1988. *The biomechanics of running.* St. Paul, MN: Motion Analysis Laboratory, University of Minnesota, Gillette Children's Specialty Healthcare.

Smith, S., and E. Russell. 2005. *A case study: A biomechanical analysis of selected parameters measured in the approach of an elite male high jumper.* Unpublished. 23.

Tellez, T. 2003. Biomechanics of sprinting. Unpublished paper.

Vaughan, C.L. 1990. Biomechanics of running gait. *Critical Reviews in Biomechanical Engineering,* 12(1), 1-48.

Vaughan, R. 1994. Independent study on velocity and center of gravity height. Personal interview. Boise State University.

Weyland, P.G., D. Sternlight, M.J. Bellizzi, and S. Wright. 2000. Faster top running speeds are achieved with greater ground forces not more rapid leg movements. *Journal of Applied Physiology,* 89, 1991-1999.

Index

Note: The italicized *f* and *t* following page numbers refer to figures and tables, respectively.

About the Editor

As head track and field coach at Boise State University in Idaho for 24 years, **Ed Jacoby** was a 3-time NCAA District Coach of the Year and 10-time Big Sky Conference Coach of the Year. He has served as assistant coach at the 1992 Olympic Games, as head coach for the 1993 world championship team, as high-jump coordinator for USA Track & Field, and as chair of the National Track & Field Development Committee.

Jacoby, a master coach, has authored three books and is sought for his expertise in biomechanics, principles of training, and training methodology. His book *The Complete Book of Jumps* was hailed by *Track & Field News* as the best book ever written on the jumping events. Jacoby is a member of the USA Track & Field and Cross Country Coaches Association Hall of Fame.

About the Contributors

Will Freeman is the head track coach at Grinnell College in Iowa. He is a sought-after clinician, instructing and speaking at clinics around the United States and the world. He has written 3 books and has authored 19 coaching videos and has served as national chairman for coaching education for USA Track & Field.

Keith Henschen is a professor in the department of exercise and sport science at the University of Utah with an area of expertise in applied sport psychology. He has published over 200 articles, 35 chapters of books, and 5 monographs. He has coauthored 5 books and has made over 400 presentations. He has consulted with numerous Olympic, professional, and world-class performers. Henschen is also the sport psychology consultant for the Utah Jazz.

Greg Hull is founder and director of Sky Athletics Vault Club in Phoenix, where he coaches elite vaulters, including 2000 Olympic gold medalist Nick Hysong. He also took over coaching duties for 2000 Olympic women's gold medalist Stacy Dragila. He serves as co-national coach for USA Track & Field Olympic Development in the pole vault.

Cliff Rovelto, Kansas State University head track and field coach, has coached 3 NCAA champions, 36 All-Americans, and 22 conference champion high-jumpers. His jumpers have won 9 national titles and he has had 4 Olympic competitors. A 6-time U.S. team staff member for international teams, Rovelto was Women's Outdoor National Coach of the Year in 2001.

Irving "Boo" Schexnayder was the jumps and multievent coach at Louisiana State University. His jumpers have won eight indoor and outdoor NCAA titles in the triple jump since 2000, and they placed 1-2-3 at the 2004 indoor championships. Schexnayder was assistant coach for Team USA at the IAAF World Junior Championships in 2007, and he also served on the USA Track & Field coaching staff for the 2008 Olympic Games.

Kyle Tellez is the associate head coach for the University of Houston. During his tenure working with Houston's jumpers and multiathletes, he has produced seven All-Americans, including two-time NCAA long-jump champion Jenny Adams.

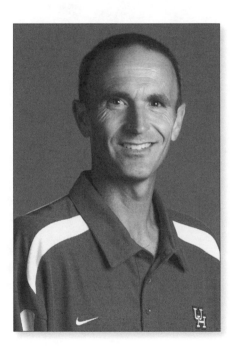

Tom Tellez has coached many elite athletes, including Carl Lewis. He coached at UCLA before becoming head coach for the University of Houston, where he coached for 22 years. Between 1984 and 1996, six of the seven U.S. sprinters who won Olympic gold medals were coached by Tellez, who served as head coach for the 1991 world championship team. Tellez is a member of the USA Track & Field and Cross Country Coaches Association Hall of Fame.

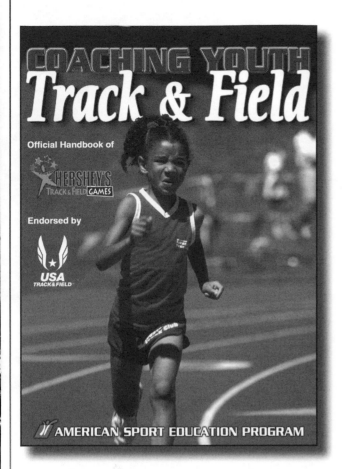